Bibliographic Control of Microforms

BY FELIX REICHMANN
AND JOSEPHINE M. THARPE
with the cooperation of
Henriette Avram, Suzanne Dodson,
Harry Gochman and Laura Jennings.

SPONSORED BY
THE ASSOCIATION OF
RESEARCH LIBRARIES UNDER
CONTRACT WITH THE OFFICE
OF EDUCATION

Greenwood Press, Inc., Publishing Division
Westport, Connecticut

Library of Congress Cataloging in Publication Data

Reichmann, Felix, 1899-
    Bibliographic control of microforms.

    Sponsored by the Association of Research Libraries
under contract with the Office of Education.
    Bibliography: p.
    1. Microforms--Bibliography. 2. Books on microfilm
--Bibliography. I. Tharpe, Josephine M., joint author.
II. Association of Research Libraries. III. Title.
Z1033.M5R43   016.02517'9   72-2463
ISBN 0-8371-6423-9

Library of Congress Catalog Card Number: 72-2463
ISBN: 0-8371-6423-0

First published in 1972
Second printing 1973

Greenwood Press, Inc., Publishing Division
51 Riverside Avenue, Westport, Connecticut 06880
Printed in the United States of America
Designed by Laurel Brown

Bibliographic
Control of
Microforms

Contents

Acknowledgments

This study was made possible through the cooperation of librarians, microform dealers, and many other interested persons throughout the world. A few names must be singled out for special acknowledgment.

The structure of the survey is the result of the suggestions and advice of the two chief officers of the Association of Research Libraries, Stephen A. McCarthy and Louis E. Martin, and the members of the Advisory Committee for the study: Samuel M. Boone, University of North Carolina Library; Helen Brown, Pennsylvania State University Library; Lyman H. Butterfield, Massachusetts Historical Society; Richard DeGennaro, University of Pennsylvania Libraries; and Allen B. Veaner, Stanford University Libraries.

Of great value was the assistance given by Suzanne Dodson, Head, Government Publications and Microforms, University of British Columbia Library; Laura L. Jennings, former Head, Catalog Department, and the Reference staff, Cornell University Libraries. Many staff members of the Library of Congress discussed the study with the authors in detail and assisted in a variety of ways. Among them, we are especially grateful to Robert Holmes and C. Sumner Spalding, administrative officers of the Technical Services; Gloria Hsia and Imre Jarmy of the Catalog Publications Division, which is responsible for the *National Register of Microform Masters;* Henriette Avram and Harry Gochman of the MARC (Machine Readable Catalog) Project of the Library of Congress contributed the paper on the Machine-Readable Index for Microsets (Appendix 2).

Seven specialists offered advice at a meeting devoted to technical operations of libraries: Michael Fitzgerald, Harvard University Libraries; F. Bernice Field, Yale University Library; John Byrum, Princeton University Libraries; Joseph Treyz, Jr., University of Wisconsin Libraries; C. Sumner Spalding, Library of Congress; Fred Blum, Catholic University of America Library; and Phyllis Richmond, Case Western Reserve University School of Library Science.

Bibliographic Control of Microforms

CHAPTER ONE

Introduction

Bibliographic control of microforms is a foremost need in today's library world. Despite the rapidly increasing quantity of materials and their bibliographic complexity, the methods for controlling microforms on all levels—local, national, and international—are inadequate. As early as 1940, Herman Fussler called attention to the peril of the situation: "The adequacy of the research collections and their accompanying reproductive services will be of little avail unless we are able to develop and distribute adequate bibliographic tools for making known our actual holdings in toto."[1] Twenty years later, George Schwegmann reiterated the warning: "A serious situation exists concerning the lack of centralized cataloging or indexing for multi-title microform projects; and, as a result, libraries are expending an unnecessary amount of duplicate effort in cataloging this form of material."[2]

The first study of microform problems for the Association of Research Libraries (ARL) fully recognized the precariousness of the situation. In a July 1969 report, the investigators criticized "the lack of an adequate system of bibliographic control of microforms which diminishes access to them and presents difficulties in their acquisition and cataloging."[3] The Association, concurring, proposed to the Office of Education a study to determine "the elements of an effective system of bibliographic control of microforms which would permit the expeditious selection, acquisition, cataloging and use of micropublication both current and retrospective."[4] The Office of Education accepted the proposal and provided funds for this bibliographic study.

As production and distribution of microforms increase, the situation becomes more critical. The upward trend that began in the early 1930s has not yet slowed. Three years ago the microform industry estimated that production would increase by 10 percent annually. The current prediction is 20 percent yearly. George Bernstein predicted that by 1978 the use of microforms would be tenfold the 1969 rate.[5] This prediction appears to be a distinct possibility, for many publishers plan to produce microfiche in addition to hard copies (see Appendix 3), and the sale of vast book collections on ultramicrofiche is increasing.

The federal government is one of the largest producers and distributors of microforms. The National Archives sold 10,200 rolls of film in 1958; nine years later, the figure was 91,800 rolls. In 1953, it used 300,000 feet of film, and in 1967, 6 million feet. Also in 1967, a selected group of government agencies used 33 million feet of film and distributed internally 12.5 million microfiche (see Appendix 1). Recently the Government Printing Office entered the field of micropublishing, adding microfiche to its letterpress output.

A substantial part of the holdings in United States libraries is on microform. The median ARL library in 1970 had 1,268,159 books and 355,490 units on microform.[6] Thus, for every 100 printed books, the library had 28 microforms, a ratio of less than four to one.

The number of microforms issued is expected to reach parity with printed books in the very near future. They will not displace books, but they will become an influential part of library holdings.

At present many libraries buy microforms (often to prove that the library is not old-fashioned), even though their use is not commensurate with the volume and cost of these acquisitions. The deplorable failure to utilize microform collections arises both from a reluctance by readers to use them and an unwillingness of librarians to process them adequately. A microform looks "strange." It has been heavily sponsored by industry and engineers, and at first glance it may appear to be nothing more than a technological curiosity, an alien visitor to the world of books and learning. The use of reading equipment demands bodily adjustments and is often inconvenient to the eye, especially to an eye with bifocals. Reader resistance to microforms is stressed in Rundell's and similar surveys of research efforts.[7] Ralph Lewis points out: "Perhaps the most basic of the problems is the reluctance of users to accept microcopies. Forty-five percent of the respondents regarded microfiche as no more than acceptable and over 30 percent thought it poor and unacceptable. Most thought that the library should have a significant amount of its collection on microfiche if the microfiche was limited to technical report materials."[8] Again, technology is regarded as microphotography's real parent, and the library as its foster home at the very best.

As microforms become "naturalized" members of the book community, conditions will improve. Reader education may well start in grade schools according to a fascinating paper, "Teaching Microforms in Grade Schools," presented by Miss Katherine B. Harmon at the twentieth convention of the National Microfilm Association in Washington, D.C., in May 1971.

The passive attitude of librarians will be more difficult to change. Their apathy is due neither to lack of education nor to unfamiliarity with the new forms but to the inadequacy of the bibliographical apparatus. It is a misleading cliché to say that "a book is a book is a book." Obviously, considering the content alone, it is immaterial whether the text is printed on letterpress or reproduced as a microimage. The bibliographic control provided for the letterpress book differs markedly from that provided for the book in microimage. For a large part of library holdings, the reader is able both to consult subject headings in the catalog and to browse in classified stacks. Microforms, of course, do not lend themselves to browsing. Most books can be identified through national bibliographies. Microforms are not cited in these tools and will not be until international copyright legislation and rules for deposit are changed. Clearly, there is no comparison between microreproduction and antiquarian reprints; reprints are classified and are frequently, though by no means consistently, entered in national bibliographies.

Libraries also use a great number of indexes to supplement the catalog. Microforms do not fit into the structure of these chronologically arranged tools, since their publication dates are meaningless. The Procrustean bed of existing bibliographic tools cannot accommodate microforms. From art history, it is clear that the use of new material demands new artistic forms. A case in point is the application of steel construction and cement in architecture. That thought can also be applied to the bibliographic problem: use of an entirely new and revolutionary production method such as microphotography demands an innovative bibliographic tool if the selection and processing of microforms are to be adequately controlled. Such a tool, combining computer and microfilm, is outlined in Appendix 2.

Notes

1. Herman H. Fussler, "Microfilms and Libraries," in William M. Randall, ed., *Acquisitions and Cataloging of Books* (Chicago: University of Chicago Press, 1940), pp. 33-54.

2. George A. Schwegmann, Jr., "Bibliographic Control of Microforms," *Library Trends* 8 (1960): 380-90.

3. Donald C. Holmes, "Determination of User Needs and Future Requirements for a Systems Approach to Microform Technology (Washington, D.C.: Association of Research Libraries, July 19, 1969). Prepared for U.S., Department of Health, Education, and Welfare, Office of Education, Bureau of Research, Contract #OEC-0-8-080786-4612(095), p. ii.

4. Ibid., p. 23.

5. George B. Bernstein, *A Fifteen-Year Forecast of Information-Processing Technology,* prepared by Research and Development Division, Naval Supply Systems Command (Detroit: Management Information Services, 1969); also available from National Technical Information Service as AD 681752.

6. John G. Veenstra, "Microimages and the Library: A Review of the Most Recent Trends in the Spreading Use of Microimage Materials in Libraries of All Types," *Library Journal* 95 (1970): 3443.

7. Walter Rundell, *In Pursuit of American History: Research and Training in the United States* (Norman: University of Oklahoma Press, 1970).

8. Ralph W. Lewis, "User's Reaction to Microfiche," *College and Research Libraries* 31 (1970): 260-68.

CHAPTER TWO

Methods and Procedures

This study of means of establishing bibliographic control of microforms began with an intensive literature search. Some 1,200 books and papers yielded only 160 items—most of them in English—with information useful to such a study.

Information on current procedures and plans came from American and foreign libraries and from microform dealers and publishers. As personal visits to a large sample of libraries would have been very time-consuming, expensive, and impractical, librarians were asked in personal letters and telephone calls to describe their bibliographic procedures. Information was solicited from 250 American libraries and scholarly organizations and about 150 foreign institutions through approximately 1,500 letters and scores of telephone calls (in many cases, inquiries had to be repeated two or three times). The responses of 190 American libraries could be tabulated and the situation sketched for 73 countries. Information on their publication plans was gathered from directories of microform dealers and publishers and, in about 50 cases, from telephone calls to or from correspondence with these businesses.

A number of experts helped to assess the information, checking the bibliography and evaluating the adaptability of the proposed controls to modern technology. Four times during the study, at one-day meetings, the ARL Advisory Committee members offered their suggestions and advice. In April 1971 seven librarians who specialize in technical services met to comment on the procedures and plans thus far devised.

Staff of the Library of Congress, especially those working on the *National Register of Microform Masters*, were consulted in a half-dozen visits and frequent exchanges of letters. A conference on the microfilming of colonial documents held at the State University of New York at Stony Brook in March 1970 and later contacts with its chairmen afforded practical guidance, as did the annual conferences of the National Microfilm Association held in San Francisco in April 1970 and in Washington in May 1971.

Reports on the progress of this study were made to the Association of Research Libraries at the midwinter meeting of the American Library Association (ALA) in 1971 and to the technical services librarians of New York City in May 1971. Also at the ALA meeting, the possibility of cooperating in the preparation of a *Guide to Microforms* was discussed with the Resources Committee of the Resources and Technical Services Division.

The staff of the ARL and the Advisory Committee for this study concur in the following definition: bibliographic control of microforms denotes effective access to material, provides the inquirer with a list of material available, indicates the location of material, and provides the necessary equipment for using the material.

Three rules govern the actual operation of a control system: (1) every item acquired has its appropriate bibliographic control, either homemade (catalogs) or store-bought (indexes); (2) bibliographic control costs money; and (3) incorrect bibliographic control is worthless.

This study is concerned with all types of microforms: microfilm, microcard, microprint, and microfiche. The materials on microform include books and periodicals, manuscripts, manuscript collections, and archival materials. The study considers bibliographic control at the local, national, and international levels.

CHAPTER THREE

Findings

LOCAL BIBLIOGRAPHIC CONTROL

The overwhelming majority of the 190 libraries that responded to the questionnaire on local bibliographic control are not satisfied with the present situation and deplore the lack of adequate control. Many expressed sharp discontent: "We are missing the goal by a far margin"; "We rely on oral tradition and on the good memory of the reference staff." Especially critical is lack of control for analyzed series. Librarians complain that many publishers furnish unusable entries, and that even when Library of Congress cards are provided, the libraries are unable to process and file them. Lack of staff is a pervasive problem. At the core of the problem is the widespread belief that microforms are "second-class citizens."

The intricacies of controlling microforms may be "truly an impossible burden" for the individual library. The solution lies in a national tool (see Appendix 2) that can supplement but never completely replace the library's own catalogs and lists and that will provide ready access for selection and processing on the broadest basis.

Following is an analysis of responses to the questionnaire, supplemented by letters and telephone calls, from all members of the Association of Research Libraries and a number of college libraries, major public libraries, state libraries, state historical societies, and library agencies in the United States and Canada. Some libraries did not answer some questions or did not state their positions clearly. The tabulations and percentages given below are based only on the number of answers that could be used.

Cataloging of Microforms

Sixty percent of the libraries catalog microforms; 40 percent make many exceptions to the general rules or do not catalog at all. The official rule is to treat microforms like books; however, both technical services and reference departments were critical of the quality of processing operations in follow-up conversations. Some libraries catalog only microforms for which no index or bibliography is available; some use analytics if they can be purchased. A number of libraries hope to improve their cataloging; others are pessimistic that they will be able to carry the burden.

Of 185 libraries responding, 9 do not catalog; 119 do catalog; 57 do catalog, but make exceptions (for example, 20 do not catalog analytics for series, 28 catalog only part of their holdings, 5 give main entry only, 4 do not catalog serials and newspapers).

Cataloging Rules Followed

The vast majority of the libraries follow standard rules for descriptive cataloging. Fifteen percent simplify, modify, or shorten the rules.

Of 181 libraries responding, 9 do not catalog; 145 follow standard Anglo-American rules; Canadian libraries follow Canadian cataloging rules; 27 vary the rules: 16 apply simplified rules and 11 modify and shorten rules.

Classification of Microforms

Almost 60 percent of those responding do not classify in the strict sense of the word but shelve microforms by sequential numbers. Films, cards, and fiche have their own sequential numbers, and continuations (series and newspapers) are kept together. Thirty percent classify fully, while 6 percent arrange by the first two letters of the Library of Congress classification or by the first three digits of Dewey. Two libraries use sequential numbers but have the cards fully classified to preserve their shelflists as classed catalogs.

There are many variations. Sometimes roll films are classified, while microcards and microfiche are arranged alphabetically. Microprint is often classified. Some libraries use sequential numbering for microfilms and full classification for all other types of microforms; others follow the opposite rule. Libraries that do not classify serials do not classify serials on microforms.

Of 173 libraries responding, 10 do not classify; 49 use full Library of Congress or Dewey classifications; 6 classify "simply," by broad subject; 11 use the first two letters of Library of Congress classification or the first three digits of Dewey, followed by a sequential number; 3 arrange microforms alphabetically by author; 94 use sequential numbering.

Separate Shelflist for Microforms

Only ten libraries do not shelflist their microforms. Of the 153 that do, 70 percent have, in addition to the general shelflist, a separate shelflist for microforms; the others are satisfied with one shelflist for all titles. One library has a separate shelflist for serials only and one a control file for sequential numbering in the catalog department.

Of 163 libraries responding, 10 do not shelflist microforms; 43 file all cards in the general shelflist; 110 have a separate shelflist for microforms.

Listing of Microforms in the
General Public Catalog

Almost 90 percent of the libraries responding file entries for microreproductions in the Public catalog, but over 40 percent list major exceptions. The largest omission is the failure to file analytics. Many libraries have a disturbingly large backlog in filing and no plan to employ more personnel or to buy more catalog cases. Broadly phrased reference cards are used as temporary stopgaps. Some libraries file all cards now but did not do so previously; others follow just the opposite practice.

Of 179 libraries responding, 15 do not file microform entries in the general catalog; 89 do file microform entries; 75 do file microform entries but make exceptions (for example, 48 do not file analytics for series, 22 do not file all cards, 5 file no subject cards).

Backlog in Cataloging

Over 60 percent of the libraries report backlogs in processing. Here, too, analytics are a major part of the problem. Generally, the processing of microforms is postponed in order to make printed books available to the patrons as quickly as possible. Some libraries report that few microforms have been cataloged during recent years.

Of 173 libraries responding, 16 have no backlog in cataloging, 75 have backlogs, 9 have very large backlogs, and 20 have small backlogs.

Special Guides for Microform Holdings

Almost 70 percent have no special guide for their microform holdings. Ten percent have a guide, and another 10 percent report one in preparation. Telephone conversations and correspondence reveal that interest in such a tool is growing. Frequently, reference departments have prepared orientation leaflets and loose-leaf binders as guides to the library's holdings.

Location of the Bulk of the Collection

Forty percent of the respondents have a caged or vaulted area in the stacks for microforms. Sixty percent have a separate room; most of these rooms are labeled "microfilm reading room," "newspaper and microcopy room," or "audiovisual center." Of 150 libraries responding, 87 have a special microfilm reading room, 2 will have a separate room in the near future, and 61 store microforms in caged or vaulted stacks.

Librarian in Charge of Microforms

Almost 30 percent of the libraries have a professional librarian in charge of their microforms. The need for microform reference librarians is slowly gaining acceptance. Twenty percent feel that they have to be satisfied with a nonprofessional staff supervised by personnel from readers' service departments. Fifty percent rely completely on nonprofessional help.

Of 168 libraries responding, 47 have a professional librarian in charge of their microform collection (3 call the position "Microform Reference Librarian"); 2 are considering appointing a professional librarian; 89 have

clerical help or student assistants in charge; 30 have a clerical staff profes-
sionally supervised by: 12, the Reference Department; 6, the Circulation
Department; 4, the Document Section; 4, the Serials Department; 4, the
Public Service Department.

Report to the National Register of
Microform Masters

Of 174 libraries responding, 105 do not report to the *National Register,* 40
report regularly, 16 promise to begin reporting, and 13 report irregularly.
Sixty percent of libraries do not report to the *National Register of Microform
Masters.* Quite a number did not know about the *Register* or did not
understand its function; often the difference between the *Register* and the
National Union Catalog was not clear. Twenty five percent do report regularly and an additional 10 percent have promised to do so.

MARC Project

Although 64 libraries expressed an interest in the extension of the MARC
(machine-readable cataloging) project to include microforms, their enthu-
siasm seemed limited. Of 99 libraries responding, 64 favored including microforms with full analytics for all titles in the MARC project in the Library of
Congress, 11 expressed a very mild interest, and 24 did not favor including
microforms in the MARC project.

Filing of Analytics for Monograph Sets Owned by the
Center for Research Libraries

Only one library files all entries for microforms held by the Center for
Research Libraries. The overwhelming majority of the libraries contacted
showed no interest in the question.

Of 20 libraries responding, 1 files all analytics of the Center for Research
libraries in its official catalog; 19 do not file but would not oppose such a
procedure.

NATIONAL BIBLIOGRAPHIC CONTROL

As early as 1936, Keyes Metcalf proposed a national file of negative microforms. In 1940, reporting on microphotography for scholarly purposes, the
Committee on Scientific Aids to Learning recommended a central listing of
microfilm negatives.[9] This recommendation was strongly endorsed at the
1946 Conference on International Cultural, Educational and Scientific Exchanges at Princeton University.[10] Except for some very valuable regional
union lists, little was done on the national level until Wesley Simonton
conducted his survey on the bibliographic control of microforms for ARL in
1962.[11] This finally led to the establishment of the *National Register of
Microform Masters* at the Library of Congress in 1965. The objectives of the
National Register are:

1. To provide a complete national register of microform masters from which libraries might acquire prints when needed and thus avoid the expense of unnecessarily making another master; and
2. To help libraries assure the preservation of our intellectual heritage by identifying those microform masters that meet the requirements for such preservation.[12]

The *Register* does not list technical reports, foreign archival manuscript collections, United States dissertations, or newspapers.

The *Register* consists of two files: master negatives and master preservation negatives. Master negatives do not circulate; they are used only to produce positive copies. Master preservation negatives must neither circulate nor serve as copying media; they must be housed in a temperature-controlled, fireproof space and must be owned by a responsible, nonprofit institution.[13]

The *Register* is a well-conceived and important bibliographic tool. Some early blemishes that made it difficult to use have been corrected, and the reports that were so laborious to fill out have been eliminated. The *Register* is one of the most distinguished bibliographic achievements of recent years; it will steadily grow in importance and usefulness. Unfortunately, many American libraries know little of the *Register* and do not understand its function. The administrators of the *Register* are aware that a major publicity campaign should be launched to explain to the book community (libraries, publishers, and readers) the objectives, scope, and applications of the *Register*.

An additional national tool is needed to supply the analytics of microform series. Listing of microform negatives in the *National Register* does not solve the need of the individual library for bibliographic control of the series it has acquired. Like the *National Union Catalog*, the *National Register* does not make the catalogs of the individual library a superfluous and redundant luxury.

Libraries cannot file the series analytics because the cost involved would more than offset the savings gained by the purchase of the inexpensive microforms. Publishers are willing to, and in many cases do, supply series indexes, but no library can combine all the series it owns into one index.

A machine-readable index that could be frequently updated should be established to supply each library a "complete index" of all the series it owns. The index should provide a variety of access points, such as author, title, subject, and series. The machine—a combination of microfilm and computer—should be capable of furnishing printouts in tape, microfilm, or book form.

The index should include archival collections, although their cataloging differs basically from the cataloging of books. Librarians can learn much from archivists about the control of microforms. Annually, archives make around 25 million negative exposures and some 150 million images in positive copies. (Reports from 40 countries on production of negatives and from 26 on dissemination of positives suggest that archives have photographed about a half-billion negatives; the distribution of positive copies is obviously a multiple of this figure.)

Archives prefer to use 35mm microfilm. The major considerations in selecting items to be microfilmed are security (most dramatically emphasized by the irreplaceable losses during World Ward II); preservation (biochemical destruction of paper); space saving; reference service (many readers are satisfied to consult a microcopy); and publication (a microfilm publication is much less expensive than letterpress copy). Both the technical quality of the film and the bibliographic preparation of files before filming starts have been carefully considered by archivists. The following rules were prepared to govern archival reproduction:

1. Indexes, registers, lists, and other finding aids should be filmed before the records they govern. Thus indexes or registers at the end of a volume are filmed before the records in a volume.
2. Blank pages should not be filmed.
3. Endorsements, numbers, and other data appearing on the back of individual documents should be filmed before the text of the document.
4. Enclosures should be filmed immediately after letters of transmittal.
5. Guide cards and folder labels should not be filmed unless the information on them is essential to the user of the film.
6. Duplicate papers, disposable items, or records of no research value should not be filmed if they can easily be separated from the records or if they may be so identified that the camera operator will not film them.
7. Since documents in a folded file (such as those folded in thirds with enclosures also folded in thirds) are apt to become disarranged or lose their relationships if they are unfolded or flattened before they are filmed, it is usually best to have them unfolded and refolded by the camera operator.[14]

Archival microforms are frequently superior to those produced for (not by) the library community. Bibliographic control of archival materials is ahead of that achieved by libraries, and the Microfilming Committee of the International Council on Archives has urged "all member nations that have lists of their master negative microfilm that are free from legal restrictions on their use to publish and widely disseminate these lists with the end of increasing scholarly use of their records. Such lists should be kept up to date through the issuance of supplements or through regular revision. The Committee also urges archives that do not have such lists to prepare and publish them."[15]

The microform bibliography included as Appendix 4 to this report mirrors the bibliographic activities of archivists, for about one-third of the titles are devoted to archives. In many cases (publications of the United States National Archives) only the scope is indicated and full analytics are not given. The bibliography could have easily been tripled if all the available material had been included.

International bibliographic control of library and archival material may differ at times. But the identical goal of both is to furnish an efficient tool for the scholarly community. Thus, firm and cordial cooperation should be established between the ARL (and later, the International Federation of

Library Associations) and the Microfilming Committee of the International
Council on Archives.

INTERNATIONAL BIBLIOGRAPHIC CONTROL

The interest in microforms is global. Almost every country has photographed
books and documents; local control is often poor, and international control is
nonexistent. During the last twenty years, two events of international signifi-
cance occurred. At the Montevideo conference of the United Nations Educational Scientific and Cultural Organization (UNESCO) in 1954, it was decided
to establish a Mobile Microfilm Unit. From 1956 through 1970, these units
were sent to twenty-four countries to film valuable archival material in danger
of destruction, to train technicians, and to encourage the establishment of
national microfilm offices. Local experts selected archival material, printed
books, engravings, and drawings that were of sufficient value to justify
microreproduction.

Two microfilm copies were made. The negative remained in the country.
The positive, property of UNESCO, was deposited in one of four regional
centers: for Latin America, the Instituto Panamericano de Geografía y Historia, Comision de Historia, Mexico City (Ex. Arzobispado, 29, Tacubaya);
for the Arab nations, the Institute of Arab Manuscripts, Cairo; for Asia
(except for the Arab states), the Centre for East Asian Cultural Studies,
Oriental Library, Tokyo (2-28-21 Honkomagone, Nunkyo-ku); and for Africa
(except for the Arab states), the Ethiopian Studies Institute of the Haile
Selassie I University, Addis Ababa.

The units operated in Algeria, Barbados, Cambodia, Ceylon, Chile, Domini-
can Republic, Ethiopia, Federation of Arab Republics, Honduras, India, Iraq,
Korea, Libya, Malaysia, Morocco, Nepal, Panama, Paraguay, Peru, Philippines,
El Salvador, Sierra Leone, Singapore, and Sudan.

In 1963 UNESCO commissioned the Bibliothèque Nationale "to prepare a
study on how information on all types of microphotographic reproductions is
secured and distributed." The Bibliothèque Nationale mailed 185 question-
naires; only 35 (less than 20 percent) were returned with all questions
answered; another 28 answers were incomplete; 122 institutions (66 percent)
did not respond.[16]

The following synopsis of bibliographical control of microforms in 73
countries is based on a follow-up survey conducted for this study. Several
hundred letters were sent to libraries, scholarly institutions, and persons
interested in microreproduction; 75 percent were answered but the information was at times contradictory. The synopsis is therefore incomplete.

Algeria

A UNESCO Mobile Microfilm Unit visited Algeria.

Angola

The Biblioteca Nacional de Angola (Box 2915, Luanda, Angola), founded
recently, has no microform collection. The Instituto de Investigacão Cientifi-
ca de Angola (provincial office of the Centro de Documentacão Científica,

Portugal) handles microforms in the same way as books, both for local catalogs and for the union catalog of scientific libraries of Angola that is being compiled. No separate printed list of microforms is available, but they are included in the quarterly bibliographic bulletin.

Argentina

No information is available on processing of microforms in Argentina.

Australia

The National Library of Australia, Canberra, catalogs microforms in the same way as books, following Anglo-American rules and Library of Congress subject headings. Catalog cards for large sets in microform are interfiled. Classification is according to current numbers. A large part of the microform collection is uncataloged. Access is by a single temporary control entry. Manuscripts are listed in a separate catalog. The microcopy reading room has an author-title catalog for staff use. If the library holds the copyright for a negative, positives are sold.

The major Australian libraries buy much material on microform. Significant purchases are mentioned in the Australian Advisory Council on Bibliographic Services, *AACOBS Supplement* to the *Australian Library Journal*. They are also listed in the *Acquisitions Newsletter* published by the National Library five or six times a year.

The Queensland University Press, Brisbane, has published a catalog of available microfilms.

Austria

The Austrian National Library has a provisional cataloging rule for microforms. Classification is by sequential numbers. Title entries are the same as for books, with technical additions about film. Microform entries in classified catalogs are the same as book entries. Separate cards for microforms are kept near reading machines.

There is no union catalog of microcopies and no central agency where microcopies can be purchased. The large libraries have microfilm apparatus. The Austrian State Archives is systematically microfilming important archival material. In addition to public and university libraries, the International Atomic Energy Agency (11 Kärntner Ring, A-1010 Vienna) supplies photocopies.

Barbados

A UNESCO Mobile Microfilm Unit microfilmed documents at the Bridgetown Public Library.

Belgium

The Royal Library follows general rules in cataloging microforms. However, technical notes concerning reductions, number of exposures, etc., are added. Classification is by sequential numbers. Positive copies of negatives made by the library's photographic department are sold. The library has a small collection of Belgian newspapers on microfilm for sale. The national bibliography reports microfilms "in principle." Microforms are generally listed in scholarly periodicals of their respective fields. The Centre d'Histoire Contemporaine, University of Ghent, has a list of Belgian newspapers on microfilm.

The national libraries of Belgium and the Netherlands have an arrangement for exchanging manuscript reproductions on microfiche.

Brazil

In addition to public and university libraries, Laboratório de Reproduções Fotográficas, Instituto Brasileiro de Bibliografia e Documentação (Avenida General Justo 171, 40 andar, Rio de Janeiro) supplies photocopies.

Bulgaria

The National Library processes microfilms exactly as it does books, following the general Bulgarian cataloging rules. All microfilms are included in the catalogs open to readers. There is also an official catalog for microfilms. Upon request, positive copies are supplied. There is no union catalog or printed list of microfilms available. The library collects microfilms; other microforms such as microcards and microfiche are not collected.

In addition to public and university libraries, the Centre for Scientific and Technical Information and Documentation (rue "7 Novembre" No. 1, Sofia) supplies photocopies.

Cambodia

A UNESCO Mobile Microfilm Unit visited Cambodia.

Canada

Canadian libraries follow, on the whole, techniques adopted in the United States. Microfilms are arranged in broad groups (monographs, government documents, serials, theses) and shelved by sequential numbers. Microcards and microfiche are filed alphabetically by main entry. Microprints are classified according to the Library of Congress system. Probably in due time the National Library of Canada will function as a Canadian bibliographic center for microforms. The best-known publication is *Canadian Newspapers on Microfilm* issued by the Canadian Library Association. Another important service is *Canadian Theses on Microfilm,* a list of 7,000 dissertations available on microfilm. No comprehensive catalog of microfilms is available.

Ceylon

A UNESCO Mobile Microfilm Unit visited Ceylon.

Chile

A UNESCO Mobile Microfilm Unit visited Chile. In Santiago, 500,000 pages were filmed.

China (People's Republic)

No information received.

China (Taiwan)

Only a small part of China's microfilm collection has been processed; however, a catalog is planned. Large collections of negative microfilms of Chinese rare books are on hand, and positive copies can be bought.

In addition to public and university libraries, the Bureau of International Exchange of Publications, National Central Library (43 Nanhai Road, Taipei, Taiwan), supplies photocopies.

Colombia

In addition to public and university libraries, the Centro Interamericano de Vivienda y Planeamiento (Apartado Aereo 6209, Bogotá) supplies photocopies.

Costa Rica

In addition to public and university libraries, the Library and Documentation Service, Inter-American Institute of Agricultural Sciences (Turrialba), supplies photocopies.

Cuba

The National Library follows book regulations for cataloging microforms; however, microforms are not classified. Cards are filed in the public catalog and in a separate departmental catalog. No union list is available.

Czechoslovakia

The National Library keeps microforms separate from printed material. Cataloging entries follow book regulations; however, catalog cards carry brief technical notes. Only the most important microforms are listed in public catalogs. Only the library staff has access to a complete catalog of microforms. No printed list is available. Positive copies are sold on demand. There is no union catalog of microforms.

Denmark

The Royal Library handles microforms in the same way as printed books; however, they are shelved separately. Microforms are listed in the public catalogs, and positive copies are sold if copyright regulations permit. All Danish newspapers will eventually be microfilmed. A provisional list is available. There is no union catalog of microfilms in Denmark. The national bibliography does not list microcopies. The best commercial establishment is Minerva Mikrofilm in Copenhagen.

Dominican Republic

A UNESCO Mobile Microfilm Unit on its visit filmed 156,000 pages in the National Archives at Santo Domingo.

Ethiopia

No microfilms are kept at the Royal Library, and no microfilms are produced in the country; however, a UNESCO Microfilm Unit operated in Ethiopia, and the Haile Selassie I University is a regional center for microform deposits. Of special interest is the national Department of Fine Arts and Culture's *Catalogue of Manuscripts Microfilmed: Ethiopian Monasteries* (Addis Ababa, 1970).

Federation of Arab Republics

The Institute of Arab Manuscripts in Cairo keeps only microfilms. Descriptive cataloging follows standard rules. Microfilms are included in the public catalog; they are shelved separately, seemingly according to sequential number. Positive copies are sold if copyright regulations permit. There is no union catalog of microforms. No complete list of microforms is available, but printed lists on Islam, linguistics, Arabic literature, and Arabic history are available.

The manuscripts microfilmed by the UNESCO Mobile Unit have not been cataloged separately but are included in the Institute's catalog of microfilmed manuscripts. The Institute is one of the four regional centers for the deposit of UNESCO's positive microfilms.

Finland

The Helsinki University Library handles microforms in the same way as books. There is a special catalog for newspapers on microfilm. A catalog of Finnish newspapers is to appear shortly, and a catalog of foreign newspapers is in preparation. Positive copies are sold by a private firm, Oy Rekolid.

In addition to public and university libraries, the Keskuslavoratorio Central-laboratorium AB [Finnish Pulp and Paper Research Institute] (P.O. Box 136, Helsinki) supplies photocopies.

France

Interest in microforms and their bibliographic control is strong. Many libraries and scholarly institutes produce microfilms—for example, Archives de France, Institut de Recherche et d'Histoire des Textes, Centre National de la Recherche Scientifique. The Bibliothèque Nationale has had an active microfilm laboratory since 1937. Microcopies are not mentioned in the *Bibliographie de la France* and very often are overlooked in scholarly periodicals.

No central agency takes care of bibliographic control, although the Service Nationale de Microfilm and the Association pour la Conservation et la Reproduction Photographique de la Presse (ACRPP), Les Appareils Controleurs, are very active. The Archives Nationales has published four catalogs of microfilms in the Archives Nationales and in the Archives Departementales.

In addition to public and university libraries, and the above-mentioned agencies, photocopies can be obtained from Centre de Documentation de la Mécanique (11, avenue Hoche, Paris 8e); Centre International de l'Enfance, Service de Documentation, Section Microfilms-Photocopies (Château de Longchamp, Bois de Boulogne, Paris 16e); Centre National de la Recherche Scientifique, Service Photographique (15 quai Anatole France, Paris 7e); Centre Scientifique et Technique du Bâtiment (4 avenue de Recteur-Poincaré, Paris 16e); Commission Internationale des Industries Agricoles, Centre de Documentation (18 avenue de Villars, Paris 7e); Institut de Recherche et d'Histoire des Textes (15 quai Anatole France, Paris 7e); Institut National de la Propriété Industrielle (26 bis, rue de Léningrad, Paris 8e); Institut Pasteur, Service de Documentation Scientifique, Microfilms (25 rue du Docteur Roux, Paris 15e); Société de Productions Documentaires (28, rue St. Dominique, Paris 8e).

For further information, see "La Microcopie en France dans les Bibliothèques et Centres de Documentation," *Bulletin des Bibliothèques de France* 4 (1959): 161-182, 222-248.

German Democratic Republic

Processing of microforms is like that of printed material. All types of microreproduction are acquired and processed. They are entered in public catalogs. Copies of films are made only on specific demand. No other type of microform can be copied. The German national bibliography lists microforms in an appendix to Series A under the title "Microeditions."

The Deutsche Bücherei (701 Leipzig, Deutscher Platz 1) is the center for German national bibliography and responsible for all methodological questions in the field of bibliography.

The Methodisches Zentrum für Wissenschaftliche Bibliotheken (108 Berlin, Universitätstrasse 7) studies the use and storage of microforms.

Germany, Federal Republic of

Generally, microform cataloging follows accepted cataloging regulations. There is a special interest in microfilming German dailies, publications of German immigration, 1933-1945, and dissertations. There is no central depository for all microforms. An important institute, the Microfilm Archive of the German Press in Dortmund, has 35mm films. German libraries generally have large microform holdings. Complete bibliographic control has not been achieved.

In addition to public and university libraries, photocopies are supplied by Max-Planck-Gesellschaft zur Förderung der Wissenschaften E.V., Dokumentationsstelle (Bunsenstrasse 18, Göttingen).

Honduras

A UNESCO Mobile Microfilm Unit filmed 186,000 pages in the National Archives and the National Library.

Hungary

Processing of microforms follows general regulations. Technical information, such as number of frames, is added to the entry. All microforms are listed in the public catalog; they are filed in the general union catalog. No central bibliographic control exists, but individual libraries have published a number of special catalogs of their holdings: a microcard catalog of the Kaufmann Collection is available; lists published by the Hungarian National Archives are devoted to specific categories, for example, Austrian archival material, Romanian documents, and Czechoslovakian materials.

The promotion of reprography, which includes microfilming, is a matter of public interest in Hungary; it is currently discussed at the sessions of the National Committee for Technical Development.

The Microfilm Department of the National Archives, working with 35mm microfilm, is the oldest microfilm laboratory in Hungary. The National Széchényi Library (the National Library), mainly concerned with microphotography for preservation purposes, has a program for microfilming Hungarian newspapers.

The Hungarian Academy of Science produces 90mm microfilm and 9cm x 12cm microfiche. The first publications were the Oriental manuscripts from the Kaufmann Collection.

The National Technical Library and Documentation Center produces microfilm and microfiche 75mm x 125 mm. The National Bureau of Statistics and the National Bank of Hungary microfilm many records.

Of special interest is a paper by Laszlo Tohes in the Microfiche Foundation *Newsletter* 21 (February 1970).

Iceland

The National Library keeps only microfilm and microfiche. Cataloging regulations are like those for printed books; however, microforms are shelved separately in classified order. Positive films are not manufactured. Microfilms of manuscripts are not listed in the manuscript catalog, but a separate list is maintained in the department of manuscripts.

India

The use of microforms is comparatively limited. Generally, processing of microforms follows that of printed books. No union list exists. No library has published catalogs of microforms. In addition to public and university libraries, photocopies are supplied by INSDOC (Indian National Scientific Documentation Centre), National Laboratory of India (Hillside Road, New Delhi 12), and Microfilm and Photocopy Service Unit, Central Research Institute (Kasauli).

A UNESCO Mobile Microfilm Unit filmed 1,308 manuscripts from 38 institutions in 12 centers in India. Altogether the unit made 142,901 exposures and deposited 189 reels. A large part of the work was done in Calcutta.

Indonesia

Very few microforms are available in Indonesia, and most of them have not been cataloged. There is no union list of microforms and there is hardly any bibliographic control.

The Inter Documentation Company (Zug, Switzerland) is reproducing the Indonesian periodical holdings of Cornell University Libraries on microfiche; the company plans to publish a sales catalog.

The Museum Library (Perpustakaan Museum, Merdeka Barat 14, Djakarta) and the Modern Indonesia Project of Cornell University are cooperating in the microfilming of Indonesian newspapers in Djakarta. The negative and one positive copy are kept by the Cornell University Library and one positive copy in Djakarta. Cornell University will lend the positive copies on interlibrary loan, but no reproduction is permitted without authorization of the Indonesian authorities. No printed catalog is available.

Iran

The National Library reports that no microforms are used.

Iraq

A UNESCO Mobile Microfilm Unit visited Iraq.

Ireland

Most microforms are copies of manuscripts. They are cataloged in the same way as the originals. Examples are given in *Manuscript Sources for the History of Irish Civilization,* 11 volumes (Boston, 1965). Queen's University, Belfast, and the National Library, Dublin, are the biggest holders of microfilms. Both libraries are prepared to sell positive copies.

Israel

The Jewish National University Library collects only microfilm and microfiche. Processing regulations follow book procedure. Cards are interfiled in the general public catalog. There is no national union catalog of microforms.

In addition to public and university libraries, photocopies are supplied by Technion—Israel Institute of Technology (P.O. Box 4910, Haifa).

Italy

Processing regulations follow closely the general rules for printed books. Microreproductions of modern books are included in the public catalog. No general union catalog exists. Complete lists of microfilms (other microforms are seldom used) are apparently available only in official catalogs. No library can sell positive copies. There is no centralized bibliographic control. (Readers often are given microfilm copies in lieu of the old printed editions.)

An impressive amount of microreproduction has been done in Italy. Most tantalizing are the microfilms owned by the Instituto di Patologia del Libro in Rome (Via Milan 76). By 1969 the Institute had microfilmed 25,489 important manuscripts from 34 libraries carefully selected by the Ministry of Education (5,969 manuscripts are from the Biblioteca Laurenziana in Florence). Eight card catalogs list the manuscripts by author, provenance, former owners, name of scribes, date, and so forth. In the distant future, this list may be published in the *Bollettino* of the Institute. The libraries retain a negative and a positive copy for internal use and interlibrary loan; the Institute has another positive copy.

The Archivio dello Stato has a "Schedario Nazionale degli Archivi Fotoriprodotti." By 1960, 36 archives had microphotographic centers. The Biblioteca Nazionale Centrale in Rome has negative microfilms of 35 Italian newspapers, mostly in broken files. The Biblioteca Nazionale in Naples is microfilming its manuscripts. The entries are filed in a special catalog available only to the personnel of the Photographic Archive. The Biblioteca Nazionale in Turin has microfilmed 1,484 manuscripts on ballet and has both a negative and a positive of each. Handwritten entries are filed in special catalogs open to the public.

In addition to public and university libraries, photocopies are supplied by Centro Italiano di Documentazione (CID) (Foro Buonaparte, 31, Milano); Centro Nazionale di Documentazione Scientifica (Piazzale delle Scienze, 7 Roma); Centro Nazionale Meccanico Agricolo (Via O. Vigliani, 104, Torino); Fondazione Mario Donati, Centre d'etudes pour la Médecine et la Chirurgie (Via Festa del Perdono 3, Milano).

Japan

Microfilms are officially processed in the same way as books. Other microforms are not processed. Japanese and Chinese literature follow 1965 Nippon cataloging rules. Western books are cataloged according to Anglo-American cataloging rules.

Microforms are shelved separately from books; they are classified according to the National Diet Library Classification Table, "Special Materials Y." Microforms are grouped by periodicals, newspapers, documents, and books. Subject cataloging is according to the National Diet Library List of Subject Headings. Catalog cards are filed in all public catalogs. Positive copies are not sold. There is no general bibliographic control, but important catalogs have been published. The National Diet Library published in 1970 *Zenkoku Shimbun Microfilm Seisaku Shozo Ichiran* (List of microfilms of newspapers). The National Bibliography lists microfilms "if the leading deposit principle has been observed." There is a strong possibility that the deposit rules are not observed and the microforms are not entered in the National Bibliography. The Japan Microfilm Service Center has published a catalog of Japanese books on microfilm. Toyo Bunko mentions a union catalog of microforms not for sale.

The organization interested in microfilms is Nihon Microfilm Association (Tokuwa Building, Uchi-Kanda, Chiyoda-ku, Tokyo).

The University of Tokyo Press expects to publish both current books and part of their backlist on microfiche.

In addition to public and university libraries, Japan Information Center of Science and Technology (15 Itibantyo, Tiyoka-ku, C.P.O. Box 1478, Tokyo) supplies photocopies.

A UNESCO Mobile Microfilm Unit visited Japan. The Center for East Asian Cultural Studies in Tokyo is a regional center for UNESCO film deposit.

Republic of Korea

A UNESCO Mobile Microfilm Unit visited the Republic of Korea. Korea Research Center has 500 reels of microfilm, mostly of Korean material.

Libya

A UNESCO Mobile Microfilm Unit visited Libya.

Luxembourg

The national library in Luxembourg does not collect microforms.

Madagascar

Cataloging and classification regulations follow rules for books. Entries are in the public catalog. Positive copies are not sold. There is no union catalog of microforms.

Malaysia

A UNESCO Mobile Microfilm Unit visited Malaysia.

Mexico

In addition to public and university libraries, photocopies are supplied by Departmento de Bibliotecas y Servicios Bibliográficos, Centro de Investigación y de Estudios Avanzados del Institute Politecnico Nacional (Enrico Martínez No. 25, Mexico 1, D.F.).

The Instituto Panamericano de Geografía y Historia, Comision de Historia, in Mexico City (Ex. Arzobispado, 29, Tacubaya) is one of the regional depositories for microfilm made by the UNESCO Mobile Microfilm Unit.

Monaco

No libraries in this territory use microforms.

Morocco

A UNESCO Mobile Microfilm Unit visited Morocco.

Nepal

A UNESCO Mobile Microfilm Unit visited Nepal.

Netherlands

The Royal Library has not cataloged any microforms. Microforms are not mentioned in the national bibliography. There is a growing stock of newspapers on negative microfilm. A list may be published in the future and positive copies may be sold.

The national libraries of the Netherlands and Belgium have an arrangement for the exchange of manuscript reproduction on microfiche.

The Netherlands is extremely interested in microfiche. The International Microfiche Center is located at 177 Rijnsburgerweg, Leiden, and the Microfiche Foundation, with headquarters at the Technical University Library, is at 76 Nieuwelaan, Delft.

In addition to public and university libraries, photocopies are supplied by Nederlands Instituut voor Documentatie en Rigistratuur (Bezuidenhoutseweg 43, s'Gravenhage).

New Zealand

The National Library answered queries only about microfilm. Microfilms are cataloged in the same way as book material; however, they are not classified but divided into sections on microfilms of printed material not in the library (micro), manuscripts (micro ms.), and material held by the library in some other form (copy micro). Entries are in the public catalog. Positive copies are sold. Microfilm copies of manuscripts are also listed in the union catalog of manuscripts.

Nigeria

The national library in Lagos reports that all microforms are cataloged in the same way as book material; however, instead of collation, exposures are recorded. Call numbers are prefixed by the term "microfilm" when appropriate. All entries are filed in the public catalogs. There is no printed list of microforms.

Norway

Cataloging and classification of microforms is no different from the processing of printed material. Microforms are shelved separately. All microforms are listed in public catalogs. There is no printed list of microforms and no union catalog. Micropublications are not recorded in the national bibliography.

Universitetsforlaget, publishers to the Norwegian universities, did not publish microforms during 1971-1972; the question was to be reconsidered for the year 1972-1973.

Panama

A UNESCO Mobile Microfilm Unit filmed 150,000 pages in the National Library, National Archives, and the University Library.

Paraguay

A UNESCO Mobile Microfilm Unit visited Paraguay. The National Archives have 200,000 pages on film.

Peru

Microforms are processed like books. The call number is prefixed by "m" to indicate microfilm (apparently, no other microforms are collected and cataloged). There is no printed list of microforms and no national union catalog. Many Peruvian libraries have microform collections.

A UNESCO Mobile Microfilm Unit visited Peru.

Philippines

Cataloging of microforms basically follows the processing of printed material, though it is often simplified. Classification is on a broad subject basis. All microforms are listed in the public catalog. There is no printed list, but the national library has a mimeographed list. The collection of microforms is comparatively small.

The University of the Philippines has a separate microfilm reading room. It plans to publish a list of Philippine materials on microfilm under the title *Filipiniana on Microfilms*. It also plans to print a list of all University of the Philippines theses and dissertations on microfilm.

A UNESCO Mobile Microfilm Unit visited the Philippines.

Poland

Cataloging and classification appear to follow the processing of printed book material. There is no union catalog. Both the National Library and the National Archives have a very extensive film program, mainly for preservation.

Polish libraries are extremely interested in microforms and have published detailed standards. The National Library has published 15 catalogs of microfilms. Other catalogs have been published by the Catholic University in Lublin, by the Polish Archives in Warsaw, and by the Polish Academy of Sciences. The Workers' Party in Poland has published *The History of the Party* in three volumes.

Portugal

The National Library in Lisbon does not collect and catalog microfilms and does not know anything about any other microforms.

In addition to public and university libraries, photocopies are supplied by Arquivo Historico Ultramarino (Calcada da Boa Hora, Palacio da Ega, Lisboa), Centro de Documentação Científica (Campos dos Martires da Pátria, Lisboa), and Laboratório Nacional de Engenharia Civil, Seccão de Documentação (Avenida do Brasil, Lisboa).

Rhodesia

Libraries follow the same standard rules for processing microforms as for books. Some libraries do not classify but shelve by sequential number.

Microforms are listed in all catalogs; however, the number of microforms is very small. The National Free Library in Bulawayo has a national union catalog for books, which also contains cards for microforms. There is no printed catalog for microforms; the National Archives of Rhodesia plans to make available a duplicate list of their microfilms.

Romania

Cataloging and classification of microforms follow standard rules for books with the addition of specific elements for microforms such as number of reels, positive or negative, and location of the original. Microforms are not listed in the public catalog but in a separate catalog in the microform reading room available to the public. There is no union catalog for microforms but the matter is being discussed.

El Salvador

A UNESCO Mobile Microfilm Unit filmed 280,000 pages in El Salvador.

Senegal

In addition to public and university libraries, photocopies are supplied by Institut Français d'Afrique Noire (B.P. 206, Dakar).

Sierra Leone

According to the Sierra Leone Library Board, microfilms are not used in any library.
  A UNESCO Mobile Microfilm Unit visited Sierra Leone.

Singapore

The National Library uses the same cataloging code for books as for microfilms. Only 35mm films are collected and processed. Where appropriate, call numbers are stamped "Available on Microfilm." All microforms are entered in public catalogs. Positive copies are sold from negatives held by the library. There is no printed list of microfilms, but special mimeographed lists are issued from time to time. The Library Associations of Singapore and Malaysia are very much interested in the microfilming technique; they are discussing joint projects to investigate microfilm resources, present microfilming programs, and coordinate with national and international libraries.
  Lists published by the Singapore National Library include *Singapore and Malaysia Newspapers in English; Straits Settlement Despatches; Straits Settlement Records; Early Singapore Imprints; Singapore and Malaysian Journals;* and *Southeast Asia Studies (nonscientific).*
  A UNESCO Mobile Microfilm Unit visited Singapore.

South Africa

The cataloging of microfilms does not differ from the processing of printed books. They are not classified but arranged by sequential number. There is no union list or printed catalog.

Spain

Little work is being done on microforms; however, the reorganization plans of the National Library include a complete photographic laboratory and a microfilm archive and reading room.

The government of Spain, the Organization of American States, and University Microfilms will microfilm the *Archivo General de Indias* (Seville).

In addition to public and university libraries, photocopies are supplied by Consejo Superior de Investigaciónes (Serrano 117, Madrid); Junta de Energía Nuclear, Servicio Documentación, Biblioteca y Publicaciónes (Ciudad Universitaria, Madrid 3).

Spain's Servicio Nacional de Microfilm issues a *Boletín* devoted to microfilm service.

Sudan

A UNESCO Mobile Microfilm Unit visited Sudan.

Sweden

The cataloging of microforms does not differ much from the handling of printed books; however, collation is omitted. Shelving follows sequential numbering by class for books, manuscripts, newspapers, microcards, and microfiche.

Microforms are listed in an alphabetical catalog and in a journal that are available to the library staff only.

Rekolid in Stockholm produces microfilms of Swedish daily newspapers.

Switzerland

Microforms are processed in the same way as printed books. In descriptive cataloging, the bibliographic data of the original are given first; film data are noted in the footnotes. Microforms are not used too much in Swiss libraries. The National Library sells positives from negatives it owns.

The microforms produced in Switzerland are listed in the national bibliography. The largest collection of microforms is in the Swiss Federal Institute of Technology in Zurich.

Thailand

The microform collection is small and has not been processed. Reorganization plans call for "a well-organized collection of microforms in the short future."

Turkey

No processing of any microforms is done in any library in Turkey.

In addition to public and university libraries, photocopies are supplied by Mikrofilm Servisi, National Library (Milli Kütüphane, Ankara).

Union of Soviet Socialist Republics

The Lenin National Library and the other major libraries of the country have important collections of microfilms. Seemingly no other type of microform is collected and kept. For preservation purposes, Soviet libraries microfilm many of their publications. They also collect microfilms of publications from other libraries.

Microfilms are processed under the same rules that apply to printed books. In a drop note, the technical description of the microfilm is given. Microfilms appear to be classified by "location number." There is no center for the bibliographic control of microforms.

The Four Continent Book Corporation in New York City accepts orders for Russian microfilms. A list has been published by this corporation.

United Kingdom

The British Museum and most other British libraries catalog both books and microforms according to standard processing regulations. A footnote is added explaining that the item is a microform. All microforms are shelved separately.

All microforms are included in the public catalog. Individual libraries have printed lists of their holdings; for example, the British Museum has a catalog of newspapers on microfilm and the National Library of Scotland has a publication *Out of Print Works and Manuscripts on Microfilm Held in the Scottish Central Library* (1962). There is no national union catalog, but the National Lending Library of Science and Technology at Boston Spa, which has a very large collection of microforms, claims to fulfill most of the functions of the United States *National Register of Microform Masters*. A National Reprographic Center for Documentation was established in 1967 at the Hatfield Polytechnic Institute, Hatfield, Hertfordshire. (See *UNESCO Bulletin for Libraries* 21, 1967, page 164.)

There is a great interest in all microforms, and individual libraries and organizations have done a great amount of microfilming. A Council for Microphotography tries to integrate microform activities. The British Public Record Office has microfilmed much archival material and is currently engaged in a number of filming projects. Many local record offices have negative microfilms and positive copies are offered for sale. For instance, a catalog has been received from the Essex County Record Office.

In addition to public and university libraries, photocopies are supplied by British Plastics Federation (47/48 Piccadilly, London, W.1); British Overseas Airways Corporation (P.O. Box 10, Hounslow, Middlesex); British Glass Industry Research Association (Northumberland Road, Sheffield 10); British Institute of Management (80 Fetter Lane, London, E.C. 4); British Scientific Instrument Research Association (South Hill, Chislehurst, Kent); Building Research Station (Bucknall's Lane, Garston, Watford, Hertford); Electrical Research Association (Cleeve Road, Leatherhead); Zinc Development Association (34 Berkeley Square, London, W.1).

Vatican City

The Biblioteca Vaticana has produced a catalog of microfilms for sale.

Venezuela

The National Library in Caracas does not collect or process microforms.

Yugoslavia

Microforms are cataloged and classified in the same way as printed books. The National Library in Belgrade has a large collection of microfilms of manuscripts. All microforms are listed in the public catalog and positive copies of negatives handled by the libraries can be sold, if copyright regulations permit.

No printed list of microfilms is available, but such a project is under discussion. There is no union catalog of microforms.

In addition to public and university libraries, Jugoslovenski Centar za Tehnicku i Naucnu Dokumentaciju (Yugoslavian Centre for Technical and Scientific Documentation) (Admirala Geprata 16, Beograd) supplies photocopies.

It is evident that a staggering amount of microphotography has been done all over the world. A very good guess would put the volume at 2 billion pages in negative exposures, and the positive copies are, of course, a multiple of this figure. One American microform publisher has microcopies of about 170 million pages in his archives; the *National Register of Microform Masters* records about 150 million pages.

Not even the rudiments of an international bibliographic control exist. The need for control is felt by librarians, archivists, and the entire scholarly community. (One isolated attempt at a coordinating mechanism is the Microfilm Committee of the International Council on Archives.) No response has been made to the following recommendations that the Bibliothèque Nationale offered in 1965:

> It is desirable, in each country, to improve the bibliographic control of microcopies, whether they be on sale or merely used for the printing of positive copies at the instance of individuals: the best means of ensuring this control appears to be the compilation by national centres of registers of master microfilms, whether developed negatives or virtual microcopies. According to the structure of its record offices and research establishments, each country could have either a single national centre or a number of centres, each specializing in one or more categories of documents. Initial information should be supplied to the national centres in standardized form by the producers. So long as such information could not be reliably obtained from the producers, it should be sought out by the national centres by

all suitable means. National centres responsible for the registers in question should issue, not less than once a year, systematic lists of completed or projected microcopies; obviously, too, there should be interchange of information between them at the international level along the same lines as between national centers for international exchanges or interlibrary loans. In a number of cases the proper place for such bodies would be attached to the national loan or union catalogue centres.[17]

Year after year, a bewildering number of microforms have been produced without any effort at coordination or care that a record of operations is widely available. Mankind is simply not rich enough to permit such a waste. At the same time that a great amount of needed microphotography of books and archival documents, both for preservation and easier access, is neglected, some titles are photographed more than once because no record exists of work done. The Association of Research Libraries, the International Federation of Library Associations, UNESCO, and other interested agencies should make every effort to promote the international bibliographic control of microforms.

Notes

9. Keyes D. Metcalf, "Care and cataloging of microfilms," *Bulletin of the American Library Association* 31 (1937): 72-74.

Irvin Stewart, "Microphotography for Scholarly Purposes," *Journal of Documentary Reproduction* 4 (1941): 44-52.

10. Edwin E. Williams, *Conference on International Cultural, Educational and Scientific Exchanges,* Princeton University, Nov. 25-26, 1946 (Chicago: American Library Association, 1947).

11. Wesley C. Simonton, "Bibliographic Control of Microforms," *Library Resources and Technical Services* 6 (1962): 29-40.

12. *National Register of Microform Masters, 1969* (Washington, D.C.: Library of Congress, 1970), p. v.

13. Ibid.

14. Albert H. Leisinger, Jr., *Microphotography for Archives* (Washington, D.C.: International Council on Archives, 1968), p. 22.

15. "Report of Microfilming Committee of the International Council on Archives, Presented . . . by Albert H. Leisinger, Jr., Secretary," *Archivum* 18 (1968): 52.

16. Bibliothèque Nationale (Paris), "Bibliographic Control of Microcopies," *UNESCO Bulletin for Libraries* 19 (1965): 136-60.

17. Ibid.

CHAPTER FOUR

Conclusions and Recommendations

Technology and its products are not a panacea, the computer does not solve all library problems, reading cannot be equated with information retrieval, and microimages will not render printed books superfluous. However, the librarian must be familiar with the computer and automation and must use machines whenever warranted; information retrieval is a significant part of library work and microforms a substantial segment of libraries' holdings.

The descriptive cataloging of microforms should follow established rules. It should be practically identical with the cataloging of the original except for notes identifying the item as a microimage. Notes designating type of microimage and number of reels or fiche are generally deemed essential.

Maurice Tauber suggested in 1940 that "cataloging of films is both desirable and necessary, classification is neither."[18] Classification of other microforms is also unnecessary, as is use of the first two letters of Library of Congress classification to split up the microform collection among departments of a library. Selection for a departmental library does not fully match library classification. Moreover, long and bitter experience has proved how dangerous it is to shortcut basic rules of processing.

Libraries cannot cope with the burden of analyzing the many large series on microform they have acquired; moreover, the size of public catalogs is increasing much too rapidly. Therefore, a national, machine-readable index of microform publications that can be broken down into a multiplicity and variety of indexes tailored to the particular needs of a given library should be established.

Libraries should be protected against inferior reproduction methods. As Allen Veaner pointed out in 1967, "the performance of many micropublishers has been far from satisfactory. Films have been sold without leaders or trailers, with unlabelled boxes; inadequately processed films have been offered; excessive reduction has been used by some stingy producers to save a few pennies worth of film. Every conceivable technical and bibliographic fault has been present in all but a few micropublications."[19] He later concluded, in his standard book on micropublications, "Individual libraries can accomplish only a small portion of the immense task of inspecting and evaluating . . . all micropublications. There is therefore a need for the establishment of a national testing and certifying agency for micropublications . . . as recommended to A.R.L."[20]

Excellent norms for controlling production have been worked out by the Copy Methods Section of the American Library Association. They have to be enforced, and every attempt should be made to reach an international agreement. Copyright legislation should be broadened to give some protection to bona fide publishers of microforms. International consistency should be sought so that microforms will be listed in national bibliographies. National microform centers must be established if bibliographic control of all microforms on a worldwide basis is to be achieved.

Specific recommendations:

1. The Library of Congress should give high priority to the processing of microforms. It should consider the inclusion of microforms and analytics for them in the MARC project.

2. Professional journals should publish papers that stress the importance of assigning adequate manpower to the processing and servicing of microforms.

3. A detailed cost and feasibility study of a machine-readable index for analytics of series in microform should be made. The national index should be capable of providing a complete index for all the series any given library possesses.

4. Every effort should be made to support the *National Register of Microform Masters.* The Library of Congress should engage in a major publicity campaign through papers in professional journals and speeches at professional meetings to explain the objectives, scope, and uses of the *National Register.* The Library of Congress should identify departments and individuals in American libraries responsible for reporting to the *National Register* and should maintain systematic contact with them.

5. A national microform agency should be established to set standards for both production and bibliographic control of microform publications. It should evaluate all forthcoming microform publications and promote the proper processing and servicing of microform collections. It should provide an up-to-date international microform bibliography and directory of microform publishers.

6. Establishment of national centers to set and enforce norms for the production and bibliographic control of microforms should be encouraged. Efforts to establish identical norms and coordination between centers all over the world should be promoted.

7. Copyright legislation should be modified to include protection of the product of bona fide publishers of microforms. Parallel legislation in all countries should be sought so that microforms may be included in national bibliographies.

8. Norms for the production and bibliographic control of microforms should be enforced.

9. Every effort should be made to have identical norms established all over the world.

Notes

18. Maurice F. Tauber, "Cataloging and Classifying Microfilms," *Journal of Documentary Reproduction* 3 (1940): 10-25.
19. Allen B. Veaner, "Developments in Reproduction of Library Materials and Graphic Communications, 1967," *Library Resources and Technical Services* 12 (1968): 203-14, 467.
20. Allen B. Veaner, *The Evaluation of Micropublications; A Handbook for Librarians,* an LTP Publication No. 17 (Chicago: Library Technology Program, American Library Association, 1971).

Appendixes

The United States Government as Microform Publisher

SOURCE: U.S. Business and Defense Services Administration. *Microforms: A Growth Industry* (Washington, D.C.: U.S. Government Printing Office, 1969).

TABLE 1

Estimate of Microfilm Consumption by Selected Government Agencies
(in thousands of feet)

Bureau of the Census (1967)	750
Internal Revenue Service (Fiscal 1967)	2,086
Library of Congress (Fiscal 1967)	7,434
National Archives and Record Services (Fiscal 1967)	6,111
National Library of Medicine (Fiscal 1967)	520
Patent Office (1967)	794
Social Security Administration (Fiscal 1968)	15,500
Total	33,195

SOURCE: Agencies named provided information.

TABLE 2

Estimate of Microfiche Sold or Distributed by Government Agencies in 1967
(number of microfiche)

Distributed Internally

    Atomic Energy Commission (Fiscal 1967)   3,000,000

    Defense Documentation Center   800,000[1]

    Educational Research Information
      Center (Office of Education)   630,000[2]

    National Aeronautics and Space
      Administration   8,000,000[3]

Sold

    Clearinghouse for Federal Scientific
      and Technical Information   1,500,000

    Educational Research Information
      Center (Office of Education)   560,000[4]

[1] 214,000 additional microfiche duplicated and sold by CFSTI.
[2] In 1966, ERIC distributed internally approximately 283,000 microfiche.
[3] In 1966, NASA distributed internally approximately 6,500,000 microfiche.
[4] Microfiche sold for ERIC by commercial contractor.
SOURCE: Agencies named provided information.

A Machine-Readable Index for Microsets

Henriette D. Avram and
Harry Gochman

SOURCE: MARC Development Office, Library of Congress

The purpose of this appendix to the report is to describe a possible method of using the computer and associated hardware devices to produce one or more indexes to be used as a finding tool to the material contained in microsets. A variety of solutions can be postulated, but in the context of this report only one has been discussed in any detail. It is important to note that costs cannot be estimated for an operation at this early stage of its development. Many variables exist which affect cost and are unknown at this time, for example, the number of data elements that make up the bibliographic description of each title, the number of titles contained in the universe of microsets, the actual computer and associated devices to be used, the location of the editors and keypunch staff (geographic location affecting salary scales), etc.

Certain assumptions had to be made to perform the analysis leading to the methodology elaborated on in this section. These assumptions are listed as follows:

1. The basic bibliographic record for each title in the microsets contains the following data elements:
   a. Author headings(s) (one or more author headings, corporate or personal, or uniform title heading associated with the work)
   b. Subject(s) (one or more subject terms)
   c. Short title
   d. Editor or translator statement when there is one
   e. Edition
   f. Imprint date
   g. Publisher
   h. Set number and item number within the set
   i. Unique number assigned to each title
2. Three indexes will be produced:
   a. Author index, a main listing in author/title sequence containing all of the data elements of the bibliographic description
   b. Subject index containing a subset of data elements of the bibliographic description
   c. Title index containing a subset of the data elements of the bibliographic description
3. The first edition will contain indexes to 100,000 titles.
4. Each title has an average of 1.6 authors (personal and corporate names and uniform title headings).[1] Therefore, the author index will contain approximately 160,000 entries with full information.
5. Each title has an average of 1.5 subjects.[2] Therefore the subject index will contain approximately 150,000 entries.
6. Each supplement of the indexes will contain entries representing corrections made to the previous issue, whether the latter was a complete

1. Based on information contained in "Selected Statistics Based on LC MARC Bibliographic Records: Cumulated Statistics for vol. 1, nos. 1-54, March 1969-March 1970" by Gerald L. Swanson. Columbia University Libraries Systems Office. September 1970. Technical note no. 2.
   2. Ibid.

edition or an earlier supplement (corrected entries will be marked with a unique symbol).

The processing required for the indexes may be considered as having three major components: (1) input and maintenance; (2) generation of indexes; (3) output.

(1) INPUT AND MAINTENANCE

It is assumed that an editorial staff exists in some institution. The staff is composed of a librarian as a supervisor, editors (a term used for individuals who explicitly identify bibliographic data elements by the addition of tags to the source document), input typists, and clerks. The number of staff required is dependent on the number of records to be processed daily and thus dictates the total elapsed time for the completion of any phase of the project, i.e., the first edition of the 100,000 titles and the continuing supplements.

The source document could take many forms—a Library of Congress catalog card, a typed worksheet, etc. The editors tag the data elements—the main entry is uniquely marked, the title, etc. If the number of data elements is minimal and the explicit tagging simple to apply, the actual tagging could be performed by the typist during the input phase. (Another method, depending on the source document and the tagging scheme, is for the typist to input the text characters without the associated tags and have the tags assigned by the computer program. The typist indicates the end of a data element and the beginning of a new data element by a series of function codes, i.e., spaces, tabs, carriage returns, etc. This method reduces the amount of manual keying and also human effort required to assign tags but increases the complexity of the input program.) The record is passed on to the typist who uses a keying device (for example, keypunch, magnetic tape inscriber, paper tape punch) to record the data into machine-readable form. The resultant media (magnetic tape, punched paper tape, punched card) is fed into the computer, a unique number is added by computer to each new record, and a proofsheet is printed via the computer printer for each title input. The proofsheet is returned to the editors for proofing the machine-readable record against the source documents. Errors are noted and corrections made on the proofsheet. The corrections are typed and input to update the affected machine-readable record. During the correction cycle, another proofsheet is produced for each title corrected but a new unique number is not added to the corrected record. This cyclic process is repeated until the record is declared error free. The record then passes from a working file to a master file of verified records, which is in unique number order.

Any time a transaction is made to a record on the working file, the computer assigns a new value to a date field (hereafter referred to as the date of last transaction). The date of last transaction is subsequently used to control by date span the records selected from the master data base to produce a particular supplement.

The process described above is a batch off-line process. New and/or correction records could be input on line. A decision as to a best method, i.e., off-line vs. on-line, is dependent on many factors that cannot be accurately evaluated at this time without a more precise definition of operating characteristics. However, based on experience at other institutions, on-line correction does facilitate the logistic problems associated with the recording of bibliographic records into machine-readable form.

(2) GENERATION OF INDEXES

This section describes a procedure for the production of the first edition of the indexes (hereafter referred to as edition 1), supplement(s) to that edition, and a second edition. The procedure described ends with the generation of tapes containing the index entries in a form suitable for publication. The publication procedure itself is described in the section labelled *Output*.

When the time arrives to publish the first edition of the indexes, each of the records on the master file is used to generate a set of index entries. The number of author index entries derived from a bibliographic record will equal the number of authors carried in the record. Similarly, the number of subject index entries will be the same as the number of subjects carried in the record. Only a single title index entry will be derived from a bibliographic record. Each type of index entry generated is written onto its own output tape: the author index entries to tape A1, the title index entries to tape T1, and the subject index entries to tape S1. Each entry contains the unique number associated with its parent bibliographic record.

Each index tape is then sorted on the key or keys[3] appropriate to it, i.e., author, title, and subject, and written onto tapes A2, T2, and S2. This last set of tapes is used to generate a set of print tapes, which become the primary input to the publication procedure used to produce edition 1.

New bibliographic records, each assigned its own unique number, are accepted into the system after the publication of edition 1 and follow the input and maintenance procedures described above. These eventually reside on the master tape. Along with these new records, corrections to old records (those which formed part of edition 1) are introduced. Each correction carries the unique number of the bibliographic record to which it is to be applied, and the incorrect record is transferred from the master file to the working file. The input, maintenance, and verification procedure applies these corrections to their associated bibliographic records and places a corrected form of the record onto the master tape. Actually what is being produced is an updated version of the master tape which eventually carries the following bibliographic records:

1. All verified records which did not have corrections applied to them;

---

3. The keys are computer generated and assume programs designed to effect the filing requirements of the published indexes. Since the index entries are displayed in a page format and not in a blind file, such as a card catalog, economics may dictate that the entries be sorted in straight alphabetic sequence.

2. The corrected forms of those records which have had corrections applied to them;
3. All new records placed onto the master tape since the publication of edition 1.

When the time arrives to publish the first supplement to edition 1 (supplement 1), the master file is scanned, and each bibliographic record whose date of last transaction falls into the date span for the supplement is selected. Each new record is used to generate its associated set of index entries, just as was done in the processing for edition 1. Each corrected record also has a set of associated index entries generated.

Each of the three types of index entries (author, title, and subject) is written onto its own output tape, tapes $A1'$, $T1'$, and $S1'$ respectively. Entries of a given type derived from new records or corrected records go onto the same tape. For corrected records, this includes both the correction entry and, under certain circumstances, a deletion entry (to remove the incorrect entry from the tape).

Each of these last-named tapes is then sorted on the key or keys appropriate to it and the sorted entries output onto tapes $A2'$, $T2'$, and $S2'$. Supplement 1 print tapes are then generated. In the course of the generation of the print tapes, deletion entries are ignored. That is, they are retained within the set of index entries but they are not transfered to the print tapes. The corrected entries contain a special character which marks•this entry as a correction to one previously published. The print tapes so produced are then used in the publication of supplement 1.

The supplement 1 procedure requires one last step. This consists of merging the new, correction, and deletion index entries which represent supplement 1 with the index entries generated for edition 1. The former reside, in sorted order, on tapes $A2'$, $T2'$, and $S2'$ while the latter, also in sorted order, are to be found on tapes A2, T2, and S2. In the course of each merge, a corrected entry causes the replacement of the incorrect entry with itself; a deletion entry simply deletes the incorrect entry from the file.

The merges produce three output tapes, Tapes A3, T3, and S3, which carry all of the index entries generated to date, with all corrections made. (A more detailed explanation of the correction technique is described in Addendum A at the end of this appendix.)

Each succeeding supplement to edition 1 is processed as described above resulting in all index entries merged into three index data files, i.e., author index file, title index file, and subject index file. These files, the most recently produced A3, T3, S3 tapes, become the data for the publication of the next edition.

In order to arrive at even a rough estimate of the computer time it would take to produce edition 1 and supplement 1 (these estimates do not include machine time for input and maintenance of new correction records or printing of the proofslips), certain assumptions had to be made. The assumptions concerning the machine configuration are stated in Addendum B, while those relating to the data itself are given in Addendum C. The resulting time estimates are as follows:

Procedure for Edition 1

To create index entries:	36 minutes
To sort index entries:	3 hours, 34 minutes
To create print images:	52 minutes
Total	5 hours, 2 minutes

Allowing some additional time for job setup and tape handling brings this estimate to: 5 hours, 15 minutes

Procedure for Supplement 1

To create index entries for new and corrected bibliographic records:	36 minutes
To sort new and corrected index entries:	12 minutes
To merge these entries with last accumulated file:	1 hour
Total	1 hour, 48 minutes

Allowing some additional time for job setup and tape handling brings this estimate to: 2 hours

(3) OUTPUT

This section discusses the principal means by which the print tapes could be converted to human-readable form. Although these techniques apply both to the major edition(s) as well as any supplement run, the calculations pertain only to the edition 1 since the calculation is based on the assumed 100,000 titles.

One method is to use a line printer to produce hard copy. The number of print lines required are based on the following calculations:

1. An author index entry requires approximately 250 print positions including spaces, or 2 print lines. The number of print line positions on a page is 66. If 3 line positions are allowed at the top of a page and 5 at the bottom as margins, and 8 line positions (including 3 for vertical spacing) for data element headers, the result is 50 data lines or 25 entries on a page. Therefore, 160,000 entries require 6,400 pages or 320,000 lines plus 32,000 (5 x 6,400) header lines, resulting in a total of 352,000 print lines.
2. A title index entry requires approximately 160 print positions including spaces, or 2 print lines. As calculated above, there are 25 entries on a page. Therefore, 100,000 entries require 4,000 pages or 200,000 data lines plus 20,000 (5 x 4,000) header lines, resulting in a total of 220,000 print lines.

3. A subject index entry requires approximately 160 print positions or 2 print lines. As calculated above, there are 25 entries on a page. Therefore, 150,000 entries require 6,000 pages or 300,000 data lines plus 30,000 (5 x 6,000) header lines, resulting in a total of 330,000 print lines.

The total for all three index runs is 902,000 print lines or 16,400 pages.

If a two-column format were adopted then, depending on the precise entry format used, it might be possible to put more entries on a page and thus reduce the number of pages required.

There are line printers (of the impact type) which are rated at 2,000 lines a minute. Such a printer would take just over 8,000 minutes (133 hours, 20 minutes) to complete the printing of the three indexes. However, printers of the type in more general use are rated at around 1,100 lines a minute. Such a device would require 242 hours to produce the indexes.

A number of printers could be used working in parallel. Each of the indexes could be segmented by alphabet into sections with a print tape being produced for each segment and the printers used simultaneously. This method would shorten print time but requires additional equipment.

The process described above produces at the most six legible (original and five carbons) copies of the indexes. For larger quantities of copies, a single hard copy can be produced on a line printer (or printers), the copy photo-reduced and then used to reproduce as many copies as desired. The cost of reproduction must be taken into account.

Another possible method makes use of microfilm techniques. The print images are formated so that they can be read (from magnetic tape) and interpreted by a Computer Output Microfilm (COM) device. This device converts these images into frames on a microfilm master. A variety of different frame sizes (number of lines per frame) are provided on most COM units. These usually vary from 32 line positions per frame (with 66 character positions per line). Thus a frame, equivalent to a standard hard copy page (66 lines positions at 132 character positions per line), is readily available. The indexes would require 16,400 frames.

A COM unit with an input tape speed of 50,000 bits per second can produce microfilm frames at the following rates:

1. For the author index entries (25 entries per frame with 227 character positions per entry, plus 250 header characters per frame), the frame rate equals 2.4 frames a second.
2. For the title index entries (same as (1) above except that there are 150 character positions per entry), the frame rate equals 2.7 frames a second.
3. For the subject index entries (same as (2) above), the frame rate equals 2.7 frames a second.

The 160,000 author index entries require 18 hours and 31 minutes of COM time; the 100,000 title index entries require 10 hours and 17 minutes; and the 150,000 subject index entries require 15 hours and 25 minutes. The total COM time is 44 hours and 13 minutes.

The cost of the original film itself as well as processing costs must be taken into account. These will run approximately one-sixth the cost of printer paper on a per frame/sheet basis. In addition, the cost of making the microfilm copies must be considered. This should run considerably lower per frame than the original microfilming. It should be noted that all facilities utilizing the microfilm must provide viewer units for their users and must maintain these units.

There are enlarger/printer devices which will produce enlarged (to normal size) hard-copy reproductions of microfilm images, at the rate of 50 copies a minute. Since the final product is hard copy, the need for microfilm viewers is eliminated. The cost associated with the enlarging/printing process and publishing the hard-copy volumes must be considered.

ADDENDUM A

The corrected records carry special information beyond the normal content of a record. They contain an indicator marking the record as a corrected record, as well as other indicators which identify the data element(s) that have been corrected. If such a data element is one which is used to derive a sort key, the incorrect value of the element is carried in the record as well as the correct value. A corrected record carries the same unique number as originally assigned to it when it was first introduced into the system.

The rules governing the generation of correction entries are the same as those which apply to new records, with the following additions:

1. If a data element which was used to generate a sort key has been corrected, a special deletion entry is generated from the incorrect version of the data element and is added to the tape of index entries for the type of entry to which this data element applies. For example, if the data element *author* has been corrected, an author index entry marked as a deletion entry is made up, using the old (incorrect) form of *author*. This deletion entry is included among the author indexes along with the author index entry(s) derived from the corrected record.
2. All other index entries from a corrected record are marked as being replacement entries. Thus in the example introduced above, an author index entry, a title index entry, and the appropriate number of subject index entries (all marked as replacements) would be generated, in addition to the deletion (author) entry already discussed. If a corrected record carried a second author as well, one which did not need correcting, then an author index entry (marked as replacement) would be derived for the second author from the corrected record. If a data element that did not generate an index entry was corrected, imprint date for example, the required number of replacement entries would be generated but no deletion entry would be required.

ADDENDUM B

The following assumptions were made concerning the computer configuration in calculating the run time for edition 1 and supplement 1:

Machine Configuration:
> IBM 360/Model 40 with 65 K bytes of memory and two selector channels.

Tape Unit Characteristics:
> Type: 2400 series, Model 4 tape drives
> Storage Density: 1600 cpi (characters per inch)
> Blocking Factor: 20 records per block
> Number of Tape Drivers Used in a Sort: 5

ADDENDUM C

In arriving at the time calculations for the edition and supplement procedures, the following assumptions were made with respect to the data being processed:

1. The length (in number of characters) of the full bibliographic record and the author index entry is 227 characters.
2. The other index entries are 150 characters in length, approximately two-thirds the length of an author index entry.
3. On the average there are: 1.6 author index entries per title and 1.5 subject index entries per title.
4. There are 100,000 bibliographic records included in edition 1.
5. There are 2,000 corrections to edition 1 processed in supplement 1.
6. There are 5,000 new bibliographic records processed in supplement 1.

American University Presses That Plan to Publish Microforms

University of Illinois Press plans to publish books in microform in the near future. The press will probably engage in retrospective publishing.

Massachusetts Institute of Technology intends to develop a number of microform projects in the very near future. Under consideration is a series in the history of science, history of technology, and history of medicine.

University of Missouri Press will undertake such publications as soon as possible, but surely nothing will be done during this fiscal year. The press will begin on a current basis and work systematically back through the list.

Montreal University Press is interested in microform publishing and considers getting into that field but not in the immediate future. They plan at the moment to publish current books only.

State University of New York Press considers the publication of books in microform in the very near future. Their plan includes both current titles and the entire backlist, including out-of-print books.

University of Pittsburgh Press has no immediate plans but considers the possibility, probably for current books only.

Smithsonian Institution Press visualizes publication of books in microform in two or three years.

University of South Carolina Press reports that it is very likely that it will engage in some form of microform publishing. It will probably concentrate on the out-of-print backlist titles. They also consider a combination of book and microfilm items; for instance, a microfilm of archival documents together with a printed book containing an index and a scholarly introduction.

Southern Methodist University Press plans to publish all books in microfiche in addition to the regular hard-bound copy. At present there are no plans for retrospective publishing.

University of Texas Press intends to publish in microfiche beginning with the fall list. At the moment only current books will be in microform. No backlist is planned at the moment.

University of Toronto Press will publish all current books simultaneously in hard cover and in microfiche. The institution intends to work back and publish also the older books on microfiche if a demand exists.

All in-print publications by the *University of Washington Press* are now available on microfiche. The press anticipates that a number of their out-of-print publications will be made available through microfiche.

Wayne State University Press intends to publish all current books both in hard cover and in microform.

Wesleyan University Press plans to issue their out-of-print titles on microfiche in the near future. They would appreciate suggestions about bibliographic control of microfiche.

A Microform
Bibliography

With the Cooperation of
Suzanne Dodson and Laura L. Jennings

We are including the Microform Bibliography in our final report with some misgivings as we are woefully aware of its shortcomings both in admissions and omissions. It was originally planned to include only guides or bibliographies which give bibliographic control in the rigorous sense of the word. In the course of the work we mellowed in the definition of "control" and included many titles which we would have rejected a year ago.

We finally decided to submit it to the profession for three reasons:

1. The bibliography mirrors the statements we have made in our analysis of the use of microforms.
2. As the first major attempt of a bibliographic compilation it may have a certain value.
3. A bibliography of microforms was suggested by our advisory committee from the very beginning of our survey.

The main credit for the work is due to Miss Tharpe. As in all aspects of our work we received the help of many of our colleagues. Many libraries sent us their guides to microforms and the Cornell University Library Reference Department gave us valuable assistance. We cannot mention all the names; but we have selected two of our colleagues to appear on the title page.

Some of us contemplate continuing the work on the bibliography and submitting it in a revised form for publication.

MICROFORM BIBLIOGRAPHY

I. Catalogs and Lists
II. Collections and Series
III. Manuscript and Archival Collections
IV. Reference Books

This sample bibliography attests both to the proliferation of microforms in the past thirty years and to the great variety of materials available in microform throughout the world at the present time.

Section I gives some idea of the ways in which the availability of microforms is publicized by commercial publishers and by libraries, associations, societies, government agencies, etc. It consists of catalogs and lists issued by commercial publishers and all the above types of institutions. Some of the publications listed in this Section merely enumerate microform publications for sale or available for use in a particular institution, but some are also valuable for their annotations or descriptive notes.

A scanning of Section I, admittedly a sample, cannot help but impress the reader with the variety of materials, both with respect to subject matter and format, which are available on microform. That more commercial publishers from English-speaking countries than from other countries around the world are represented is quite noticeable. We tried to secure catalogs from every country but with relatively little success. The number of microform publishers in the United States is of interest. There are the old established companies, but also there are many relatively new names, both large and small producers.

Section II includes microform series, frequently referred to as collections, sets, or projects. Almost as soon as microfilm was introduced into the library picture, publishers conceived the idea of issuing series or collections of materials. One of the earliest microform projects (University Microfilms, 1938) was *Early English Books, 1475-1640* based on Pollard and Redgrave's *Short-title Catalogue,* which is still in progress. Publishers have continued this practice of basing a collection on a standard bibliography as the numerous collections of this type found in Section II testify. Another practice of the microform publisher has been to employ a scholar or group of scholars to select materials for a collection. This practice is likewise illustrated several times in Section II as is the practice of reproducing a special collection found in a library, historical society, in the possession of an individual, etc.

In Section II, if a series is based on a published bibliography, the bibliography, not the title of the series, is cited as the entry; if a guide to a series has been specially prepared and published, the guide is cited as the entry rather than the series. Otherwise, with a few exceptions, the series is entered under the name of the publisher. A few items in this Section are not series in the usual sense, i.e., a group of related monographic or serial publications, but are simply (1) photoreproductions of out-of-print serial titles or multivolumed works, e.g., the *Proceedings of the U.S. Congress, 1789-1964,* and the *American State Papers* or (2) guides or indexes to newly published material available in microform, e.g., *Research in Education,* which lists and provides résumés of research sponsored by the Bureau of Research, U.S. Office of Education and indicates which reports are available on microfiche from EDRS (ERIC Document Reproduction Service), and *Nuclear Science Abstracts,* which indexes Reports of the U.S. Atomic Energy Commission deposited in microform in 65 depositories or the *Government Reports Index,* which is an index to various government reports, which are made available in microform as well as in paper copy.

Examining carefully the microform series, the bibliographies on which they are based, and the guides accompanying them, one is led to the conclusion that there are a relatively small number of microform series for which wholly adequate access is provided. Few libraries have been able to provide series analytics in their catalogs and few have been able to develop the reference aids necessary for an enlightened use of their microform collections. Microform publishers frequently provide reel guides for the material in a shipment, but not always do they issue consolidated or cumulative lists as successive shipments of material are made. Publishers certainly should be exhorted and encouraged to furnish not only easily usable reel contents lists but guides providing background and descriptive notes.

Section III comprises manuscript and archival collections in microform. For the majority of these collections there are guides or indexes, varying quite naturally, but providing background information, including biographical and historical material plus detailed reel contents notes. Several of the indexes were mechanically produced. All the indexes to Presidential Papers were produced by the use of key punched cards which were sorted and printed mechanically, and the index to the William Beaumont manuscript collection (Washington University School of Medicine Library, St. Louis) was also produced by computer.

As in Section II, if there is a guide or index, it is cited as the entry.

Otherwise, the collection is listed under the name of the publisher or institution owning the collection.

A glance at Section III reveals that a large number of the microform collections of manuscripts are from U.S. government agencies or were at least partially funded by government money. The Manuscript Division of the Library of Congress has almost completed the project of microfilming and indexing the Papers of the Presidents. The National Historical Publications Commission has truly stimulated historical societies, archives, and rare book departments of libraries to microfilm their manuscript collections and prepare guides for using the microfilm edition. Mention should be made here also of the guides prepared by the National Archives for their microfilm publications. There are now over 500 of them. For examples of these guides see in Section I, U.S. National Archives. *List of . . . Microfilm Publications.*

A very interesting commercial microfilm publication of manuscript materials, which is in progress, is *British Records Relating to America* (Micro Methods Limited, East Ardsley, Yorkshire). Introductions to each group of manuscripts making up this collection have been written by leading scholars, but unfortunately they are not separately published, appearing only on the film itself.

Granted that manuscript collections and collections of large numbers of printed works present slightly different problems, on the surface it appears from our sample that a larger number of microform manuscript collections have *adequate* guides or indexes than do microform collections of printed materials. It must be admitted, of course, that there are probably numerous manuscript collections in microform for which no guide or index has every been published. In fact, a rapid scanning of Hale's *Guide to Photocopied Historical Materials* verifies this assumption.

Only a few reference books dealing directly with microforms have been compiled or developed. They are listed in Section IV with brief annotations. It is these books which provide a measure of bibliographic control for microforms in the United States.

I. CATALOGS
AND LISTS

1. AMS Press, Inc.

    Microfilm catalogue, Spring 1971. Important serial publications on 35mm positive microfilm. New York, 1971. 12 p.

    1. Type of microform: Microfilm
    2. Availability: Publications available at prices listed.
    3. Orders: AMS Press, Inc., 56 East 13th Street, New York, New York 10003.
    4. An alphabetical listing of newspapers, magazines, monograph series, and catalogs, covering a wide variety of subjects.

2. American Theological Library Association. Board of Microtext.

    List of microfilms available. Revised Autumn 1968. New Haven [1968] 31 1.
    ————————. Supplement. 1969. 5 1.
    ———— List of films produced. 1969-1970. VII 1.

    1. Type of microform: Microfilm.
    2. Availability: Positive microfilm of the titles listed can be supplied at the prices indicated. Xerox copy can be supplied. Estimates of cost can be provided upon application.
    3. Orders: Mr. Raymond P. Morris, Chairman, ATLA Board of Microtext, 409 Prospect Street, New Haven, Connecticut 06510.

    Film is shipped directly from the Photoduplication Department of the University of Chicago Library with an accompanying invoice; but payment should be made to the American Theological Library Association, Board of Microtext, and mailed to Mr. Morris at the above address.

    4. Lists manuscripts, monographs, and periodicals which have been filmed by the ATLA Board of Microtext which operates a nonprofit educational program to produce microfilm and Xerox copy for the benefit of the Association and others.

    The materials filmed are primarily those required for research in theology. In addition to individual titles, the *List* gives the contents of the ten units (35 reels) comprising the "Microfilm Corpus of American Lutheranism."

    Association des Universités Partiellement ou Entièrement de Langue Française.

    Catalogue des éditions miniaturisées de l'Aupelf. Mai 1970. [Montreal, Canada, 1970] 11 p.

    1. Type of microform: Microfiche
    2. Availability: Available at prices listed in the catalog.
    3. Orders: A. U. P. E. L. F., Université de Montréal, B. P. 6128, Montréal 101, Quebec, Canada, *OR* Bureau Européen de l'AUPELF, 173 Bd. Saint-Germain, 75-Paris VIe, France.
    4. Two lists of books, those already available and those to be edited by subscription, classified under broad headings: Histoire des lettres et des sciences humaines, Histoire des sciences, Histoire de France, Histoire du droit, Histoire de la médecine et de la pharmacie.

4. Association of Research Libraries. Center for Chinese Research Materials.

    Materials available at the Center. (In its Newsletter. no. 6- Dec. 1970-)

    1. Type of microform: Microfilm

2. Availability: All items listed are available at prices quoted.

3. Orders: Center for Chinese Research Materials, Association of Research Libraries, 1527 New Hampshire Avenue, N.W., Washington, D.C. 20036.

4. The Center was formed in 1968 for the purpose of acquiring, reproducing, and distributing Chinese research materials, especially those relating to twentieth-century China. The materials available at the Center, listed in its *Newsletter,* are reproductions by offset, Xerox, or on microfilm. Many items may be had either on microfilm or in Xerox copies. They are listed under four main headings: newspapers, periodicals, research aids, and monographs, the last being further broken down by subject. Each title is listed in Romanized Chinese, with English translation, imprint and collation of the original, and title in Chinese characters.

5. Association pour la Conservation et la Reproduction Photographique de la Presse.

Catalogue de microfilms reproduisant des périodiques, journaux et revues. no. 9 [Paris] 1971. 159 p.

1. Type of microform: Microfilm

2. Availability: The ACRPP supplies, subject to permission from the copyright-holders, positive, nonperforated 35mm microfilms at prices listed.

3. Orders: Association pour la Conservation et la Reproduction Photographique de la Presse, 4, rue Louvois, Paris (2ᵉ), France.

4. The *Catalogue* is divided into two main parts. First is given an alphabetical list of newspapers and periodicals. Following are lists of newspapers by the following categories: short-lived newspapers published during the Revolution; short-lived newspapers, 1848-1849; newspapers published during the Commune; newspapers from Algeria; and newspapers from Indochina. The newspapers listed in these five categories are also represented in the alphabetical list, either in the form of complete entries or as cross-references.

The second part includes the following groups of material: official gazettes of France; official gazettes in French; French parliamentary publications; underground periodicals, 1939-1945; newspapers published by German prisoners of war in France, 1946-1948; various publications; and addenda. The titles in this second part are not incorporated in the general alphabetical list.

Whenever possible, entries include the name of the editor or founder of the periodical, place of publication, frequency, and the call number in the Bibliothèque Nationale or the library which lent the periodical for microfilming.

6. Balle, Povl.

Avisit atuagagssiatdlo kalâtdlisût agdlagsimavfiat 1861-1968 ved Povl Balle. Fortegnelse over grønlandske aviser og periodica 1861-1968. Index of Greenlandic newspapers and periodica 1861-1968. [Udarb. af] Povl Balle [og Helge Tønnesen] København, Minerva Mikrofilm A/S [1969] 19 p.

1. Type of microform: Microfilm.

2. Availability: May be purchased but no prices are given.

3. Orders: Minerva Mikrofilm A/S, Ehlersvej 27, Hellerup, Denmark.

4. Lists alphabetically by place, and alphabetically under place, newspapers of Greenland, giving dates covered. Following this brief listing is an

alphabetical title list, giving Danish translation, place of publication, brief description, editors and exact holdings.

7. Bell and Howell Company. Micro Photo Division.
    Duopage book reproductions. General works, part 1: author catalog. May 1969 edition. Wooster, Ohio, 1969. 80 p.
    1. Type of microform: Microfilm.
    2. Availability: All books listed can also be ordered in positive microfilm form at approximately one-quarter the listed Duopage price. Minimum order for microfilm copy, $6.00.
    3. Orders: Micro Photo Division, Bell & Howell Company, Old Mansfield Road, Wooster, Ohio 44691.
    4. Alphabetical listing of books available in Duopage (and microfilm) with Duopage prices.
    At the end of the catalog are listings of mathematics books which have been added since issuance of the *Mathematics Duopage Catalog,* January 1968; religion books which have been added since issuance of the *Religion Duopage Catalog,* April 1967; and Russian books which have been added since issuance of the *Russian Duopage Catalog* [in 1968].

8. Bell and Howell Company. Micro Photo Division.
    Mathematics: Full size book reproductions available by Duopage. Cleveland, Ohio, 1968. 32 p.
    1. Type of microform: Microfilm.
    2. Availability: All books listed can also be ordered in positive microfilm form at approximately one-quarter the listed Duopage price. Minimum charge, $3.00.
    3. Orders: Micro Photo Division, Bell & Howell Company, Old Mansfield Road, Wooster, Ohio 44691.
    4. Lists mathematics books available in Duopage (and microfilm) with Duopage prices.
    An additional listing of titles added since issuance of this catalog appears at the end of Bell & Howell, Micro Photo Division, *Duopage book reproductions. General works. Part 1: Author catalog.* May 1969 edition.

9. Bell & Howell Company. Micro Photo Division.
    Newspapers along America's great trails. [Cleveland, 1968?] 40 p.
    1. Type of microform: Microfilm.
    2. Availability: This is not a collection. A microfilm of each newspaper may be purchased separately. However, the prospective purchaser is asked to check with the publisher for quotations on specific titles and dates.
    3. Orders: Micro Photo Division, Bell & Howell, Old Mansfield Road, Wooster, Ohio 44691.
    4. This is a catalog of microfilmed newspapers selected from Micro Photo's archival collection. The papers were selected because of their special interest to students of the American frontier. The catalog is organized around thirteen trails that played an important part in America's history. There are interesting historical notes about each trail, followed by a list of newspapers published in cities and towns along the trail, arranged alphabetically first by

state and then by city. In some cases a historical note about a particular newspaper is also given. Although dates are given, the publisher asks that before ordering, the prospective purchaser check for quotations on specific titles and dates.

10. Bell and Howell Company. Micro Photo Division.
    Newspapers of the Civil War on 35mm microfilm. Wooster, Ohio [1970] [8] 1.
    1. Type of microform: Microfilm.
    2. Availability: Available at prices quoted.
    3. Orders: Micro Photo Division, Bell & Howell Company, Old Mansfield Road, Wooster, Ohio 44691.
    4. Lists alphabetically by state, and under each state by city, the newspapers available, with period covered by each and prices. This list includes additional items added since the issuance of Bell & Howell, Micro Photo Division, *Special Collections* (1970), which contained a list of newspapers of the Civil War.

11. Bell and Howell Company. Micro Photo Division.
    Newspapers on microfilm. Catalog and price list. 1971. 25th anniversary edition. [Wooster, Ohio, 1971] 130 p.
    1. Type of microform: Microfilm.
    2. Availability: May be purchased on 35mm microfilm rolls. Price list included for current subscriptions and for separate list of Civil War newspapers. Quotations on specific titles and dates will be supplied.
    3. Orders: Micro Photo Division, Bell & Howell Company, Old Mansfield Road, Wooster, Ohio 44691.
    4. Geographical listing of newspapers of the U.S., followed by an alphabetical list of foreign newspapers, which includes a few periodicals.
    The first section of the catalog is devoted to "Selected American Newspapers." Practically every one of the thirteen titles included is accompanied by descriptive historical notes. Similar sections on "Newspapers of Early America," "Newspapers of the Civil War," "Asian Newspapers," and "Other Foreign Newspapers" follow. Next come several miscellaneous collections, such as "Newspapers of the Black Community," "The Assassination of John F. Kennedy," etc. Then "American Newspapers" (current and backfile) are listed alphabetically by state and under state alphabetically by city. Frequency and dates available are indicated, and a symbol shows whether current issues are being microfilmed. "Foreign Newspapers" (current and backfile) are listed alphabetically by country and under country alphabetically by city. Information noted is similar to that given for American newspapers. The section, "Leading Newspapers of the Black Community" (current and backfile) is followed by a current subscription price list.

12. Bell and Howell Company. Micro Photo Division.
    Religion. Full size reproductions available by Duopage. Cleveland, Ohio, 1967. 65 p.
    1. Type of microform: Microfilm
    2. Availability: All books listed can also be ordered in positive microfilm

form at approximately one-quarter the listed Duopage price. Minimum charge, $3.00.

3. Orders: Micro Photo Division, Bell & Howell Company, Old Mansfield Road, Wooster, Ohio 44691.

4. Lists alphabetically the books on religion available in Duopage (and microfilm) with Duopage prices; there is a separate section for editions of the Bible.

An additional listing of titles added since issuance of this catalog appears at the end of Bell & Howell, Micro Photo Division. *Duopage book reproductions. General works. Part 1: Author catalog.* May 1969 edition.

13. Bell and Howell Company. Micro Photo Division.

Russian newspapers, periodicals and books reproduced in microfilm [and] book form. Cleveland, Ohio, Micro Photo Division, Bell & Howell Company, [1968?] ii, 31 p.

1. Type of microform: Microfilm.

2. Availability: All books listed can also be ordered in positive microfilm form at approximately one-quarter the listed Duopage price. Minimum charge, $3.00.

3. Orders: Micro Photo Division, Bell & Howell Company, Old Mansfield Road, Wooster, Ohio 44691.

4. Lists Russian-language books and books about Russia in western language with Duopage prices, and Russian newspapers, periodicals, miscellaneous Russian works, and historical sources on 35 mm microfilm with film prices.

An additional listing of titles added since issuance of this catalog appears at the end of Bell & Howell, Micro Photo Division. *Duopage book reproductions. General works. Part 1: Author catalog.* May 1969 edition.

14. Bell and Howell Company. Micro Photo Division.

Special collections, newspapers, periodicals and records in microform. Wooster, Ohio [1970] 139 p.

1. Type of microform: Microfilm, microfiche.

2. Availability: Most items are available at prices listed.

3. Orders: Micro Photo Division, Bell & Howell, Old Mansfield Road, Wooster, Ohio 44691.

4. Selected lists of American newspapers, newspapers of early America, newspapers of the Civil War, Asian newspapers, Russian newspapers and periodicals, other foreign newspapers, periodicals on 35mm microfilm, periodicals on microfiche, personal papers, government records, and miscellaneous collections.

15. Books in English, a Bibliography Compiled from UK/US MARC Sources.

A prepublication announcement by the British National Bibliography describes briefly the pilot project used to test the viability and acceptability of an ultrafiche bibliography produced from a computer-held MARC data base and outlines the 1972 publication program which calls for six progressively cumulated issues per year (Jan.-Feb., Jan.-Apr., Jan.-Jun., Jan.-Aug., Jan.-Oct., Jan.-Dec.). This new bibliography published on high-reduction microfiche will list "in one single sequence of authors and titles every book in the English language currently cataloged by the British National Bibliography and the Library of Congress." The main entry will carry full bibliographic description together with DC and LC classification, LC subject headings, LC card number, BNB number, and other national bibliography identifications. The index entries will give essential bibliographic information under additional authors, titles, and series. The BNB will commit itself to an ongoing publication program if initial orders reach a "break-even" level of 250 subscriptions. In midsummer order forms for the subscription service were in press. PCMI readers may be purchased or rented.

16. British Museum Newspaper Library.
    Microfilms made by the British Museum Newspaper Library. (In Microdoc, 1966. Vol. 5, no. 3, p. 58-64)
    1. Type of microform: Microfilm.
    2. Availability: Positive microfilm copies can be supplied.
    3. Orders: Photographic Service, British Museum, Great Russell Street, London, W. C. 1, England.
    4. Alphabetical listing of certain newspapers selected for filming either for their importance or because the originals were deteriorating. In two sections, United Kingdom newspapers and overseas newspapers, giving for each title the frequency, dates covered, and number of reels or feet.

17. British Museum Newspaper Library.
    Newspapers and journals on microfilm. [London, 1969?] [10] p.
    1. Type of microform: Microfilm.
    2. Availability: Copies can be supplied on 35mm positive microfilm.
    3. Orders: Photographic Service, British Museum, Great Russell Street, London, W. C. 1, England.
    4. In two main sections, British Isles and overseas countries, the list gives for each title the frequency, dates covered, and number of reels or feet.

18. Budapest. Országos Széchényi Könyvtár.
    Az Országos Széchényi Könyvtár Mikrofilm. Cimjegyzekei. 1-   Budapest, 1963-

    None published since no. 3 (1964) according to letter of 12 Dec. 1970 from National Széchényi Könyvtár.

    List of microfilms in the National Széchényi Library. No. 1 lists in separate alphabets microfilms of newspapers and journals in the holdings of the National Széchényi Library and microfilms of newspapers and journals in the holdings of other domestic or foreign libraries. No. 2 lists microfilms of volumes of manuscripts in Hungarian, with a name index and subject index. No. 3 lists microfilms of analects and letters, with a separate section on material of the Festetics family's archives. There is a name index.

19. Canada. Department of Labour. Library.
    Canadian labour papers on microfilm in Department of Labour Library . . . Sept. 30, 1969. [Ottawa, 1969] 13 1. (*Its* Library bulletin)

1. Type of microform: Microfilm.
2. Availability: Positive copies may be borrowed on interlibrary loan or bought. Only complete reels are sold.
3. Orders: Canada Department of Labour, Ottawa 4, Ontario, Canada.
4. An alphabetical list by title of microfilm copies of Canadian labor periodicals and papers in the Library of the Department of Labour of Canada. Holdings are indicated.

20. Canadian Library Association. Microfilm Committee.
    Canadian newspapers on microfilm; Catalogue. Compiled under the supervision of Sheila A. Egoff. Ottawa, Canadian Library Association, 1959- (looseleaf)
    1. Type of microform: Microfilm.
    2. Availability: Positive copies of Canadian newspapers filmed by the Canadian Library Association are available at the prices given. Inquiries concerning positive copies of Canadian newspapers filmed or held by other institutions or commercial publishers may be secured from the holder of the negative. Price not given.
    3. Orders: Canadian Library Association, 63 Sparks Street, Ottawa 4, Canada.
    4. The *Catalogue* published in loose-leaf form to provide continuous, up-to-the-minute revision consists of two parts. Part I is a cumulative catalog of Canadian newspapers filmed by the Canadian Library Association, plus a few foreign newspapers and periodicals which the Association has filmed. The newspapers are arranged by province. Part II lists by province Canadian newspapers filmed by other institutions or commercial publishers. There is a title index for each section.
    Supersedes Canadian Library Association. *Newspaper microfilming project; catalogue.* Pt. 1-6, 1948-57.

21. Catholic Microfilm Center.
    List 1-
    Note: Lists are undated.
    1. Type of microform: Microfilm.
    2. Availability: Negative microfilms may be purchased at the prices given. Positive copies may be purchased at a 10 percent increase in price.
    3. Orders: Catholic Microfilm Center, Graduate Theological Union Library, 2451 Ridge Road, Berkeley, California 94709.
    4. These lists indicate titles available. Materials are grouped under broad subjects. For instance, in List III and IV we have "Reformation Period" which appears to mean "Reformation Authors," "Roman Catholic Reformation Authors," and "Titles without Authors." Under each heading the arrangement is alphabetical. Information given for each book includes author's full name, birth and death dates in some, but not all, cases, enough of the title for identification, imprint (not always complete but usually the date of publication is given), and price of negative film. In some instances, the length of the film or the number of rolls is given. The four figure item numbers are apparently internal control numbers.

22. Central Archives of Fiji and the Western Pacific High Commission.
    Catalogue of microfilm. Archives series. Rev. and enl. Suva, Fiji, 1970. 11, iii 1.
    1. Type of microform: Microfilm.
    2. Availability: Copies of microfilm may be purchased.
    3. Orders: The Central Archives of Fiji and the Western Pacific High Commission, Box 2025, Post Office, Government Buildings, Suva, Fiji.
    4. The *Catalogue* consists of a table of contents, the catalogue proper which shows the government publications available on microfilm, and an index. Most items listed are serial in nature. For each item are given essential bibliographical information, number of frames, kind of microfilm (negative or positive), price in Fijian currency, and a brief descriptive annotation.

23. Central Archives of Fiji and the Western Pacific High Commission.
    Catalogue of microfilm. Library series. Rev. and enl. Suva, Fiji, 1970. 19, iii 1.
    1. Type of microform: Microfilm.
    2. Availability: Copies of microfilm may be purchased.
    3. Orders: The Central Archives of Fiji and the Western Pacific High Commission, Box 2025, Post Office, Government Buildings, Suva, Fiji.
    4. This *Catalogue* comprises a table of contents, the catalogue proper, which gives for each item essential bibliographical information, number of frames, kind of microfilm (negative or positive), price in Fijian currency, notation showing date microfilm was made, and the location of the original manuscript or book, and a brief descriptive annotation. Finally, there is an author and title index.

24. Chicago. University. Library. Department of Photoduplication.
    Doctoral theses of the University of Chicago on positive microfilm. Chicago, 1949. 22 1.
    ———— ————. Supplementary list. no. 1-   January 15, 1950-   Chicago, 1950-
        28 nos. published 1950-69.
    1. Type of microform: Microfilm.
    2. Availability: Positive microfilm copies or Xerox copies available at prices stated.
    3. Orders: Photoduplication Service, University of Chicago Library, Chicago, Illinois 60637.
        All remittances should be made payable to "The University of Chicago Libraries." Remittance should be by check, money order, or cash. Stamps are not acceptable.
    4. The basic list includes only doctoral dissertations. Beginning with *Supplementary list*, no. 4 (January 14, 1952), master's theses, as well as doctoral dissertations, are included, and with no. 15 (September 1958) miscellaneous long-run serials on film are included. The long-run serials listed are those filmed for the Board of Microtext of the American Theological Library Association (see item 2). Also listed are the books, monographs, and manuscripts filmed for the ALTA Board of Microtext. No. 22 (September

1963) through no. 24 (July 1965) only include theses from Chicago Teachers College.

25. Chung yang t'u shu kuan, T'ai-pei.
    List no. 1-   Taipei, National Central Library [1967?] -
    1. Type of microform: Microfilm.
    2. Availability: All items available.
    3. Orders: Bureau of International Exchange of Publications, National Central Library, 43 Nanhai Road, Taipei, Taiwan, China.
    4. The first two lists consist of the collected works of individual authors available for purchase on positive microfilm. List no. 3, 1969, and List no. 4, 1970, offer a more varied selection of history and artworks available on positive microfilm for exchange or purchase. Prices are in United States dollars.

26. Commonwealth Microfilm Library, Limited.
    Newspapers, periodicals, rare books marketed in microform. 1970-71 edition. Calgary [1970?] 24 p.
    1. Type of microform: Microfilm.
    2. Availability: Titles are available at prices stated.
    3. Orders: Commonwealth Microfilm Library, Ltd., #436 700-6 Avenue, S. W., Calgary 1, Alberta, Canada.
    4. This publisher's catalog is organized under two headings: "Canadian Collection" and "Rare Books." Under "Canadian Collection" are listed newspapers and periodicals. The newspapers are arranged alphabetically by province and city, while the periodicals are in a single alphabet. Under "Rare Books" are Slavonic books printed in the fifteenth to eighteenth century, arranged according to date of publication.

27. Diaz, Albert James.
    Selected list of microreproduced material relating to Latin America. Submitted for the ninth Seminar on the Acquisitions of Latin American Library Materials, Washington University Libraries, St. Louis, Missouri, June 25-27, 1964. [n.p., 1964?] 10 1. [Seminar on the Acquisitions of Latin American Library Materials. 9th, Washington University, St. Louis, Missouri, 1964. Working paper, no. 6]
    1. Type of microform: All types included.
    2. Availability: Type of microform and price given for each title.
    3. Orders: Publisher of microform given for each title.
    4. A selected list, alphabetically arranged by author, of materials available on various types of microform from fourteen commercial firms and institutions in the United States.

28. Disciples of Christ Historical Society.
    Publications: Microfilms, books, and pamphlets. 1970 edition. Nashville, Tenn., [1969] 15 p.
    1. Type of microform: Microfilm.
    2. Availability: Available at prices listed, with two percent discount allowed for cash with orders. Minimum order, $5.00.

3. Orders: Marvin D. Williams, Jr., Director of the Library and Archivist, Disciples of Christ Historical Society, 1101 Nineteenth Avenue, South, Nashville, Tennessee 37212.

4. Microfilms of periodicals, minutes, church records, and personal papers are listed on pp. 10-13, giving dates covered and price, and notation if descriptive brochure is available.

29. Duke University, Durham, N.C. Library.
Periodicals and other serials in the libraries of Duke University. Durham, N.C., 1971. 2 v.
1. Type of microform: Microfiche.
2. Availability: Inquire.
3. Orders: Assistant Librarian for Technical Services, William R. Perkins Library, Duke University, Durham, North Carolina 27706.
4. Duke University Library announces publication of the two-volume set, containing over 50,000 entries for titles held in the Duke University libraries (excluding the Medical Center Library) as of January 31, 1971, for $35.00. Librarians interested in acquiring a microfiche set (at 42x reduction ratio) with comprehensive index should inquire at the above address.

30. Essex, Eng. Record Office. Microfilm Service.
List No. 1-   February 1962 -
1. Type of microform: Microfilm.
2. Availability: Available for purchase at prices stated.
3. Orders: The County Archivist, Essex Record Office, County Hall, Chelmsford, Essex, England.
4. Lists archival records, giving for each group: date range, brief description of original format, description of content, number of reels, and price.

31. Ethiopia. Department of Fine Arts and Culture.
Catalogue of manuscripts microfilmed: Ethiopian monasteries. [Addis Ababa, 1970] unpaged.
1. Type of microform: Microfilm.
2. Availability: According to UNESCO regulations, the negative microfilm is the property of the institution owning the original, while the positive microfilm is placed in the regional depository designated by UNESCO. This *Catalogue* gives no indication of the location of positive and negative films.
3. "This catalogue lists the manuscripts microfilmed by the UNESCO Mobile Microfilm Unit during its five-month mission in Ehtiopia, from 8 September 1969 to 12 February 1970, in collaboration with the Ministry of Education and Fine Arts, Department of Fine Arts and Culture.
"Only readily ascertainable details about each manuscript are provided in this catalogue, which has been prepared at great speed, simultaneously with the microfilming of the documents."
A total of 368 manuscripts (103,699 pages) from twelve institutions, including libraries and churches, were filmed. The manuscripts are listed under the names of the institutions in which they are located. An index is provided.

32. Field, Henry.
     List of documents microfilmed: 1941-1955. [Coconut Grove, Florida]
     1956. 32 p.
     1. Type of microform: Microfilm.
     2. Availability: Positive microfilm may be purchased at currently pub-
     lished prices.
     3. Orders: Photoduplication Service, Library of Congress, Washington,
     D.C. 20540.
     4. Lists the microfilmed material placed in the American Documentation
     Institute, c/o Photoduplication Service, Library of Congress, by Henry Field,
     well-known physical anthropologist. Consisting of original contributions, ar-
     ticles, statistical tables, maps and photographs, most of the material is
     supplementary to Field's publications on Southwestern Asia. Arrangement is
     under ten regional categories: Southwestern Asia, Northeast and East Africa,
     Union of Soviet Socialist Republics, Europe, China, Caribbean, Mexico,
     South America, Miscellanea, West Pakistan. Descriptive notes accompany
     many entries.

33. Foundation for Reformation Research. Library.
     Acquisition list: microfilm. (In its Bulletin. v. 3, no. 1-   March 1968-   )
     1. Type of microform: Microfilm.
     2. Availability: Available on interlibrary loan.
     3. Orders: Foundation for Reformation Research, 6477 San Bonita Ave-
     nue, St. Louis, Missouri 63105.
     4. Lists in the order they were acquired the books and manuscripts for
     which FRR holds master negative microfilms.

34. Four Continent Book Corporation.
     List of available microfilms. No. 2 (Revised) May, 1971. New York, 1971.
     8 l.
     1. Type of microform: Microfilm.
     2. Availability: Commercially published.
     3. Orders: Four Continent Book Corporation, 156 Fifth Avenue, New
     York, New York 10010.
     4. This *List* indicates the contents of the forty-five rolls of microfilm
     which the publisher has in stock. Catalog cards are also available. In addition
     to the titles in stock, orders for monographs in the Lenin and Saltykov-
     Shchedrin Libraries are accepted by the Four Continent Book Corporation.

35. Fuji Book Company, Inc., Tokyo.
     A catalogue of Japanese books and periodicals, microfilm publications,
     reprint & newly [revised] editions and complete sets, back-files. Social and
     humanities sciences. List no. F-811, Jan. 1971. Tokyo, 1971. Unpaged.
     1. Type of microform: Microfilm.
     2. Availability: Available at prices listed.
     3. Orders: Fuji Book Company, Inc., Hachiya Building, No. 2-1, Kudan
     Kita 1-chome, Chiyoda-ku, Tokyo, 102 Japan.
     4. The first thirteen items in the catalog are microfilm publications, and
     include Kyubakufu Hikitsugi-sho (Edo Bakufu Documents for the Transfer of

Administration), which is a collection of historical materials on the politics, economy, manners and customs, institutions, society and culture of the Edo period. The original manuscript in 7,000 volumes is owned by the National Diet Library. There is an explanatory text of about 70 pages by Dr. Minami Kazuo, containing abstracts of text, index, and contents. Other items include newspapers, a magazine, and a multivolume monograph on the conditions of social movement.

36. General Microfilm Company.
    Publications on microfilm: catalog and price lists. Cambridge, Mass. [1970?] Unpaged, loose-leaf.
    1. Type of microform: Microfilm.
    2. Availability: Most offerings are large projects in process, available on a subscription basis or in groups at prices listed.
    3. Orders: General Microfilm Co., 100 Inman Street, Cambridge, Massachusetts 02139.
    4. General Microfilm Company offers collections of various types of material on microfilm and intends to continue the microfilming for each series that has been started until the source of material is exhausted. Proposed collections will be started as soon as response to them indicates there is enough interest to support whatever must be invested to put a collection together. Catalog cards will be available.

37. Godfrey Memorial Library, Middletown, Conn.
    Consolidated microcard catalog. (*Its* Bulletin no. 59, March 1968. 19 p.)
    1. Type of microform: Microcard (and microfiche).
    2. Availability: Microcard editions available at prices listed.
    3. Orders: Godfrey Memorial Library, 134 Newfield Street, Middletown, Connecticut 06457.
    4. The bulletin lists the Godfrey Library's publications on microcards under the following headings: general works [on genealogy], family genealogy (alphabetically by family), and local history (alphabetically by state).
    A revised publication and price list effective January 1, 1971, lists additional publications: U.S. chemical patents (microcard edition only) at 35¢ per side; and U.S. *Federal register, New York law journal,* corporation annual reports (New York Stock Exchange and American Stock Exchange) at 35¢ per side for the microcard edition, and 40¢ per negative for the microfiche edition.

38. Gt. Britain. Public Record Office.
    Film catalogue. [London] 1970. 1 v. unpaged
    Not seen by compiler.

39. Hebrew Union College - Jewish Institute of Religion. American Jewish Periodical Center.
    Jewish newspapers and periodicals on microfilm, available at the American Jewish Periodical Center. Cincinnati, 1957. 56 p.
    ——— ——— Supplement. 1st-   Cincinnati, 1960-
    Note: The First Supplement, by Herbert C. Zafren is reprinted

from *Studies in Bibliography and Booklore.* v. 4, no. 2 (December 1959).

1. Type of microform: Microfilm.

2. Availability: Positive copies available on interlibrary loan. The Center maintains a file of master negatives for making positive copies. "When the Center acquires a positive film from another negative holder, it makes another copy as a master, unless it is assured that the holder of the negative is giving it master negative care."

3. Orders: American Jewish Periodical Center, Hebrew Union College, Jewish Institute of Religion, 3101 Clifton Avenue, Cincinati, Ohio 45220.

4. Lists American Jewish newspapers and periodicals microfilmed by the Center through 1959. The goal of the Center's microfilming program is to film through 1925 all Jewish newspapers and periodicals published in the United States, regardless of language. For the period after 1925, only a selected group of serials will be filmed.

The arrangement is alphabetical by state and city, with a division by language under city. Bibliographic details given are those essential for identification. In many instances useful notes are added. In the basic list, location of the original is not given. Although the first supplement does not identify all owners of the originals, those whose files were used in filming are indicated. The supplement also provides a statement of missing numbers, gives the approximate number of feet of film if less than one reel, and corrects errors in the basic list.

40. Helsinki. Yliopisto. Kirjasto.
Suomen sanomalehtien mikrofilmit. Mikrofilmade tidningar i Finland. Microfilmed newspapers of Finland. Helsinki, 1971. 154 p.

1. Type of microform: Microfilm.

2. Availability: The Helsinki University Library owns both a negative and positive of all newspapers listed. Microfilms are available for loan.

3. Orders: Helsingin Yliopstan Kirjasto, Unioninkatu 36, Helsinki 17, Finland.

4. This catalog lists all the newspapers published in Finland or in the Finnish language abroad which had been filmed by the end of 1970. The Finnish-language papers published abroad are in a separate list at the back of the catalog. The arrangement of both lists is alphabetical by title with call numbers for each roll. No detailed bibliographical information is given since the primary purpose of the catalog is to make the borrowing and lending of films easier and quicker.

41. Illinois. State Historical Library. Springfield.
Newspapers in the Illinois State Historical Library, edited by William E. Keller. [Springfield, 1970] 489-602 p.
"Reprinted . . . from Illinois Libraries, June 1970."

1. Type of microform: Microfilm.

2. Availability: Copies may be borrowed on interlibrary loan or purchased.

3. Orders: Illinois State Historical Library, Centennial Building, Springfield, Illinois 62706.

4. Since 1959 the Illinois State Historical Library has been engaged in a comprehensive program of microfilming Illinois newspapers. By June 1, 1970, the collection had grown to approximately 37,000 reels of positive microfilm in which files from all 102 counties are represented. In addition to Illinois papers, the list includes the following sections: Out-of-state Papers; Foreign Papers; Soldier and Ordnance Papers; Campaign Newspapers. There is also a useful Illinois File by Countries, and, finally, a listing of missing issues divided into two groups: Illinois and Out-of-state.

42. Inter Documentation Company, Zug.
   Africa. Catalog 1969. Microfiche-editions. [Zug] Switzerland, 1969. 16 p.
   1. Type of microform: Microfiche.
   2. Availability: All listed items are available for immediate delivery.
   3. Orders: Inter Documentation Company AG, Poststrasse 14, Zug, Switzerland.
   4. The majority of titles in the catalog are from a checklist prepared for the Africa Project by Peter Duignan, Hoover Institution, Stanford University. Items are listed under the following headings: Periodicals, Reference Works, Description-Travel-History, and Ethnographic Studies.

43. Inter Documentation Company, Zug.
   Arctica [by] Robert Petersen. Catalog 1969. Microfiche-editions. [Zug] Switzerland, 1969. 16 p.
   1. Type of microform: Microfiche.
   2. Availability: All items available at prices listed.
   3. Orders: Inter Documentation Company AG, Poststrasse 14, Zug, Switzerland.
   4. Alphabetical listing of books and journal articles on microfiche, giving place of publication, date, and collation of the originals, and price of microfiche in Swiss francs. Updated by new listings in IDC's *Newsletter.*

44. Inter Documentation Company, Zug.
   Asia. East Asia, Inner Asia, South Asia, Southeast Asia, Near East. Catalog 1971. Microfiche-editions. [Zug] Switzerland, 1971. [73] p.
   1. Type of microform: Microfiche.
   2. Availability: Items available separately at prices listed.
   3. Orders: Inter Documentation Company AG, Poststrasse 14, Zug, Switzerland.
   4. The introduction discusses briefly the various segments of the Asia Project which is at present by no means complete. A section of the *Catalog* is devoted to each of the geographical areas indicated in its subtitle. Typical are the headings for South Asia: Newspapers, Periodicals and Government Publications, Legislative Series, Monographs, India Catalogues of Books, Development Plans, Archaeology Series, Periodicals, General.

45. Interdocumentation Company, Zug.
   Arts: original sources, emblem books, modern handbooks, catalogs, periodicals and series. Checklist 1969. Microfiche-editions [by] J. van der Wolk [and] J. Landwehr. [Zug] Switzerland, n.d. [40] p.

1. Type of microform: Microfiche.
2. Availability: Not completely available at the time the *Checklist* was published. Items which were available are accompanied by an asterisk. Prices listed for items not available are estimated.
3. Orders: Inter Documentation Company AG, Poststrasse 14, Zug, Switzerland.
4. This *Checklist* was prepared as the basis for a long-term micropublishing program in the field of art. Titles were chosen for their usefulness in research and their nonavailability on the market. The *Checklist* is divided into three categories: (1) monographs, including original sources, emblem books, and modern handbooks; (2) catalogs of museums and libraries; (3) periodicals and series. Emblem books are keyed to four bibliographies: *Studies in Seventeenth-Century Imagery*, by Mario Praz (Roma: Edizioni di Storia e Letteratura, 1964), *Dutch Emblem Books*, by John Landwehr (Utrecht: Haentjens Dekker & Gumbert, 1962), *Andrea Alciati and his Books of Emblems*, by Henry Green (London: Trübner, 1972), and *Les Livres à Gravures du XVIᵉ Siècle. Les Emblèmes d'Alciat*, by George Duplessis (Paris: Librairie de l'Art, 1884).

46. Inter Documentation Company, Zug.
    Botany. Zug, Switzerland, 1968. 47 p. (Basic collections in microedition)
    1. Type of microform: Microfiche.
    2. Availability: All priced items are available for immediate delivery. Further information about unpriced items will be supplied upon request.
    3. Orders: Inter Documentation Company AG, Poststrasse 14, Zug, Switzerland.
    4. This catalog supersedes the 1964 edition. Greatly enlarged, it is useful not only for ordering microfiche but also as a reference guide, since it was compiled by a scholar whose purpose was to list those works deemed essential to institutions maintaining collections for postgraduate work. Material is listed under the following headings: (1) herbaria; (2) pre-Linnean; (3) Linnaeus; (4) general works; (5) medical; (6) orchids; (7) phanerogams; (8) travels; (9) floristic works (divided geographically); (10) cryptogams; (11) periodicals.

47. Inter Documentation Company, Zug.
    Botany. Catalogue 1971. Microfiche-editions. F. A. Stafleu and L. Vogelenzang, editors. [Zug] Switzerland, 1971. 88 p.
    1. Type of microform: Microfiche.
    2. Availability: Most of the priced items are available from stock for immediate delivery.
    3. Orders: Inter Documentation Company AG, Poststrasse 14, Zug, Switzerland.
    4. The Botany Project, started over thirteen years ago, now comprises about 2,100 titles essential to institutions maintaining collections for postgraduate research in botany. The *Catalogue* is alphabetically arranged under two headings: monographs and periodicals, and series.

48. Inter Documentation Company, Zug.

Checklist of literature for microfiche publication: Russian dictionaries and encyclopediae, 1627-1917. Zug, Switzerland, n.d. 12 p.

1. Type of microform: Microfiche.

2. Availability: Not yet available at the time the *Checklist* was published.

3. Orders: Inter Documentation Company AG, Poststrasse 14, Zug, Switzerland.

4. The *Checklist* is an alphabetical list of Russian dictionaries and encyclopedias. Sufficient bibliographic data are provided for identification.

49. Inter Documentation Company, Zug.

Checklist of literature proposed for microfiche publication: Collected works of Russian authors. Zug, Switzerland, n.d. 8 p.

1. Type of microform: Microfiche.

2. Availability: Not yet available at the time the *Checklist* was published.

3. Orders: Inter Documentation Company AG, Poststrasse 14, Zug, Switzerland.

4. Labelled "preliminary list no. 1," this *Checklist* includes 200 Russian authors. References are to specific editions of their collected works; however, only place, date, and pagination, or number of volumes are given.

50. Inter Documentation Company, Zug.

Checklist of literature proposed for micro-publishing: East Asia [compiled by] T. H. Tsien. Zug, Switzerland, n.d. Various paging.

1. Type of microform: Microfiche.

2. Availability: At the time this *Checklist* was published none of the items was available. Subsequently many items have been copied and listed in IDC sales catalogs.

3. Orders: Inter Documentation Company AG, Poststrasse 14, Zug, Switzerland.

4. This *Checklist* was prepared by Professor T. H. Tsien of the University of Chicago at the suggestion of IDC. The materials included were selected on the basis of their applicability to research and their nonavailability on the book market. They are listed under the following headings: (1) periodicals in Western languages; (2) periodicals in the Chinese language; (3) periodicals in the Japanese language; (4) local gazetteers: China. The introduction to the *Checklist* notes a number of other categories which will eventually be included in the project.

51. Inter Documentation Company, Zug.

Communist Party of Indonesia documents on microfiche. [Zug, Switzerland, 1969] 14 p. (*Its* Special announcement, 1)

1. Type of microform: Microfiche.

2. Availability: Entire collection available. Periodicals may be ordered separately, but individual pamphlets cannot be supplied.

3. Orders: Inter Documentation Company AG, Poststrasse 14, Zug, Switzerland.

4. Publications in this collection include those issued by the Communist

Party of Indonesia, PKI (Partai Komunis Indonesia) and by its peasant and labor organizations during the years 1952-1965. If papers have been translated into English, both versions are included. The collection does not pretend to be complete, since it is almost impossible to determine even the titles of all PKI publications issued during the years covered.

The basic arrangement is chronological. For each item, there is a translation of the title into English or a brief English explanatory note. Also given is a number which refers to a list kept at the Internationaal Instituut voor Sociale Geschiedenis, Azië-Afrika Department at Amsterdam, by means of which the original can be located.

52. Inter Documentation Company, Zug.

European studies: Catalog 1969. Microfiche-editions. [Zug] Switzerland, 1969. 22 p.

1. Type of microform: Microfiche.

2. Availability: All items listed available at prices listed.

3. Orders: Inter Documentation Company AG, Poststrasse 14, Zug, Switzerland.

4. Alphabetical list of monographs on widely varying subjects, ranging from the fifteenth to the twentieth century, followed by an alphabetical list of periodicals; imprints and collations of the originals are given for each title, and price of the microfiche in Swiss francs.

53. Inter Documentation Company, Zug.

Geology, mineralogy, palaeozoology, palaeobotany. Zug, Switzerland, 1967. 7 p. (Basic collections in microedition)

1. Type of microform: Microfiche.

2. Availability: All priced items are available for immediate delivery. Further information about unpriced items will be supplied upon request.

3. Orders: Inter Documentation Company AG, Poststrasse 14, Zug, Switzerland.

4. This greatly enlarged catalog supersedes the 1964 edition. It should be a valuable aid not only for ordering works in microfiche but also as a reference guide, since the works included in it were selected by a scholar whose purpose was to include only those works considered essential for postgraduate research. The catalog lists materials under the two headings: monographs and periodicals.

54. Inter Documentation Company, Zug.

Government publications of Australia. List of literature proposed for microfiche publication. Zug, Switzerland, n.d. 22 p.

1. Type of microform: Microfiche.

2. Availability: A list of publications proposed for microfiche.

3. Orders: Inter Documentation Company AG, Poststrasse 14, Zug, Switzerland.

4. This list is a reprint from the *List of the Serial Publications of Foreign Governments, 1815-1931*, edited by Winifred Gregory (New York: Wilson, 1932) and distributed as a preliminary survey to explore the extent of the demand for the government publications listed.

55. Inter Documentation Company, Zug.
    History of art; original sources, emblem books, handbooks, catalogs, periodicals and series [edited by J. van der Wolk] Catalogue 1971. Microfiche-editions. [Zug] Switzerland, 1971. [40] p.
    —————— —————— New microfiche editions. no. 1-   1971-
    1. Type of microform: Microfiche.
    2. Availability: Each title is available at the price listed. The 204 emblem books listed may be purchased as a unit as may the 574 monographs.
    3. Orders: Inter Documentation Company AG, Poststrasse 14, Zug, Switzerland.
    4. According to the editor's note, the titles in the *Catalogue* "were selected primarily on the basis of their usefulness for research and their non-availability on the antiquarian market." Material is listed under two headings: monographs, and periodicals and series. IDC plans to make all known emblem books available in microfiche editions. With this in mind, each emblem book in this *Catalogue* bears a reference to the standard bibliography in which it appears. Two supplementary lists adding seventy-one titles to the 1971 list have been published.

56. Inter Documentation Company, Zug.
    Horticulture. Monographs, periodicals, seed lists [compiled by L. Vogelenzang] Catalogue 1970. Microfiche-editions. [Zug] Switzerland, 1970. 17 p.
    1. Type of microform: Microfiche.
    2. Availability: All items available for immediate delivery at prices listed.
    3. Orders: Inter Documentation Company, Poststrasse 14, Zug, Switzerland.
    4. This second catalog of horticultural literature in microfiche includes many newly added titles. The materials are grouped under the headings: monographs, periodicals, seed lists.

57. Inter Documentation Company, Zug.
    India. Census, 1872-1951, a check list and index. Zug, Switzerland [c1966] 18 p. (Basic collections in microedition)
    1. Type of microform: Microfiche.
    2. Availability: The complete collection or part of the reports of a particular census may be purchased. The smallest unit sold is the microbox which contains approximately forty-five to fifty microfiches.
    3. Orders: Inter Documentation Company AG, Poststrasse 14, Zug, Switzerland.
    4. A brief but interesting essay by Asok Mitra giving useful background material on the census of India serves as an introduction to the microfiche edition of the census of India publications. The index can also serve as a checklist and guide for anyone working with the census reports. It indicates the contents of the volumes of each census, the place and publication date of each volume, the number of microfiche, and the microbox number.

58. Inter Documentation Company, Zug.
    India. Gazetteers: imperial series, provincial series, district series; a check

list and index. Zug, Switzerland [1964?] 32 p. (Basic collections in micro-editions)

    1. Type of microform: Microfiche.

    2. Availability: The complete collection, individual series or single volumes may be purchased. The smallest unit sold separately is a microbox which contains approximately forty-five to fifty microfiches.

    3. Orders: Inter Documentation Company AG, Poststrasse 14, Zug, Switzerland.

    4. This checklist lists the imperial, provincial, and district gazetteers of India, indicating all issues and volumes with date of publication for each. Inclusion of the microfiche numbers and the microbox number for each volume makes the checklist a useful finding guide.

59. Inter Documentation Company, Zug.

    Insects. Catalogue 1970. Microfiche-editions. [Zug] Switzerland, 1970. [31] p.

    ———— New microfiche editions. no. 1-   1970-

    1. Type of microform: Microfiche.

    2. Availability: All items available for immediate delivery at prices listed.

    3. Orders: Inter Documentation Company AG, Poststrasse 14, Zug, Switzerland.

    4. This *Catalogue* on insects lists material under the following headings: general zoological works; travels-zoology; monographs-insects; general zoological periodicals; and periodicals-insects. At least five listings of new titles have been issued, supplementing the 1970 *Catalogue.*

60. Inter Documentation Company, Zug.

    Joint microfiche project: Indonesia. Checklist 1969. Microfiche-editions. Joint project of the Royal Institute of Linguistics and Anthropology at Leiden, The Netherlands and I. D. C., Switzerland. [Zug] Switzerland [1969] 23 p.

    1. Type of microform: Microfiche.

    2. Availability: The complete collection, partial sets, and individual series may be purchased.

    3. Orders: Inter Documentation Company AG, Poststrasse 14, Zug, Switzerland.

    4. The Royal Institute of Linguistics and Anthropology in Leiden and IDC are engaged in making a large library of Indonesian material available on microfiche. The library will include periodicals, government (nonserial) publications, and monographs. This particular *Checklist* indicates the Indonesian serials at Cornell University Libraries selected for microreproduction. The numbers used refer to items listed in *A Guide to Indonesian Serials, 1945-1965, in the Cornell University Library,* by Yvonne Thung and John M. Echols (Ithaca, N.Y.: Modern Indonesia Project, Southeast Asia Program, Department of Asian Studies, Cornell University, 1966). Criteria for selection were: (1) only publications dating from 1945-1968; (2) publications issued within the territory of the present Republic of Indonesia; (3) mainly publications in Bahasa Indonesia but also some in Javanese, and foreign languages; (4) in general, publications in the social sciences and humanities.

61. Inter Documentation Company, Zug.
    Kinshasa-Congo [compiled by Benoit Verhaegen] Catalogue 1970. Micro-fiche-editions. [Zug] Switzerland, 1970. 19 p.
    1. Type of microform: Microfiche.
    2. Availability: Titles available at prices indicated.
    3. Orders: Inter Documentation Company AG, Poststrasse 14, Zug, Switzerland.
    4. This *Catalogue* "presents the first phase of a vast project which started in 1966 and will take several years to complete." The principal aim of the project is to make available basic documentation on the Congo. It has been divided into three time periods: (1) 1960-1970 (publications relating to the Congo since its independence); (2) 1940-1960 (starting with the outbreak of the war and ending with independence); (3) pre-1940 (colonial period). This *Catalogue* represents the first phase of the project (1960-1970). Materials are listed under: monographs; series and periodicals; newspapers; government publications; specific documentation; and bibliographies.

62. Inter Documentation Company, Zug.
    Law. Catalogue 1970. Microfiche-editions. [Zug] Switzerland, 1970. 15 p.
    1. Type of microform: Microfiche.
    2. Availability: All items available at prices listed. A minimum amount for an order is set at Sw. fr. 43.00. For an order amounting to less than this figure, an additional charge of Sw. fr. 9.00 is made for handling.
    3. Orders: Inter Documentation AG, Poststrasse 14, Zug, Switzerland.
    4. This is IDC's first catalog of law titles. It lists outstanding works in the field of law and related sciences under: (1) international law, which is subdivided into collections of treaties and jurisprudence and monographs and periodicals; (2) East-European law, which is subdivided into official gazettes and publications and monographs, bibliographies, and periodicals; (3) Anglo-American law (including former colonies); and (4) miscellanea. The publisher intends to extend the list of law books as rapidly as possible.

63. Inter Documentation Company, Zug.
    List of literature proposed by Charles B. Osburn for microfiche publication: French periodicals. Zug, Switzerland, n.d. [10] p.
    1. Type of microform: Microfiche.
    2. Availability: Dependent upon demand. Prices given are estimates.
    3. Orders: Interdocumentation Company AG, Poststrasse 14, Zug, Switzerland.
    4. This is an annotated alphabetical list of twenty-nine periodicals, the majority of them French, concerned with French language and literature, European linguistics, folklore, book reviews, etc., which IDC proposed to microfiche, provided there was a demand.

64. Inter Documentation Company, Zug.
    List of literature proposed for microfiche publication: Agricultural periodicals. Zug, Switzerland [197? 4 p.]
    1. Type of microform: Microfiche.
    2. Availability: Dependent upon demand. Prices given are estimates.

3. Orders: Inter Documentation Company AG, Poststrasse 14, Zug, Switzerland.

4. This is an alphabetical list of twenty-six agricultural periodicals which IDC proposed to microfiche if there was immediate demand.

65. Inter Documentation Company, Zug.
    List of literature proposed for microfiche publication: Geological publications. Zug, Switzerland, n.d. [2] p.
    1. Type of microform: Microfiche.
    2. Availability: Dependent upon demand. Prices given are estimates only.
    3. Orders: Inter Documentation Company AG, Poststrasse 14, Zug, Switzerland.
    4. An alphabetical list of eleven geological periodicals which IDC proposed to microfiche if there was a demand.

66. Inter Documentation Company, Zug.
    Medicine. Catalogue 1970. Microfiche-editions. [Zug] Switzerland, 1970. 28 p.
    ——— ——— New microfiche editions. no. 1-   1970?-
    1. Type of microform: Microfiche.
    2. Availability: All items available at prices listed. A minimum amount for an order is set at Sw. fr. 43.00. For orders amounting to less than this figure a charge of Sw. fr. 9.00 is made.
    3. Orders: Inter Documentation Company AG, Poststrasse 14, Zug, Switzerland.
    4. This is IDC's first catalog of titles in the field of medicine. One of the authoritative sources used for selection of titles was Garrison and Morton's *Medical Bibliography* (London, 1954). Works listed in this *Catalogue* bear the Garrison-Morton number for convenience. First are listed monographs and then periodicals. The publisher intends to extend the list of medical materials as rapidly as possible. Two supplementary lists make eighty-five more monographs available.

67. Inter Documentation Company, Zug.
    Medicine. Checklist 1969. Microfiche-editions. Checklist of literature proposed for microreproduction. [Zug] Switzerland, n.d. [6] p.
    1. Type of microform: Microfiche.
    2. Availability: Not available at time the *Checklist* was published.
    3. Orders: Inter Documentation Company AG, Poststrasse 14, Zug, Switzerland.
    4. IDC is establishing a microfiche library of outstanding works in the field of medicine and related subjects, comprising books, papers, and runs of periodicals. This first *Checklist* includes 152 monographs, all of them from the *Medical Bibliography*, by F. H. Garrison and L. T. Morton (3d ed., Philadelphia: Lippincott, 1970). The Garrison-Morton number is given in the *Checklist* and will also appear on the microfiche edition of each work selected from the Garrison-Morton *Medical Bibliography*.

68. Inter Documentation Company, Zug.
      Modern period—Central Asia; checklist of literature proposed for micro-
publishing [compiled by] Garé Lecompte. [Zug, Switzerland] n.d. 18 p.
      1. Type of microform: Microfiche.
      2. Availability: At the time of publication of the bibliography, IDC asked
customers to let them know if they had need of one or more items in the
bibliography, stating that such items would receive searching and filming on a
priority basis.
      3. Orders: Interdocumentation Company AG, Poststrasse 14, Zug, Swit-
zerland.
      4. This bibliography constitutes the basis for a long-term micropublica-
tion program by IDC. The materials are listed under several headings: (1)
periodicals; (2) bibliography; (3) political history, Civil War; (4) literature; (5)
geography; (6) state organization and law; (7) party; (8) economy.

69. Inter Documentation Company, Zug.
      Mollusca. Catalogue 1970. Microfiche-editions. [Zug] Switzerland, 1970.
23 p.
      1. Type of microform: Microfiche.
      2. Availability: All items are available at prices listed.
      3. Orders: Inter Documentation Company AG, Poststrasse 14, Zug, Swit-
zerland.
      4. The materials on mollusca are listed under the following headings: (1)
monographs; (2) periodicals mollusca; (3) periodicals insects; (4) periodicals
general.

70. Inter Documentation Company, Zug.
      Musicology. Catalogue 1970. Microfiche-editions. [By] Åke Davidsson.
[Zug] Switzerland, 1970. 20 p.
      1. Type of microform: Microfiche.
      2. Availability: All items are available at prices listed.
      3. Orders: Inter Documentation Company AG, Poststrasse 14, Zug, Swit-
zerland.
      4. This is IDC's first catalog of musicological titles. It is based on a
selection made by Åke Davidsson in Uppsala. The publisher intends to extend
this list as rapidly as possible. Indeed, the two supplementary lists already
published add sixty-seven new titles. The *Catalogue* and the supplementary
lists arrange materials under the headings: monographs and periodicals.

71. Inter Documentation Company, Zug.
      Russian-Soviet law. Microfiche project—Preliminary checklist. W. E. Butler,
editor. Zug, Switzerland, n.d. 24 p.
      1. Type of microform: Microfiche.
      2. Availability: Not yet available at the time the *Checklist* was published.
Prices are given for some items, but if IDC is following its usual practice,
these prices are only estimates.
      3. Orders: Inter Documentation Company AG, Poststrasse 14, Zug, Swit-
zerland.

4. IDC is undertaking a microfiche project devoted to important and rare works on Russian and Soviet law, including international law. The project, under the editorship of Dr. W. E. Butler, Reader in Comparative Law at the University of London, will include bibliographies, treaties, monographs, periodicals, serials, and collections of legislation and treaties from both the Tsarist and Soviet periods. Materials in this *Checklist* are grouped under the following headings: (1) indexes and bibliographies; (2) legislative, judicial, and arbitrazh materials; (4) Tsarist law: treatises and textbooks; (5) Soviet law: treatises and textbooks; (6) international.

72. Inter Documentation Company, Zug.
Slavonics: Bibliographies. Catalogue 1970. Microfiche-editions. [Zug] Switzerland, 1970. 32 p.
1. Type of microform: Microfiche.
2. Availability: The complete set of 642 titles is available. Individual items at prices listed.
3. Orders: Inter Documentation Company AG, Poststrasse 14, Zug, Switzerland.
4. The selection of this material was based in part on *Bibliographies and Books on Librarianship Printed in Russian Characters in the Helsinki University Library*, by Yrjö Aav, nr. 7 in the IDC series *Bibliotheca Slavica-Original Publications* (Zug, 1970. 171 p.). The list is alphabetical and gives place, date of publication, and collation of the original, with price of each microfiche in Swiss francs. Updated by new listings in IDC's *Newsletter.*

73. Inter Documentation Company, Zug.
Slavonics: monographs. Zug, Switzerland, 1966. 31 p. (Basic collections in microedition)
1. Type of microform: Microfiche.
2. Availability: Priced items are available for delivery. On request further information about unpriced items will be supplied.
3. Orders: Inter Documentation Company AG, Poststrasse 14, Zug, Switzerland.
4. This enlarged catalog supersedes the 1964 edition. Based on selective bibliographies prepared by well-known scholars, it includes those works considered essential for postgraduate study and research. Monographs are arranged by author in one alphabetical sequence.

74. Inter Documentation Company, Zug.
Slavonics: periodicals. Catalog 1969. Microfiche-editions. [Zug] Switzerland, 1969. 42 p.
1. Type of microform: Microfiche.
2. Availability: All items listed available at prices indicated.
3. Orders: Inter Documentation Company AG, Poststrasse 14, Zug, Switzerland.
4. Alphabetical listing of Slavic periodical titles available, giving place of publication, period covered by each, notation of any missing volumes, and price in Sw. fr. A catalog card is supplied with each microfiche. Updated by new listings in IDC's *Newsletter.*

75. Inter Documentation Company, Zug.
    Slavonics: Symbolism, futurism, acmeism, imaginism. 1971 catalogue. Microfiche-editions. [Zug] Switzerland, 1970. 43 p.
    1. Type of microform: Microfiche.
    2. Availability: The entire set is available. Each complete group may also be purchased separately.
    3. Orders: Inter Documentation Company AG, Poststrasse 14, Zug, Switzerland.
    4. Under "symbolism" monographs/periodical and joint publications items are listed alphabetically by author. Next follows a list of monographs and periodical publications; about symbolism ". . .". A similar arrangement is found under the headings: futurism, acmeism, and imaginism. No separate listing is made of articles contained in journals for which a complete run is supplied.

76. Inter Documentation Company, Zug.
    Slavonics: Zemstvo publications [compiled by] Basile Kerblay. Catalogue 1970. Microfiche-editions. [Zug] Switzerland, 1970. 20 p.
    1. Type of microform: Microfiche.
    2. Availability: Available separately at prices listed, or as a complete set.
    3. Orders: Inter Documentation Company AG, Poststrasse 14, Zug, Switzerland.
    4. "The object of this collection is to achieve a systematic microfilm edition of the statistical publications of the Zemstvo [provincial administrative bodies set up after the Reform of 1861] held by the principal Western libraries (525 titles . . .) to be supplemented by loans from Soviet libraries (74 titles)." The arrangement is alphabetical by province and within each province alphabetical by title, giving dates covered and collation of the original. Updated by new listings in IDC's *Newsletter*.

77. Inter Documentation Company, Zug.
    Social and economic development plans. Catalogue 1970. Microfiche-editions. [Zug] Switzerland, 1970. 55 p.
    1. Type of microform: Microfiche.
    2. Availability: Complete set and individual titles available. It is planned to keep the collection up to date. Standing orders are accepted and may be limited to those specific countries designated by the purchaser.
    3. Orders: Inter Documentation Company AG, Poststrasse 14, Zug, Switzerland.
    4. This second cumulative *Catalogue* lists 759 plans from 161 countries, whereas the first listed 323 plans from 113 countries. The arrangement is alphabetical by country.

78. Inter Documentation Company, Zug.
    South East Asia [by] M. A. Jaspan. Checklist of literature proposed for micropublishing. [Zug, Switzerland] n.d. 41 p.
    1. Type of microform: Microfiche.
    2. Availability: At the time the *Checklist* was published, only a small percentage of the items were available.

3. Orders: Inter Documentation Company AG, Poststrasse 14, Zug, Switzerland.

4. This *Checklist* is a preliminary compilation of serial publications concerning South East Asia. It is intended to serve as a bibliography from which items may be selected for a microfiche publication program and also as the first step in producing a standard catalog of all South East Asia serial publications, together with relevant information about the location and completeness of each series. The arrangement of the *Checklist* is by country. Symbols of twenty-two libraries indicate known long or complete runs of many of the serial titles listed.

79. Inter Documentation Company, Zug.
Taxonomic literature [by] F. A. Stafleu. Catalog 1969. Microfiche-editions. [Zug] Switzerland, n.d. 21 p.
1. Type of microform: Microfiche.
2. Availability: All items are available for immediate delivery at listed prices.
3. Orders: Inter Documentation Company AG, Poststrasse 14, Zug, Switzerland.
4. This *Catalog* lists those books described by Stafleu in his *Taxonomic Literature, a Selective Guide to Botanical Publications with Date, Commentaries and Types* (Utrecht: International Bureau for Plant Taxonomy and Nomenclature; Zug, Switzerland: Inter Documentation Co., 1967) which have been made available on microfiche.

80. Inter Documentation Company, Zug.
Zoology. Zug, Switzerland, 1966. 16 p. (Basic collections in microedition)
1. Type of microform: Michrofiche.
2. Availability: Separate items are available at prices listed.
3. Orders: Inter Documentation Company AG, Poststrasse 14, Zug, Switzerland.
4. This 1966 catalog supersedes the 1964 edition. Based on materials selected by scholars in the field, it provides a list of works deemed essential for postgraduate study and research. Monographs are listed under the headings: (1) travels; (2) general works; (3) mammals; (4) birds; (5) fish and reptiles; (6) insects; (7) other invertebrates. Next are twenty-four periodicals followed by a final section devoted to addenda.

81. Kassel. Deutsches Musikgeschichtliches Archiv.
Katalog der Filmsammlung. Hrsg. von Harold Heckmann. Bd. 1- Frühjahr 1955- Kassel, Bärenreiter, v. 1 (1955-63) (issues 1-6); v. 2, no. 1-2 (1965-1967) (issues 7-8)
1. Type of microform: Microfilm.
2. Availability: Positive copies are available.
3. Orders: Deutsches Musikgeschichtliches Archiv, Ständeplatz 16, Kassel, Germany.
4. The main goal of the Archiv is a collection of source material on microforms. Buyers of film must ask permission of the Archiv before they publish large portions of unpublished source material. Further, they cannot

sell or duplicate the films. Volume 1 lists 2,241 titles and volume 2, so far, 1,021.

82. Kokuritsu Kokkai Toshokan, Tokyo. (Japan. National Diet Library, Tokyo.)
Zenkoku shinbun microfilm seisaku shozō ichiran. Tokyo, 1970.

A letter from the National Diet Library reported the publication in 1970 of the above *List of Japanese Newspapers on Microfilm in Japan*. Not seen by compiler.

83. Leasco Systems and Research Corporation.
Now you can get the corporate reports you use regularly—without a hassle. [Bethesda, Md., 1970?] Unpaged (*Its* Report no. DB2)
1. Type of microform: Microfiche.
2. Availability: Various annual subscription packages are available. Single items may also be ordered. Fast delivery of reports (approximately ten days) is a major advantage of the program.
3. Orders: Leasco Information Products, Inc., 4827 Rugby Avenue, Bethesda, Maryland 20014.
4. Disclosure, the name of the financial information service described in this pamphlet, has been in operation since 1966. The Securities and Exchange Commission has contracted with Leasco to disseminate reports in the commission files to the general public. Both companies which report to the Securities and Exchange Commission and those traded over-the-counter and on regional exchanges are covered. For a list of companies, see the annual *Directory of Companies Filing Annual Reports with Securities and Exchange Commission* (Washington: Government Printing Office). The types of reports provided are briefly described in the above publication, namely, 10K annual reports, 8K and 9K current and semiannual reports, annual report to shareholders, proxy statements, registration statements, final prospectuses, and N-1Q quarterly reports and N-1R annual reports of registered management investment companies.

84. Levin, Alfred.
Microfilm materials from the Slavic Division of the Helsinki University Library in the Oklahoma State University Library. Prepared by Research Foundation, Oklahoma State University, Stillwater, Oklahoma, Marvin T. Edmison, Director. [Stillwater] 1960. 18 1.
1. Type of microform: Microfilm.
2. Availability: Copies of microfilm are available on interlibrary loan, with the exception of a few rolls which have become fragile.
3., Order: Interlibrary Loan Service, Oklahoma State University Library, Stillwater, Oklahoma 74074.
4. Lists the contents of fifty-three rolls of microfilm. The preface points out that the numbers of journals and newspapers cited are not necessarily complete. Primarily, they include only the pages containing information on Duma debates or organization or articles which throw some light on these matters. Included also are books and parts of books, pamphlets, and brochures.

85. Library Microfilms.
    Annual, 1968. Materials on microfilm. Palo Alto [1968?] 56 [1] p.
    1. Type of microform: Microfilm; microfiche and hard-copy reprints can also be supplied.
    2. Availability: All titles are available at the prices listed.
    3. Orders: Library Microfilms, 4009 Transport Street, Palo Alto, California 94303.
    4. The 1968 catalog lists material under a total of twenty-one headings. These headings are not arranged alphabetically but the final page of the catalog does list them in alphabetical order with page references. The catalog includes a wide variety of material with an emphasis on California and the West.

86. Library Resources, Inc.
    The microbook library series. [Chicago, 1970?] 16 p.
    1. Type of microform: Ultramicrofiche.
    2. Availability: Commercial publication.
    3. Orders: Library Resources, Inc., 201 East Ohio Street, Chicago, Illinois 60611.
    4. This booklet describes the long-range plans Library Resources has for producing an extensive series of library collections in ultramicrofiche. The first of the series, "The Library of American Civilization," contains over 12,000 titles selected by a group of advisers known for their preeminence in American studies. Catalogs in several forms are available for the series: (1) bound book catalog, (2) microfiche catalog, and (3) set of standard catalog cards for each title. Topical bibliographies called "Biblioguides" will further increase the value and usefulness of the series.
    The publisher lists the titles of sixteen future microbook libraries, among them: "Library of European Civilization" (divided into three parts), "Library of English Literature," "Library of French Literature," "Library of African Studies," "Library of Oriental Studies," etc.

87. Lublin (City) Uniwersytet. Ośrodek Archiwow Bibliotek i Muzeów Kościelnych.
    Katalog mikrofilmów Osrodka, Archiwów, Bibliotek i Muzéow Kościelnych przy Katolickim Uniwersytecie Lubelskim. Lublin, 1963-66. 2 v.
    No. 1 was published in *Archiwa; biblioteki i muzea kóscielne.* v. 6, p. 67-153. 1963, and no. 2 was reprinted from the same periodical, v. 13, 1966. Not seen by compiler.

88. Luther, Frederic, Company.
    Micropublications in print, a catalogue of out of print materials republished in microfilm. Indianapolis, n.d. various paging; spiral binding
    1. Type of microform: Microfilm.
    2. Availability: Items available at prices listed.
    3. Orders: The Frederic Luther Company, Box 20224, Indianapolis, Indiana 46220.
    4. This catalog includes material in the fields of genealogy and local history, limited primarily to the Midwest. Some Indiana newspapers, local

histories, and directories are listed, plus the records of several Quaker Meetings.

89. Malaysia. National Archives.
Catalogue of microfilm, 1968 (as at 30th June) [Kuala Lumpur, 1968] 6 1.
    1. Type of microform: Microfilm.
    2. Availability: Copies of film may be purchased.
    3. Orders: Director, National Archives of Malaysia, Jalan Sultan Petaling Jaya, Malaysia.
    4. The *Catalogue* lists newspapers, government publications, and private archives, including church records, diaries, etc.

90. Michigan. Bureau of Library Services.
Michigan newspapers on microfilm, with a description of the "Michigan Newspapers on Microfilm" project. [2d ed.] Lansing, Mich., Michigan Department of Education, Bureau of Library Services [1970] Unpaged.
———— ———— Additions, Feb. - Sept. 1970. 2 1.
    1. Type of microform: Microfilm.
    2. Availability: Available for use at the state library or via interlibrary loan.
    3. Orders: Interlibrary Loan Service, Michigan State Library, 735 East Michigan Avenue, Lansing, Michigan 48913.
    4. A listing, alphabetically by city, town, or village, of newspapers filmed commercially or by the state library in coöperation with seven leading libraries of the state, members of the Michigan Newspapers on Microfilm Project formed in 1962 to preserve valuable historical records. A third and much enlarged edition is being prepared.

91. Micro Methods Limited.
Catalog 1970. Genealogy and heraldry, Section D. [East Ardsley, Yorkshire] 1970. 9 p.
    1. Type of microform: Microfilm, microfiche, microcard.
    2. Availability: All items available at prices listed.
    3. Orders: Micro Methods Limited, East Ardsley, Wakefield, Yorkshire, England.
    4. This sales catalog lists materials in the field of genealogy and heraldry under four headings: (1) original parish registers and transcripts; (2) Moravian church registers; (3) monumental inscriptions; (4) general. Geographical breakdowns are employed under the headings where applicable.

92. Micro Methods Limited.
Catalogue 1970. History, Section A. [East Ardsley, Yorkshire] 1970. 28 p.
    1. Type of microform: Microfilm, microfiche, microcard.
    2. Availability: All items available at prices listed.
    3. Orders: Micro Methods Limited, East Ardsley, Wakefield, Yorkshire, England.
    4. This sales catalog lists materials in the field of history under seven headings: (1) Europe; (2) America; (3) Africa; (4) Asia & the Middle East; (5) ecclesiastical history; (6) voyages, exploration, trade & miscellaneous; (7)

library indices relating to history. Materials listed under headings 1-5 are subdivided.

93. Micro Methods Limited.
    Catalogue 1971. Illuminated manuscripts, books on art, social history, etc., Section H. [East Ardsley, Yorkshire] 1971. 17 p.
    1. Type of microform: Microfilm, color microfilm, microfiche, film-strips, color slides.
    2. Availability: All items available at prices listed.
    3. Orders: Micro Methods Limited, East Ardsley, Wakefield, Yorkshire, England.
    4. This sales catalog lists materials relevant to studies in art and the history of art and background studies in social history under seven headings: (1) Holkham Hall manuscripts in the collection of the Earl of Leicester; (2) The Bodleian Library; (3) university libraries and college libraries; (4) libraries, public and private collections; (5) museums; (6) cathedral libraries; (7) miscellaneous sources including printed material. Subdivisions are used under the above headings where applicable.

94. Micro Methods Limited—S. R. Publishers Limited.
    Major projects in microform and full size reprints. [East Ardsley, Yorkshire] 1970. Unpaged; some pages folded.
    1. Type of microform: Microfilm, color microfilm, microfiche.
    2. Availability: Priced items are available.
    3. Orders: Micro Methods Limited, East Ardsley, Wakefield, Yorkshire, England.
    4. This sales catalog lists not only projects such as "British Records Relating to America" and "Religious and Missionary Records," but also types of material available in microform, e.g., theses, newspapers, journals. It includes useful historical and explanatory notes. In some instances, all materials included in a project are not listed. For example, only a few of the materials included in the project *British Records Relating to America,* (see item 345) are given. There is, however, the statement, "full catalogue available on request."

95. Microcard Editions, Inc.
    Catalog. no. 1-   July 1959-
    Washington.   Annual.
    Latest edition: Catalog 12, 1971-72.
    1. Type of microform: Microfiche, microfilm, micro-opaques.
    2. Availability: Priced publications are available for immediate delivery. Publications designated as "in production" were being filmed at the time the catalog went to the printer and will be available within the next few months. The term "inquire" is used for those publications for which reprint plans have definitely been made but which are not yet actually in production.
    3. Orders: Order Processing Department, NCR/Microcard Editions, 365 South Oak Street, West Salem, Wisconsin 54669.
    4. An alphabetical listing of books and serials available or to be available in microform, a separate one-page list of newspapers on 35mm microfilm, and

a subject index. Most entries include a brief description of the publication, and all give type of microform.

96. Microfile (Pty.) Ltd.
[Catalogue] Johannesburg [1971?] [12] l.
1. Type of microform: Microfilm.
2. Availability: Commercially published.
3. Orders: Microfile (Pty.) Ltd., A.F.C. House, P.O. Box 4552, Johannesburg, Republic of South Africa.
4. The catalog lists the South African newspapers and periodicals available on microfilm. For each newspaper a brief history is given. Other groups of materials available are briefly described, but no indication of the extent of material in each group is noted.

97. Microfilm Center, Inc.
Microfiche editions (4 x 6 format) of classics and j[unio]r classics. Dallas, 1971. 1 p.
1. Type of microform: Microfiche.
2. Availability: Commercially published. Single book or a group of books may be purchased.
3. Orders: Microfilm Center, Inc., 2043 Proctor Street, Dallas, Texas 75235.
4. A title list of forty-four books available on microfiche.

98. Microfilm Center, Inc.
Micropublications in print; a catalogue of out-of-print materials republished in microfiche form. Dallas, 1971. 2 p.
1. Type of microform: Microfiche.
2. Availability: Commercially published.
3. Orders: Microfilm Center, Inc., 2043 Proctor Street, Dallas, Texas 75235.
4. This *Catalogue* lists eighty out-of-print titles concerned with Texas and the Southwest. Each book is entered under title followed by author, publisher, and date. The publisher states that he plans to add a section on Midwest Americana and a section on Western Americana.

99. Microfilm Center, Inc.
Southwestern newspapers and historical material on microfilm. 1969-1970 edition. Dallas [1969?] 39 p.
1. Type of microform: Microfilm.
2. Availability: Commercially published.
3. Orders: Microfilm Center, Inc., 2043 Proctor Street, Dallas, Texas 75235.
4. The list includes newspapers from eleven states, historical and genealogical material, primarily from Texas, the *American State Papers*, and Mexican diplomatic notes and dispatches.

100. Microlibrary Canisianum.
Catalogue. Maastricht, 1966. Various paging

1. Type of microform: Microfiche.
2. Availability: "Our library is willing to put its microfiches at the disposal of other libraries *for purposes of scientific study only.* This offer is made to libraries of theological and philosophical faculties, seminaries and colleges, and of universities which have theological or philosophical departments.

"The microlibrary is also willing to print microfiches of books and manuscripts on request, even if it does not need such microfiches for its own purposes."

3. Orders: Microlibrary Canisianum, Tongersestraat 53, Maastricht, The Netherlands.
4. This *Catalogue* of approximately a hundred pages is arranged by subject groups preceded by a listing of the periodicals available. The subject groups are: Arabica, canon law, church history, dogmatics, exegesis, liturgy, missiology, Orientalia Christiana, patrology, and philosophy. Following the subject groups are listed the volumes of the *Sitzungsberichte* der Königlich-Preussischen Akademie der Wissenschaften, Berlin, available, and six pages of varia. There is no index.

101. Microprint Publications, Ltd.
    The law; a new service of microreproduction. Catalogue of microreproductions. London, 1962. [9] p.
    1. Type of microform: Microcards.
    2. Availability: Commercially published
    3. Orders: Microprint Publications, Ltd., 287 Streatham High Road, London, S. W. 16, England.
    4. This brief catalog lists nine legal titles of both monographic and serial nature. Microprint Publications is no longer producing microforms. This 1962 catalog was the last issued.

102. Mikrofilmarchiv der deutschsprachigen Presse, e. V. [Microfilm Archives of the German Language Press. Dortmund] 1970. 113 p.
    1. Type of microform: Microfilm.
    2. Availability: All items are available at prices given. Orders for film titles not yet in the files will be accepted.
    3. Orders: Institut für Zeitungsforschung, Wissstrasse 4, Dortmund D-46, Germany.
    4. The Microfilm Archives of the German Language Press, located with the Institute for Newspaper Research in Dortmund, collects periodicals, especially those of the nineteenth and twentieth centuries, records them on microfilm, registers the films, and makes them available, primarily to research and educational institutions. This catalog lists titles under six headings: (1) before 1918; (2) 1918-1933; (3) 1933-1945; (4) post-1945 (in this section there are two lists, one under Federal Republic of Germany and the other under German Democratic Republic); (5) exile press; (6) labor movement to 1933. An index provides an approach to specific titles.

103. Minerva Mikrofilm A/S, Copenhagen.
    Fortegnelse over danske aviser 1648-1967 med angivelse af de mikro-

filmede. Index of Danish newspapers 1648-1967 including register of micro-filmed volumes. [Udarbejdet af H. Tønnesen] København [1967] 35 p.

    1. Type of microform: Microfilm.

    2. Availability: May be purchased; no prices given.

    3. Orders: Minerva Mikrofilm A/S, Ehlersvej 27, Hellerup, Denmark.

    4. An alphabetical listing of Danish newspapers, giving years covered and designation "Mikrofilm" for those on microfilm. The newspapers outside Denmark are listed separately, alphabetically under Faerøerne, Grønland, Dansk Vestindien, and Slesvig-Holsten.

104. Minnesota Historical Society.

    Catalog of microfilms for sale by the Minnesota Historical Society [St. Paul] 1970. 30 p.

    1. Type of microform: Microfilm.

    2. Availability: 35mm Kalvar positive microfilms are offered for sale. Where specific prices are not shown, the price is based on footage. Average price per reel would be $17.50.

    3. Orders: Microrecording Service, Minnesota Historical Society, 1500 Mississippi Street, St. Paul, Minnesota 55101.

    4. The first six titles represent manuscript collections prepared under grants of funds from the National Historical Publications Commission; the second grouping lists for the most part materials in the society's library. The third and largest grouping represents newspapers filmed since the program began in 1948. Minnesota newspapers are listed first, followed by newspapers from other states, and those of other countries. Arrangement within each category is alphabetically by town.

105. Modern Language Association of America.

    Reproductions of manuscripts and rare printed books. Short title list (complete to January 1, 150) (In PMLA v. 65, no. 3 (1950) p. 289-338)

    1. Type of microform: Microfilm.

    2. Availability: On deposit at the Library of Congress and may be borrowed on interlibrary loan. Microfilm copies of the rotographs and of the master films may ordinarily be purchased.

    3. Orders: Photoduplication Service, Library of Congress, Washington, D.C. 20540.

    4. Lists the rotographs or microfilms of the manuscripts and rare printed materials purchased with the proceeds of the Fund for Photographic Reproductions collected by the Modern Language Association. Film reproductions are indicated by the addition of "F" to the serial number. The number of sheets is given for rotographs, and the number of frames for films. There are two indexes: (1) location of manuscripts and books, and (2) authors, or titles when anonymous. This list supersedes the pamphlet of the same title issued by the Modern Language Association in 1942.

106. New York. Public Library.

    Publications in print and titles available on microfilm. New York, 1970. 27 p.

1. Type of microform: Microfilm.
2. Availability: Positive copies are available. Prices available upon request.
3. Orders: Photographic Service Division, New York Public Library, Fifth Avenue & 42nd Street, New York, New York 10018.
   Payment required in advance. Purchase orders for amounts over $10.00 will, however, be accepted from libraries and academic institutions.
4. "Selected List of Titles Available on Microfilm" which appears on pp. 18-27 contains primarily periodicals. "Hebraica and Judaica" are listed separately on pp. 20-21, while "official Government Gazettes" are listed on pp. 21-27.

107. Nihon Maikuro Shashin Kabushiki Kaisha, Tokyo.
Maikuro-firumu-ban kanko goannai. [Tokyo, 1970?] [4] p.
A publisher's list which includes several runs of Japanese newspapers, account reports of 1,500 Japanese companies, and important basic materials for sociological studies.

108. Nihon Maikuro Shashin Kabushiki Kaisha, Tokyo.
Nyushu kano shiryo annai. [Tokyo] 1970. [7] 1.
A publisher's catalog which lists microfilm publications in the following fields: history, political science, law, economics, socialism, industry, education, women, religion, culture, plus newspapers and materials of general interest.

109. North Carolina. University. Library.
Agricultural and manufacturing census records of fifteen southern states for the years 1850, 1860, 1870, and 1880. A microfilm project of the University of North Carolina Library under a grant from the National Science Foundation [Chapel Hill] 1966. 15 p.
1. Type of microform: Microfilm.
2. Availability: Positive copies of master negatives held by the University of North Carolina Library may be purchased. Price for each reel and for all reels for each state given. If the University of North Carolina does not own the negative, information is given about how copies may be secured.
3. Orders: Photographic Service, University of North Carolina Library, Chapel Hill, North Carolina 27514.
4. Indicates the contents of 300 reels of microfilm containing the agricultural and census records of Alabama, Arkansas, Delaware, Florida, Georgia, Kentucky, Louisiana, Maryland, Mississippi, North Carolina, Tennessee, Texas, South Carolina, Virginia, and West Virginia for the years 1850, 1860, 1870, and 1880.

110. Orion Books.
Kicho bunken maikuro firumu. [Microfilms of historical documents] Tokyo [1970] p. 11-[16]
1. Type of microform: Microfilm, microfiche.
2. Availability: Documents listed are available, and prices will be quoted upon request.
3. Orders: Orion Books, Orion Service & Trading Co., Inc., 1-55 Kanda, Jimbacho, Chiyoda-ku, Tokyo, Japan 101.

4. Lists documents available under following subjects: philosophy, history (includes geography and local gazetteers), social sciences (includes law, military history, political science, foreign relations), physical sciences, industry and agriculture, and philology. Some items are Chinese, but most are Japanese.

111. Ottawa. National Library.
Canadian theses on microfilm. Catalogue—Price list. Thèses Canadiennes sur microfilm. Ottawa, 1969. 251 p.
————— ————— Supplement no. 1-   June 1969-   Ottawa, 1969-
   1. Type of microform: Microfilm.
   2. Availability: Theses listed are available for purchase.
   3. Orders: Canadian Theses on Microfilm, Cataloging Branch, Room 414, National Library of Canada, Ottawa, Ontario, Canada.
   4. Lists through March 1971, 6,865 theses selected by participating Canadian universities to be published in microfilm form and sold by the National Library. The arrangement is by series number, which also serves as an order number. There is no index.

112.   Ouvrages cyrilliques concernant les sciences sociales; liste des reproductions disponible. Cyrillic publications concerning the social sciences; current list of reproductions. Paris, Mouton, 1964-65. 2 v. (Cahiers du monde russe et soviétique. Supplément, 1-2.
   1. Type of microform: Microfilm, microcard, microfiche. The *Liste* includes also Duopage and offset works.
   2. Availability: Available from publisher indicated.
   3. Orders: Orders must be placed with individual microform publisher.
   4. This *Liste*, though somewhat out of date, is still valuable. It shows which Russian books and periodicals in the fields of the social sciences were available in 1964 in offset or some type of microform. "Social sciences" is used in the broadest sense, including languages, literature, arts, theater, etc. The chapters are devoted to types of material, e.g., "reference works and bibliographies" or "periodicals" or to subject areas, e.g., "languages," "arts and theater," "philosophy and religion," etc.

113. PCMI library collections: catalog no. 1-   Dayton, National Cash Register Co., Educational Products Dept. [1970]
   1. Type of microform: Ultramicrofiche.
   2. Availability: All or any one of the five collections (literature-humanities, social sciences, American civilization, science and technology, and government documents) may be purchased.
   3. Order: NCR, Educational Products Dept., 1000 Cox Plaza, 3131 South Dixie Drive, Dayton, Ohio 45439.
   4. For Section 1 (literature-humanities), there is given first a list of bibliographic sources from which the books in this collection were chosen. Then follows a list of topics covered in the collection, arranged according to Library of Congress classification numbers, and last, an author-title index of books in the collection, which includes the number of the PCMI ultrafiche for

each book. The same type of information is provided in turn for Section 2 (social sciences), Section 3 (American civilization), Section 4 (science and technology) and Section 5 (government documents). The price of each collection includes a full set of Library of Congress cards for each title.

114. Pan American Institute of Geography and History. Commission on History.
Guía de los documentos microfotografiados por la Unidad Móvil de Micro-film de la Unesco. México, 1963. 317 p. (*Its* [Publicación] 112. Fuentes documentales para la historia de America. Guías 1)
Instituto Panamericano de Geografía e Historia, Publicación 269.
1. Type of microform: Microfilm.
2. Availability: A positive film was left in the country where the docu-ments were photographed, and a negative was deposited with the Pan Amer-ican Institute of Geography and History, which can supply copies on request (cf. "The Unesco Microfilm Unit in Latin America" *Unesco Bulletin for Libraries*. v. 16, pp. 182-86. July-August 1962).
3. Order: Comisión de Historia, Instituto Panamericano Geografía e His-toria, Ex-Arzobispado 29, Tacubaya, México, D. F., México.
4. In 1954 UNESCO established a Mobile Microfilm Unit for the use of any member state requesting its services in microfilming valuable material (manu-scripts, printed matter, engravings, etc.) in danger of deterioration or possible destruction. The material to be filmed was selected by experts in each country visited.
This general guide to the documents filmed in several Latin American countries gives useful background material in the introduction on the Unidad Móvil de Microfilm and then the lists (by roll number) of the documents filmed in Peru, Paraguay, Panama, Honduras, Barbados, El Salvador, and the Dominican Republic. The lists vary in arrangement; some are provided with indexes.

115. Pan American Institute of Geography and History. Commission on History.
Barbados, guía des documentos; microfotografiados por la Unidad Móvil de Microfilm de la Unesco. México, 1965. 141 p. (*Its* [Publicación] 113. Fuentes documentales para la historia de América, Guías 2)
Instituto Panaméricano de Geografía e Historia. Publicación no. 270.
1. Type of microform: Microfilm.
2. Availability: A positive film was left in the country where the docu-ments were photographed, and a negative was deposited with the Pan Ameri-can Institute of Geography and History, which can supply copies on request (cf. "The Unesco Microfilm Unit in Latin America" *Unesco Bulletin for Libraries*. v. 16, pp. 182-186. July-August 1962).
3. Orders: Comision de Historia, Instituto Panamericano de Geografía e Historia, Ex-Arzobispado 29, Tacubaya, México, D. F., Mexico.
4. "Between 1960 and September 1961, the programme for the Survey and preservation of Archives in the West Indies, formulated by the University College of the West Indies with a grant from the Rockefeller Foundation, was put into operation in Barbados. . . .
"During six months of the survey microfilming was also carried out. In 1960 a UNESCO mobile microfilm unit also operated in Barbados. . . .

"In selecting materials for filming by the U. C. W. I. unit, the work already done by UNESCO was naturally taken into consideration."

This guide begins with checklists of printed government serials in Barbados and in University College of the West Indies, Jamaica, showing locations. Then comes a serial list of microfilm reels, followed by groupings of various types of archives, e.g., ecclesiastical archives, which include records of the Methodist and Moravian churches; private archives, which include the Barbados Chamber of Commerce, Barbados General Agricultural Society, records of businesses, etc. For each category the reel number is cited.

116. Pan American Institute of Geography and History. Commission on History.
    Honduras. Guía de los documentos microfotografiados por la Unidad Móvil de Microfilm de la Unesco. Mexico, 1967. 245 p. (*Its* [Publicación] 120. Fuentes documentales para la historia de América, Guías 3)
    Instituto Panamericano de Geografía e Historia. Publicación no. 307.
    1. Type of microform: Microfilm.
    2. Availability: A positive film was left in the country where the documents were photographed, and a negative copy was deposited with the Pan American Institute of Geography and History, which can supply copies on request. (cf. "The Unesco Microfilm Unit in Latin America." *Unesco Bulletin for Libraries.* v. 16, pp. 182-186. July-August 1962).
    3. Orders: Comision de Historia, Instituto Panamericano de Geografia e Historia, Ex-Arzobispado 29, Tacubaya, México, D. F., México.
    4. In 1954 UNESCO established a Mobil Microfilm Unit for the use of any member state requesting its services in microfilming valuable material (manuscripts, printed matter, engravings, etc.) in danger of deterioration or possible destruction. The material to bc filmed was selected by experts in each country visited. This guide gives a detailed listing of the contents of each of the 100 reels filmed in 1958/59 by the Mobile Unit. An index of personal and place names completes the guide.

117. Paoletti, Odette.
    Périodiques et publications en série concernant les sciences sociales et humaines, liste de reproductions disponibles dans le commerce (microformes et réimpressions). Periodicals and serials concerning the social sciences and humanities, current list of available reproductions (microforms and reprints). Paris, Maison des Sciences de l'Homme, Service Bibliothèque-Documentation, 1966. 2 v.
    ———— ———— Supplement, 1967/68. Paris, Maison des Sciences de l'Homme, Service Bibliothèque-Documentation [1968?] 2 v.
    1. Type of microform: All types.
    2. Availability: Prices cited are taken from publishers' catalogs of ca. 1966.
    3. Orders: Orders should be sent to publisher.
    4. This list is the result of activities carried on over a three-year period by the Service Bibliothèque-Documentation of the Maison des Sciences de l'Homme in building up an extensive collection of periodicals and serials in the social sciences and humanities.
    Arrangement is alphabetical by title. The following information is given for

each title: place of publication; years reproduced; process of reproduction (reprint, microfilm, microfiche, microprint, microcard); publisher; current prices (i.e., those taken from the catalogs of 64 publishers).

The 1967/68 *Supplement* based on publishers' catalogs or notices received between January 1967 and January 1968 adds 1,330 new titles and 30 new publishers, giving a total of 1,855 titles available from 94 publishers.

118. Pascoe (W. & F.) Pty. Ltd.
Australian newspapers and periodicals on microfilm, 1970. Catalogue. Milson's Point, N. S. W., 1970. [4] p.
1. Type of microform: Microfilm.
2. Availability: Available at prices listed.
3. Orders: W. & F. Pascoe Pty. Ltd., 2a Glen Street, Milson's Point, N. S. W. 2061, Australia.
4. The listing is alphabetical by place and gives years covered, footage, and price in Australian dollars.

119. Philippines (Republic) National Library. Filipiniana Division.
A list of microfilms. Manila [1969] 13, 2 p.
This *List* includes newspapers, periodicals, and historical documents of the Philippines which the National Library holds in microfilm.

120. Poland. Naczelna Dyrekcja Archiwów Państwowych.
Katalog mikrofilmów i fotokopii poloniców z archiwów zagranicznych. Warszawa, 1965-69. Zesz. 1-2.
A catalog of microfilms and photocopies by Poles from foreign countries. Not seen by compiler.

121. Poland. Naczelna Dyrekcja Archiwów Państwowych. Archiwum Dokumentacji Mechanicznej w Warszawie.
Katalog mikrofilmów archiwalnych. Warszawa, 1961-62. 2 v.
Catalog of microfilmed mechanical documentation in Warsaw. Not seen by compiler.

122. Polska Akademia Nauk. Ośrodek Dokumentacji i Informacji Naukowej.
Katalog mikrofilmów sprowadzonych z zagranicy w latach . . . 1954-1968. Warszawa, 1963-69. [5 v.]
Catalog of microfilms from foreign countries. Not seen by compiler.

123. Polska Zjednoczona Partiia Robotnicza. Komitet Centralny. Zaklad Historii Partii.
Informator o zasobie mikrofilmowym. Warszawa, 1964-66. 3 v.
Guide to microfilm resources. Not seen by compiler.

124. Princeton Microfilm Corporation.
Congressional record directory, 1789-1968, and other micropublications. Microfilm catalog 36. [Princeton, N. J., 1969] 23 p.
1. Type of microform: Microfilm.
2. Availability: All items available at prices listed.

3. Orders: Princeton Microfilm Corporation, Alexander Road, Princeton, New Jersey 08540.

4. The catalog lists each reel, giving volume numbers, parts, pages, sessions, years, and cost per reel. The other microfilm publications (pp. 22-23) are a selection of journals and other United States documents.

125. Queensland. University, Brisbane. Press.
    Microform catalogue, 1969-70. [Brisbane, Savage & Company, Pty., 1969] 23 p.
    1. Type of microform: Microfilm (positive).
    2. Availability: Positive prints available at prices stated.
    3. Orders: Orders should be placed with: University of Queensland Press, Microform Division, Santa Lucia, Brisbane, Australia.

Orders originating in the United Kingdom and Europe should be directed to: Christopher Hurst, 13 James Street, London, W. C. 2, England.

Orders originating in the United States and Canada should be directed to: Richard Abel & Co., Inc., Box 4245, Portland, Oregon 97208, U.S.A.

    4. The Microform Division of the University of Queensland Press "was established in 1968 to help disseminate important research material." The 1969-70 *Catalogue* lists monographs, publications issued in series, government documents, theses, serials, and newspapers. All materials thus far available relate directly to Australia.

126. Quezon, Philippines. University of the Philippines. Library.
    Filipiniana on microfilms. [Quezon City] 1970. (*Its* Research guide, no. 18)
    Information supplied by a letter from National Library of the Philippines. Not seen by compiler.

127. Readex Microprint publications, 1969-70. New York, Readex Microprint Corporation [1969] 168 p.
    1. Type of microform: Microprint.
    2. Availability: All items are available at stated prices.
    3. Orders: Readex Microprint Corporation, 5 Union Square, New York, New York 10003.
    4. This catalog provides excellent background information on the collections of government publications, literature, and newspapers available from Readex Microprint. Also listed are bibliographies, catalogs, and indexes published singly. There is a useful index.

128. Rhistoric Publications, Inc.
    Catalog - Fall 1970. Philadelphia, 1970. 23 p.
    1. Type of microform: Microfilm, microfiche.
    2. Availability: Some items in process of being filmed, but most are available at prices listed.
    3. Orders: Rhistoric Publications, Inc., 302 North 13th Street, Philadelphia, Pennsylvania 19107.
    4. The catalog lists, under the headings Americana, ethnology, sociology and genealogy, and English history, items available for purchase, mostly on 35mm microfilm, but a few on microfiche or printed. Material offered

includes manuscript collections of individuals or societies, some with printed guides, tax lists, parish registers, early American newspaper series, Africana, etc.

129. St. Thomas Public Library.
    Catalog of microfilms [available in the] Von Scholten Collection. 1967 - St. Thomas, V. I., Bureau of Libraries and Museums. Not seen by compiler.

130. St. Willibrords Abbey, Slangenburg-Doetinchem, Netherlands.
    Microlibrary. Slangenburg-Doetinchem [1971?]
    1. Type of microform: Microfiche.
    2. Availability: Microfiche supplied "for scientific purposes only, subject to approval of editors concerned."
    3. Orders: Microlibrary, St. Willibrords Abbey, Slangenburg-Doetinchem, The Netherlands.
    4. The abbey reproduces on microfiche for its own use scientific works and periodicals. The *Microlibrary* lists according to form, e.g., periodica and collectiones, and according to subject, e.g., philosophia, exegesis, theologia, liturgia, etc.

131. Schnase Microfilm Systems.
    Akademie der Wissenschaften, Berlin, 1710-1949. Complete collection of all serial publications. Scarsdale, N. Y., 1971. [4] p.
    1. Type of microform: Microfilm.
    2. Availability: Available at prices listed.
    3. Orders: Schnase Microfilm Systems, A Division of Annemarie Schnase Organization, 120 Brown Road, P.O. Box 119, Scarsdale, New York 10583.
    4. Lists chronologically the serial publications of the Akademie and of its Mathematisch-Naturwissenschaftliche Klasse and its Philosophisch-Historische Klasse, giving the period covered and number of reels for each title.

132. Scottish Central Library, Edinburgh.
    Out-of-print books and mss. on microfilm held in the Scottish Central Library. Edited by Miss J. A. Adams. 2d ed. Lawnmarket, Edinburgh, 1965. 69 p.
    1. Type of microform: Microfilm.
    2. Availability: Positive prints, enlarged document paper prints, or Xerographic copies available.
    3. Orders: Photographic Department, Scottish Central Library, Lawnmarket 1, Edinburgh, Scotland.
    4. Lists out-of-print books and manuscripts for which the Scottish Central Library has made a master microfilm negative. Arranged by the following groups: (1) general works; (2) Scottish family history and biography; (3) Scottish music; (4) Scottish social and economic history; (5) Scottish travel and description; (6) Scottish miscellany. Within each group, arrangement is alphabetical by author. For each item, a brief annotation is given. There is no index.

133. Seminar on the Acquisition of Latin American Library Materials.
    Microfilming Projects newsletter, edited by Suzanne Hodgman.
    No. 1-   1964-   Madison, Wis., Memorial Library, University of Wisconsin.
    Latest on hand: no. 12, June 1970
    Published semiannually, 1964-1968, annually since 1969, the newsletter
    lists microreproduction projects recently completed, in progress, and planned.
    It is based on questionnaires returned by members, and is confined to
    projects related to Latin America, organized according to the publishing
    library or firm. It is not cumulative.

134. Singapore (City) National Library.
    National library holdings on microfilm. [Singapore] 1970. 5 p. "NL
    200/62"
    This list is divided into two parts: early Singapore imprints and Singapore
    and Malaysian journals.

135. Singapore (City) National Library.
    National library holdings on microfilm. Singapore & Malaysian newspapers
    in English. [Singapore] 1969. 4 p. "NL 249/62"
    Not seen by compiler.

136. Singapore (City) National Library.
    National library holdings on microfilm. Straights Settlements Despatches,
    1861-1931. [Singapore] 1969. 4 p. "NL 249/62"
    Not seen by compiler.

137. Singapore (City) National Library.
    National Library holdings on microfilm. Straits Settlements Despatches,
    1867-1915. [Singapore] 1968. 7 p. "NL 103/62"
    Not seen by compiler.

138. Singapore (City) National Library.
    National library holdings on microfilm. Straits Settlements Despatches,
    1916-1941. [Singapore] 1969. 3 p. "NL 103/62"
    Not seen by compiler.

139. Singapore (City) National Library.
    National library holdings on microfilm. Straits Settlements Records,
    1800-1867. [Singapore] 1968. 13 p. "NL 103/62"
    Not seen by compiler.

140. Singapore (City) University. Library.
    Microfilm holdings in the field of Southeast Asia studies (non-scientific),
    1963. (Provisional list) [Singapore, 1963?] 11 p.
    This alphabetical list includes books, periodicals, government publications,
    and manuscripts.

141. Société Canadienne de Microfilm, Inc.
     Catalogue. Montreal, n.d. various paging; looseleaf
     1. Type of microform: Microfilm.
     2. Availability: Available at prices listed.
     3. Orders:Société Canadienne de Microfilm, Inc., 19, rue LeRoyer, ouest, Montreal 125, Quebec, Canada.
     4. The *Catalogue* provides several approaches to newspapers of Quebec which it has microfilmed: an alphabetical title list, a chronological list, and a list by city of publication. In addition, there is a list of Canadian newspapers published outside Quebec and a list of Canadian newspapers published in the United States available on microfilm.

142. Stanford University. Hoover Institution on War, Revolution and Peace.
     Chinese communist periodicals and newspapers.
     [no. 1]-   July 1969-   List no. 7 is dated May 1971.
     1. Type of microform: Microfilm.
     2. Availability: Positive prints are available for purchase. The material is also available in Xerox form when this form of reproduction is technically possible.
     3. Orders: Hoover Institution Press (Microfilms), Stanford University, Stanford, California 94305.
     4. List nos. 1-4 contain only post-1949 Communist periodicals. Beginning with list no. 5 (March 1970), not only periodicals but newspapers as well are included. Many of the periodicals and newspapers listed are thus made accessible for the first time outside mainland China. The lists are alphabetical by transliterated title. Following the transliterated title come place of publication, English translation of title, volumes and issues, and price.

143. Stanford University. Hoover Institution on War, Revolution and Peace.
     Journals on microfilm. Stanford, Calif., 1965. 32 p.
     1. Type of microform: Microfilm.
     2. Availability: Both entire runs of periodical issues filmed and portions of runs are available.
     3. Orders: Hoover Institution Press (Microfilms), Stanford University, Stanford, California 94305.
     4. The journals are listed alphabetically by title in four groups: German, French, English, and Russian. The Hoover Institution points out that the prices quoted are no longer in effect.

144. Stanford University. Hoover Institution on War, Revolution and Peace.
     Hoover Institution microfilms: Modern China, List 1, March 1971- Stanford, Calif., 1971-
     1. Type of microform: Microfilm.
     2. Availability: Each title is separately priced.
     3. Orders: Hoover Institution Press (Microfilms), Stanford University, Stanford, California 94305.
     4. This list of thirty-four titles is divided into the six following categories: (1) diplomatic periodicals; (2) diplomatic documents of China; (3) Shanghai

foreign settlements; (4) Afro-Asian People's Solidarity Conference; and (6) Chinese Communist biographical information.

145. Stanford University. Hoover Institution on War, Revolution and Peace.
      Russian language journals and books on microfilm (including some other East European publications). Stanford, Calif. 35 p.
      1. Type of microform: Microfilm.
      2. Availability: Both entire runs of periodical issues filmed and portions of runs are available.
      3. Orders: Hoover Institution Press (Microfilms), Stanford University, Stanford, California 94305.
      4. This guide lists the Russian, Czech, Polish, and Yugoslav books and journals which are available on microfilm. There is an alphabetical list of journals and a list of books arranged alphabetically by author. Prices are noted for journals but not for books; however, the Hoover Institution points out that the prices quoted are no longer in effect.

146. Stanford University. Hoover Institution on War, Revolution and Peace. Press.
      Microfilms, 1971. Stanford, Calif., 1971. 28 p.
      1. Type of microform: Microfilm.
      2. Availability: Available for purchase.
      3. Orders: Hoover Institution Press (Microfilms), Stanford, California 94305.
      4. This catalog lists selected journals and newspapers in Russian, French, German, Spanish, Arabic, and English. Dates covered, missing issues, and total number of reels and price per title are given. Also included are brief descriptive or explanatory notes. The journals are presented in four groups: Eastern Europe and the Soviet Union; Western Europe; Africa and the Middle East; Latin America. There is a title index.

147. Temple University. School of Law. Library.
      Microfilm series: 1970 publications list. [Philadelphia, 1970] 11 1.
      1. Type of microform: Microfilm.
      2. Availability: Available at cost.
      3. Orders: Microfilming Service, Temple University School of Law Library, 1715 North Broad Street, Philadelphia, Pennsylvania 19122.
      4. "In the interest of preserving certain legal materials which have become difficult to obtain," the Law Library of Temple University has microfilmed a number of titles, and in this *1970 Publications List* gives all necessary order information.

148. Tennessee. State Library and Archives, Nashville.
      Tennessee newspapers; a cumulative list of microfilmed newspapers in the Tennessee State Library, August 1969. Progress report. Nashville, 1969. 127 p.
      1. Type of microform: Microfilm.
      2. Availability: The library holds negatives of most titles and is prepared to supply positive copies. In a few instances the holders of negatives are other institutions or commercial firms, who also can supply positive film.

3. Orders: Restoration and Reproduction Division, Tennessee State Library and Archives, Nashville, Tennessee 37219.

4. "In 1957 the Tennessee State Library launched its program for the acquisition and microfilming of all available newspapers ever published in Tennessee." This latest cumulative list of microfilms of newspapers published in Tennessee contains 1,518 titles (12,503 reels of film). The analysis of holdings given refers to the positive microfilm collection maintained by the State Library Division and serviced by the Reference Section. The *List* indicates the location of the master negative for each title. Reports on titles are made to the Microfilm Clearing House at the Library of Congress, and appropriate holdings are included in *Newspapers on Microfilm*.

149. Tennessee. State Library and Archives, Nashville. Restoration and Reproduction Division.

Negative microfilm in the Restoration and Reproduction Section, Tennessee State Library and Archives. Nashville, Tennessee State Library and Archives [1965?] 22 l.

1. Type of microform: Microfilm.

2. Availability: Positive copies may be purchased.

3. Orders: Restoration and Reproduction Division, Tennessee State Library and Archives, Room 208, Nashville, Tennessee 37219.

4. This is a listing of the 35mm nonperforated microfilm that the Tennessee State Library and Archives had available for study and research at the time the list was published. Included are newspapers, county records, county tax lists, unpublished histories, theses, genealogical material, and out-of-print books. Materials are grouped under the following headings: newspapers on microfilm; county records; county tax lists; and miscellaneous material.

150. 3M IM/Press.

A catalog of popular titles available on microfilm. 1970-1971 edition. [New York, 1970?] 56 p.

1. Type of microform: Microfilm.

2. Availability: All items are available at the prices stated.

3. Orders: Orders should be addressed to a convenient 3M Business Products Center (a list of these centers is found at the end of the *Catalog*) or to: 3M IM/Press, Box 720, Times Square Station, New York, New York 10036.

4. "This catalog contains English titles on microfilm published in the United States and abroad, plus foreign language titles published in the United States. These titles are from the New York Public Library Collections and the 3M International Microfilm Press Collections." The items are arranged in one alphabetical sequence, with a subject index, which includes a listing of all entries under place of publication. There is also a decade index indicating titles published within a particular decade.

151. 3M IM/Press.

A catalog of titles available on microfilm. 1969 edition. [New York, 1969?] 76 p.

1. Type of microform: Microfilm.

2. Availability: All items are available at the prices stated.

3. Orders: Orders should be addressed to a convenient 3M Business Products Center (a list of these centers is found at the end of the *Catalog*) or to: 3M IM/Press, Box 720, Times Square Station, New York, New York 10036.

4. "This catalog contains selected titles on microfilm from The New York Public Library Collections, plus other titles on microfilm from 3M IM/Press, 3M Company's International Microfilm Press." The body of the *Catalog* consists of an alphabetical listing plus a subject index, which includes a listing of titles under place of publication.

152. 3M IM/Press.
Foreign official gazettes of six continents. St. Paul, Minn., 1971. 6 pts.

1. Type of microform: Microfilm.

2. Availability: Either negative or positive 35mm microfilm available in thirty days from receipt of order.

3. Orders: 3M Company, 3M Center, St. Paul, Minnesota 55101.

4. The strong collection of official gazettes, (national, state, provincial, and a few municipal) of the New York Public Library is made available on microfilm by 3M International Microfilm Press. The arrangement is alphabetical by place within each of six categories: North America, South America, Europe, Asia, Africa, and Oceania.

153. Tung, Shih-kang.
Chinese microfilms in Princeton University: a checklist of the Gest Oriental Library. Washington, Center for Chinese Research Materials, Association of Research Libraries, 1969. 57 p. (Association of Research Libraries. Center for Chinese Research Materials. Bibliographical series, no. 2)

1. Type of microform: Microfilm, microfiche.

2. Availability: Positive copies are available.

3. Orders: Mr. Shih-Kang Tung, Assistant University Librarian for Asian Collections, Gest Oriental Library, Princeton University, Princeton, New Jersey 08540.

4. The *Checklist* "consists of three hundred and sixty-one items, arranged alphabetically by title. . . . Under each entry, title in Chinese follows the romanized title, then comes the author in Chinese . . . [followed by] imprint (place, publisher, and date of original publication)." Notations indicate whether the film is negative or positive, the place of origin, the agent making the film, and date of filming. Noted also are the number of volumes or pages in one reel and the total number of reels, plus an indication of whether the title being described was filmed with another title. Finally is given the call number. Similar information is recorded for microfiche. The final pages are devoted to an author index.

154. U.S. National Archives.
Federal population censuses, 1790-1890; a catalog of microfilm copies of the schedules. Washington, 1971. 90 p. (*Its* Publication no. 71-3)

1. Type of microform: Microfilm.

2. Availability: Positive prints available at prices quoted. Enlargements from microfilm copies also available. Prices furnished on request.

3. Orders: Use of one of the detachable order forms (GSA form 6784A) from the *Catalog* will speed processing of an order. Check or money order made payable to General Services Administration (NATS) should be sent to: Cashier, National Archives (GSA), Washington, D.C. 20408.

4. This *Catalog* lists copies of the original federal population census schedules for 1800-1890, the volumes published by the Bureau of the Census in 1907-1908 giving the names of heads of families as shown in the 1790 census schedules, a card index to those entries in the 1880 census schedules relating to households including a child aged ten or under and the 1890 special census schedules enumerating Union veterans and widows of Union veterans of the Civil War.

Arranged chronologically by census year and then alphabetically by name of state or territory, and next, in general, alphabetically by county. For each microfilm publication is given microcopy number, total number of rolls and their price, price of the microfilm for each state and territory, and a complete list of microfilm rolls showing numbers, contents, and price.

155. U.S. National Archives.
List of National Archives microfilm publications. 1947-   Washington (*Its* Publication)
Latest edition: 1968 (108 p.)

1. Type of microform: Microfilm.

2. Availability: Positive prints may be purchased. For most microfilm publications, the National Archives can also furnish electrostatic (Xerox) paper copy of entire rolls of microfilm.

3. Orders: Orders should ordinarily be made on General Services Administration Form 6784, Microfilm Order, or on institutional purchase order forms. Detachable copies of GSA Form 6784 are found in the *List*.

Orders accompanied by remittances (check or money order made payable to the General Services Administration[NATS]) should be sent to: Cashier, National Archives and Records Service, Washington, D.C. 20408.

All other correspondence concerning the microfilm publications program of the National Archives should be addressed to: Publications Sales Branch (NATS), National Archives and Records Service, Washington, D.C. 20408.

4. Lists and describes in a brief fashion the numerous series of records in the National Archives now available as microfilm publications. Over 130,000 rolls of master negative microfilm were available by January 1, 1968. Arranged for the most part according to the organization of the government, the *List* is accompanied by an appendix, a numerical list of microfilm publications with corresponding page numbers, and an index, which provides a subject approach.

"For many microfilm publications title pages and introductory materials have been prepared and filmed with the records. The National Archives now issues pamphlets reproducing these introductions to microfilm publications, many helpful indexes or lists, and roll-by-roll descriptions and price lists.

Microfilm publications for which these pamphlets are available are indicated [in the *List*] by the symbol AP after the price."

The National Archives has been issuing these pamphlets since 1951 and today there are well over five hundred of them. Several examples are cited below.

U.S. National Archives and Records Service.
Registers and letters received by the Commissioner of the Bureau of Refugees, Freedmen, and Abandoned Lands, 1865-1872. Washington, 1969. 9 p. (National Archives microfilm publication. Pamphlet accompanying microcopy no. 752.)
Provides the user with a brief description of the organization and work of the Bureau of Refugees, Freedmen and Abandoned Lands, an explanation of the records reproduced in Microcopy no. 752, including references to related records in the same and other record groups, and roll notes giving description, dates, and price of each of the 74 rolls of microfilm.

U.S. National Archives and Records Service.
Return from U.S. military posts, 1800-1916. Washington, 1968. 81 p. (National Archives microfilm publication. Pamphlet accompanying microcopy no. 617.)
Explains the nature of the records reproduced, both the monthly post returns made to the Adjutant General and related reports and papers. It discusses the organization and arrangement of the records for filming, points out related records in the National Archives, provides a list of cross-references indicating the names of posts under which returns were consolidated, including names of posts whose returns were filed under two or more names and roll notes giving content, dates, and price of each of the 1,550 rolls of microfilm.

U.S. National Archives and Records Service.
Dispatches from United States consuls in Shanghai, 1847-1906. Washington, 1965. 4 p. (National Archives microfilm publications. Pamphlet accompanying microcopy no. 112.)
Discusses briefly the nature of consular dispatches, notes related records in the same Record Group 59 and in Record Group 84, and gives the contents of each of the 53 rolls of microfilm, namely, the dates covered.

The National Archives, in addition to the *List . . . of Microfilmed Publications,* which is not issued with a stated degree of regularity, also puts out helpful lists of microfilm publications relating to a particular geographic area. The following are examples of recently published lists of this nature.

U.S. National Archives.
National Archives microfilm publications relating to Africa and the Near East. [Washington, D.C., 1970] 9 p.
Lists alphabetically by country dispatches received by the Department of State from United States consuls, diplomatic instructions of

the Department of State, records of the Department of State relating to internal affairs and political relations of the countries. This is followed by records of the Department of State relating to the internal affairs and political relations of the European countries that held colonies in Africa and the Near East. Those films with accompanying pamphlets available are indicated by the symbol "AP" after the price.

U.S. National Archives.
National Archives microfilm publications relating to Latin America. [Washington, D.C., 1970] 17 p.
Lists alphabetically by country dispatches received by the Department of State from United States consuls, diplomatic instructions of the Department of State, records of the Department of State relating to internal affairs and political relations of the countries. This is followed by a list of miscellaneous pertinent material. Those films which have accompanying pamphlets available are indicated by the symbol "AP" after the price.

U.S. National Archives.
National Archives microfilm publications relating to territories of the United States. [Washington, D.C., 1970] 25 p.
Lists alphabetically by territory the various territorial papers, journals, letters, records, etc., in the National Archives now available as microfilm publications. Those which have accompanying pamphlets available are indicated by the symbol "AP" after the price.

156. U.S. National Historical Publications Commission.
Catalog of microfilm publications. 4th ed. Washington, 1970. 26 p.
————————— Supplement, August 1971. [Washington] 1971. 2 p.
1. Type of microform: Microfilm.
2. Availability: Available at price stated in *Catalog*.
3. Orders: An order for positive copies should be sent to the address indicated at the end of an entry. To this address also should be sent an order for the pamphlet only or for certain rolls of a microfilm publication or a request for an interlibrary loan.
4. Lists the eighty-five microfilm publications of twenty-six participating repositories available as of May 1970 and the pamphlets describing them. Listed in the addendum are additional microfilm publications produced independently of the commission but wholly or substantially meeting its standards.
The *Supplement* lists five more publications issued and ten titles in preparation, plus two related microfilm publications.

157. University Microfilms, Ann Arbor, Mich.
Serials on microfilm. [Ann Arbor, Mich., 1968-   ] Annual.
Latest issue: 1971. 450 p.
1. Type of microform: Microfilm.
2. Availability: Positive or negative microfilm available at prices listed.

Prices shown are for positive 35mm film. Approximately 500 periodicals are also available on 16mm microfilm.

3. Orders: University Microfilms, 300 North Zeeb Road, Ann Arbor, Mich. 48106 *OR* University Microfilms Limited, St. John's Road, Tylers Green, Penn, Buckinghamshire, England.

4. Lists alphabetically nearly 6,000 periodicals on microfilm, giving title, city of publication, backfile volumes available, current volumes, Xerographic permissions, external printed indexes, publishers' indexes, and notes of bibliographic interest where appropriate. This is followed by a subject listing and a list of periodicals on 16mm microfilm.

158. Vatican. Biblioteca Vaticana.
   Riproduzioni in microfilm positivo di libri esauriti. Listino di vendita. Città del Vaticano, 1957-
   Numero 11 (1° Gennaio 1969) contains [146] p.
   1. Type of microform: Microfilm.
   2. Availability: All titles listed are available on positive microfilm.
   3. Orders: Reparto Fotografico, Biblioteca Apostolica Vaticana, Rome, Italy.
   4. List no. 11 is divided into two parts: I, out-of-print publications of the Vatican Library, and II, other out-of-print books in the Vatican Library collection. Part I lists only seven titles, while Part II runs from pp. 7-144. The arrangement in Part II is alphabetical by author. Complete bibliographic information is given: name of author in full, title, place, publisher, date, and pagination. At the end of each citation, cost of a positive microfilm is indicated.

159. Warsaw. Biblioteka Narodowa. Stacja Mikrofilmowa.
   Katalog mikrofilmów. r. 1-   (zesz. 1-   ) 1951-   Warsaw.
   Fifteen numbers published through 1969. Primarily manuscripts and early printed books. *Katalog mikrofilmów muzycznych* v. 2 (see item 235) has series note: Biblioteca Narodowa. Katalog Mikrofilmów, nr. 2. Not seen by compiler.

160. Washington (State) State Library, Olympia.
   Washington newspapers and historical materials on microfilm in the Washington State Library. Olympia, Wash., 1966. 27 p.
   1. Type of microform: Microfilm.
   2. Availability: All of the positive microfilm in the State Library's collection, with a few minor exceptions, may be borrowed on interlibrary loan. Positive copies of any of the State Library's negative microfilm of Washington newspapers may be ordered directly from Bell & Howell, Micro Photo Division, where the negative newspaper microfilm is in storage. Inquiries regarding purchase of positive copies of the library's negative film of historical materials should be sent to the State Library.
   3. Orders: Micro Photo Division, Bell & Howell Company, Old Mansfield Road, Wooster, Ohio 44691 *OR* Washington State Library, Olympia, Washington 98501.
   4. Lists the newspapers alphabetically by city, giving the period covered,

whether negative or positive, location, and length of film in feet or rolls. This is followed by a listing of microfilmed historical materials relating to Washington Territory and State, giving description and location of the originals, whether negative or positive film, location of film and length in feet or rolls.

161. Wisconsin. University. Press.
Publications of the University of Wisconsin Press. [Madison] 1971. 31 p.
1. Type of microform: Microcards.
2. Availability: Microcard copies may be purchased at the prices given.
3. Orders: University of Wisconsin Press, Box 1379, Madison, Wisconsin 53701.
Outside the United States, orders should be placed through local bookstores and not sent directly to the University of Wisconsin Press.
4. This complete list of University of Wisconsin publications includes on p. 29 the series *Microcard Publications in Archaeology and Anthropology* and on p. 30 the series *Microcard Publications in Language and Literature.*

162. World Council of Churches. Commission on Faith and Order.
Official pamphlets and publications. Series I. 1910-1948; II. 1948-1969.
1. Type of microform: Microfilm.
2. Availability: Commercially published.
3. Orders: Ecumenism Research Agency, Box 761, Estes Park, Colorado 80517.
4. The publisher has indicated that an index to Series I containing a checklist of both Series I and II is being prepared in Lausanne, Switzerland.

163. World Microfilms.
Sectional catalogue—economics, accountancy and commerce. 1970-71 catalogue of microfilm publications on economics, accountancy and commerce. [London, 1970l] [5] p.
―――― Sectional catalogue—political science. 1970-71 catalogue of microfilm publications on art, architecture, film studies, music and theatre. [London, 1970?] [5] p.
―――― Sectional catalogue—political science. 1970-71 catalogue of radical journals and publications on microfilm. [London, 1970?] 9 p.
―――― Sectional catalogue—religious studies. 1970-71 catalogue of religious journals and publications on microfilm. [London, 1970?] [5] p.
1. Type of microform: Microfilm.
2. Availability: All items available at prices stated.
3. Orders: World Microfilms, Distribution Division, 62 Queen's Grove, London, N. W. 8, England *OR* World Microfilms, EAV Inc., Pleasantville, New York 10570.
4. The materials available show a great variety—collections of manuscript papers, newspapers, periodicals, rare books, reference works, and collections of books concerning a particular subject.

164. Yu lien yen chiu so, Kowloon.
Catalogue of mainland Chinese magazines and newspapers held by Union

Research Institute. 3d ed. Kowloon, Union Research Institute, 1968. 149 p.

1. Type of microform: Microfilm.

2. Availability: Positive microfilm of all listed titles is available.

3. Orders: Union Research Institute, 9 College Road, Kowloon, Hong Kong.

4. "This catalogue lists mainland Chinese magazines and newspapers held by the Union Research Institute, covering, with a few exceptions, the period of October 1949 to December 1966." In addition, the appendix lists seventy-six titles of miscellaneous publications that do not fit precisely the definition of a magazine or newspaper.

165. Yunesuko Higashi Ajia Bunka Kenkyū Sentā, Tokyo.

List of microfilms deposited in the Centre for East Asian Cultural Studies. Part 1. Malaysia (reels 4001 to 4152) and Part 2. Malaysia (reels 1-216) (In East Asian Cultural Studies. v. 7, p. 76-98, March 1968; v. 8, p. 41-52, March 1969)

1. Type of microform: Microfilm.

2. Availability: Positive microfilm is at the disposal of researchers at the center. Prints will be made available on request at cost.

3. Orders: Centre for East Asian Cultural Studies, c/o The Toyo Bunko, Honkomagome 2-chome, 28-21, Bunkyo-ku, Tokyo, Japan.

4. The Centre for East Asian Cultural Studies, at the request of UNESCO, is acting as a depository for microfilms of important historical documents filmed by the UNESCO Mobile Microfilm Unit in Asian countries. This is a rough list of the Malaysian microfilms deposited at the Centre. The listing is by reel and gives a complete catalog entry for the original. Included in Part 1 are government documents, periodicals, books, and pamphlets, primarily in English. In Part 2 there are mostly newspapers, government reports, and some manuscripts and personal journals.

166. Yunesuko Higashi Ajia Bunka Kenkyū Sentā, Tokyo.

List of microfilms deposited in the Centre for East Asian Cultural Studies. Part 3. Cambodia (reels 1 to 71). (In East Asian Cultural Studies. v. 8, p. 53-74, March 1969)

1. Type of microform: Microfilm.

2. Availability: Positive film is at the disposal of researchers at the Centre. Prints will be made available on request at cost.

3. Orders: Centre for East Asian Cultural Studies, c/o The Toyo Bunko, Honkomagome 2-chome, 28-21, Bunkyo-ku, Tokyo, Japan.

4. The Centre for East Asian Cultural Studies at the request of UNESCO is acting as a depository for microfilms of important historical documents filmed by the UNESCO Mobile Microfilm Unit in Asian countries. This is a reel contents list of the microfilms of Cambodian materials deposited in the Centre. Included are the *Journal officiel de l'Indochine francaise*, 1904-1915, analytics in periodicals, and monographs, mostly in French.

167. Yunesuko Higashi Ajia Bunka Kenkyū Sentā, Tokyo.

List of microfilms deposited in the Centre for East Asian Cultural Studies.

Part 4. The Philippines. (In East Asian Cultural Studies. v. 9, p. 57-107, March 1970)

1. Type of microform: Microfilm.

2. Availability: Positive film is at the disposal of researchers at the Centre. Prints will be made available on request at cost.

3. Orders: Centre for East Asian Cultural Studies, c/o The Toyo Bunko, Honkomagome 2-chome, 28-21, Bunkyo-ku, Tokyo, Japan.

4. The Centre for East Asian Cultural Studies at the request of UNESCO is acting as a depository for microfilms of important historical documents filmed by the UNESCO Mobile Microfilm Unit in Asian countries. The unit worked at the Bureau of Records Management of the Republic of the Philippines in Manila and microfilmed the Spanish records in the following subject areas: educational institutions (reels 1-83); Spanish Manila (reels 1-54); control of gambling (reels 1-38); and Malacañang Palace (reels 1-21).

In addition to the list of materials filmed, Part 4 includes introductory historical notes and descriptions of the arrangement of the records filmed, prepared for each of the four series. These notes and descriptions are in Spanish and English.

168. Yunesuko Higashi Ajia Bunka Kenkyū Sentā, Tokyo.

List of microfilms deposited in the Centre for East Asian Cultural Studies. Part 5. India. (In East Asian Cultural Studies. v. 10, p. [53]-85, March 1971)

1. Type of microform: Microfilm.

2. Availability: Positive microfilm is at the disposal of researchers at the Centre. Prints will be made available on request at cost.

3. Orders: Centre for East Asian Cultural Studies, c/o The Toyo Bunko, Honkomagome 2-chome, 28-21, Bunkyo-ku, Tokyo, Japan.

4. The Centre for East Asian Cultural Studies at the request of UNESCO is acting as a depository for microfilms of important historical documents filmed by the UNESCO Mobile Microfilm Unit in Asian countries. This is a contents list of ninety-one reels of old rare handwritten books in Arabic, Persian, Sanskrit, and other languages spoken in India, photographed at the libraries, archives, and institutions in Gauhati, Hyderabad, Jammu, New Delhi, Patna, and Poona, and deposited at the Centre. Name of author, title of book, language, style of writing, date of manuscript, and number of exposures are given for each item.

A list of the remaining reels deposited, from Calcutta, Madras, Thanjavur and Trivandrum, will appear in the next issue of *East Asian Cultural Studies.*

169. Yushodo Microfilm Publications, Ltd., Tokyo.

General catalogue 1970-71. [Tokyo, 1970] Unpaged.

1. Type of microform: Microfilm.

2. Availability: All items available at prices listed.

3. Orders: Yushodo Microfilm Publications, Ltd., 29 Sanei-cho, Shin-juku-ku, Tokyo, Japan.

4. Lists family papers, newspapers, periodicals, government documents, annual reports of companies, etc., all important for the study of the history and modernization of Japan. A few items are in Chinese, but most are Japanese.

II. COLLECTIONS AND SERIES

170. ACRL Microform Series-Abstracts of Title [no. 1-170] In *College and Research Libraries.* v. 15, p. 356-61, July 1954; p. 483-84, October 1954; v. 16, p. 117-18, January 1955; p. 225-26, April 1955; p. 325, July 1955; p. 433-34, October 1955; v. 17, p. 359-61, July 1956; p. 533-34, November 1956; v. 18, p. 343, July 1957; v. 19, p. 260-61, May 1958; p. 428-30, September 1958; v. 20, p. 260, May 1959; v. 21, p. 186-88; March 1960; p. 406, September 1960; v. 22, p. 314-15, July 1961; p. 488, November 1961; v. 23, p. 267, May 1962; v. 24, p. 333, 344, July 1963; v. 25, p. 54, January 1964; v. 26, p. 159, 175, March 1965; p. 410, 441, September 1965 and in *ACRL News; a Supplement to College and Research Libraries.* No. 2, p. 29-31, April 1966; no. 6, p. 134-135, June 1967.

1. Type of microform: Microcard, microfiche. The first 170 studies may be purchased as a group or separately. Standing orders may be placed for the series.

2. Availability: Available as group or separately.

3. Orders: Microcard Editions, 901 Twenty-sixth Street, N.W., Washington, D.C. 20037.

4. Until the end of 1968, this series was known as *ACRL Microcard Series* and was published by the University of Rochester Press. The first 170 titles are abstracted in the issues of *College and Research Libraries* and its news supplement as indicated. Included in the series are theses, reports, studies, etc., in the fields of library and information science and historical, descriptive and enumerative bibliography. Beginning with no. 171, Microcard Editions took over the publication of the series and changed its name to *ACRL Microform Series.* Studies included in this series are selected by a special editorial committee of the Association of College and Research Libraries. No. 171-181 were published in 1969.

171. American Antiquarian Society, Worcester, Mass.
Index to the *Early American Newspapers* published by the American Antiquarian Society on Microprint. [Worcester, Mass.] n.d. [7] 1.

Shelf List of *Early American Newspapers* published by the American Antiquarian Society on Microprint. [Worcester, Mass.] n.d. [6] 1.

1. Type of microform: Microprint.

2. Availability: The complete series, *Early American Newspapers, 1704-1820,* will contain a larger number of titles than the number held by the American Antiquarian Society. The complete series or individual titles may be purchased.

3. Orders: Readex Microprint Corporation, 5 Union Square, New York, New York 10003.

4. The *Index* is actually an alphabetical list of newspaper titles, showing for each the dates covered. The *Shelf List* is an alphabetical listing by place of publication, with an indication under each place of papers published there and the dates covered. Readex plans to incorporate in this collection all the available newspapers in Clarence Brigham's *History and Bibliography of American Newspapers, 1690-1820.* 2 v. (Wooster, Mass.: American Antiquarian Society, 1947). "When complete, the project will include all obtainable issues of more than two thousand newspapers covering 130 years of historical research material."

172. American periodicals, 1800-1850, a guide to the microfilm collection: 18th century, reels 1-33; 1800-1850, years 1-15, reels 1-640. Ann Arbor, Mich., University Microfilms, n.d. 136 p.

———, a guide to the 16th-20th year of the microfilm collection: 1962-1966, reels 641-816. Ann Arbor, Mich., University Microfilms, n.d. 51 p.

———, a guide to the 21st year of the microfilm collection: 1967, reels 817-845. Ann Arbor, Mich., University Microfilms, n.d. 8 p.

1. Type of microform: Microfilm.

2. Availability: *American Periodicals of the 18th century (1741-1800)* available as a unit. *American Periodicals (1800-1850)* available at an annual subscription rate.

3. Orders: University Microfilms, 300 North Zeeb Road, Ann Arbor, Michigan 48106.

4. These guides provide all the data needed for the identification of the periodicals filmed. Entries for the 1741-1800 periodicals are in one alphabetical sequence. The rest of the periodicals are arranged in groups, alphabetically by title, according to the year in which they were filmed. Each entry shows the volumes and dates filmed, provides necessary history notes, and indicates the microfilm reel number. Beginning with the list for the sixteenth year, editorial notes and comments from volume 1 of Frank Luther Mott's *A History of American Magazines, 1741-1850* (Cambridge: Harvard University Press, 1930-38, 3 v.) accompany many entries.

172a. American periodicals, 1850-1900—Civil War and Reconstruction, a guide to years 1-10 of the Microfilm collection with title index, reels 1-313. Ann Arbor, Michigan, University Microfilms, 1971. 60 p.

1. Type of microform: Microfilm.

2. Availability: Individual titles or entire unit may be purchased. Price of individual titles is given in University Microfilms' *Serials on Microfilm*, 1971. Price of unit may be secured from the publisher.

3. Orders: University Microfilms, 300 North Zeeb Road, Ann Arbor, Michigan 48106.

4. "Entries in the guide give bibliographic information from the *Union List of Serials*, notes on the film, and annotations based on Frank Luther Mott's *A History of American Magazines*. Titles are arranged in the order in which they appear on the Microfilm." A title index adds to the usefulness of the guide. No prices are given.

173. American Studies Association. Committee on Microfilm Bibliography.

Bibliography of American culture, 1439-1875. Compiled and edited by David R. Weimer. Ann Arbor, Michigan, University Microfilms, 1957. 228 p.

1. Type of microform: Microfilm.

2. Availability: The "American Culture" series, published as a single unit in 1941 by University Microfilms, consists of 250 items of Americana. "American Culture II," a continuation of the original series, is a combined microfilm-bibliographical enterprise which proposes to microfilm 5,000-6,000 scarce books pertaining to American civilization which were published before 1876. Approximately 100,000 pages per year are furnished as positive microfilm. An annual subscription may be placed. As they are filmed, the books

and pamphlets in this series are also available in enlarged size, reproduced on regular book paper by Xerography.

3. Orders: University Microfilms, 300 North Zeeb Road, Ann Arbor, Michigan 48106.

4. A selective basic bibliography of American books and pamphlets published before 1876 arranged by major categories such as art and architecture, history, politics and law, mathematics, etc., each major category in turn being subdivided. With this arrangement, an author and title index would have been very useful.

Limited to publications in English except for a few foreign-language items of special importance and, limited also primarily, but not exclusively, to works written by Americans and published in the United States.

Publications filmed in the original series (1941) are designated by the abbreviation *ACS* preceding the entry, while books and pamphlets published before 1876 but reissued after 1900 and not included in "American Culture II" are designated by an asterisk preceding the entry.

174. Association pour la Conservation et la Reproduction Photographique de la Presse.
Journaux publiés par les prisonniers de guerre allemands en France, 1946-1948. (In its Catalogue de microfilms reproduisants des périodiques, journaux et revues. no. 9 [Paris] 1971. p. 48-49.)
1. Type of microform: Microfilm.
2. Availability: Complete collection of sixty titles may be purchased.
3. Orders: ACRPP, 4, rue Louvois, Paris 2e, France.
4. Alphabetical title list of the newspapers published by German prisoners of war in France, 1946-48. No information about holdings is given; presumably each file is complete.

175. Association pour la Conservation et la Reproduction Photographique de la Presse.
Périodiques clandestins, 1939-1945. (In its Catalogue de microfilms reproduisants des périodiques, journaux et revues. no. 9 [Paris] 1971. p. 139-147.)
1. Type of microform: Microfilm.
2. Availability: Entire collection of approximately 200 titles available. Each title is also priced separately.
3. Orders: ACRPP, 4, rue Louvois, Paris 2e, France.
4. The list which appears in the *Catalogue* is an alphabetical title list of French resistance newspapers published during World War II (1939-1945). The collection also includes a number of "périodiques clandestins" in foreign languages (Armenian, Spanish, Italian, Polish, Romanian, Russian, etc.), plus other interesting items from the days of the German occupation.

176. Bächtold-Stäubli, Hanns, ed.
Handwörterbuch des deutschen Aberglaubens ... Bd. 1. (Berlin, 1927.) cols. xiv - lxxi: Literaturverzeichnis.
1. Type of microform: Microfilm.
2. Availability: As of March 1970, 424,508 pages on 171 rolls were available. Catalog cards may be purchased.

3. Orders: General Microfilm Company, 100 Inman Street, Cambridge, Massachusetts 02139.

4. This microfilm collection, *Literature of Folklore,* originally reproducing titles listed in the "Literaturverzeichnis" of the *Handwörterbuch,* will ultimately include other basic works.

177. Bell and Howell Company. Micro Photo Division.
. . . The Bell & Howell black culture collection, selected, organized, and prepared from the collections of the Atlanta University Library. [Wooster, Ohio] n.d. [2] p.
1. Type of microform: Microfilm, book reproduction.
2. Availability: The collection is divided into four major categories: I. Africa: Africa and African-American Publications; II. The Black Experience in America since the 17th Century; III. The Black Experience in South America and the West Indies; IV. Slavery in History. The entire collection or any one of these categories may be purchased.
3. Orders: Micro Photo Division, Bell & Howell Company, Old Mansfield Road, Wooster, Ohio 44691.
4. This collection makes available the most relevant and significant areas of the black history and sociology sections of Atlanta University's Trevor-Arnett Library. It consists of approximately 7,000 books and pamphlets and other papers dealing with all aspects of the black experience, many of them from other special collections in the library. The selection of material for the microform library was the responsibility of the fellows of the Center for African and African-American Studies at Atlanta University.
The publisher states, "A comprehensive, hard-copy Book Catalog, prepared by reproducing the Trevor-Arnett Library's catalog cards for the titles included, will accompany each microfilm category at no additional charge." Each of the four hard-bound book catalogs is also available separately. From the catalogs, titles may be selected for hard-copy xerographic book production.

178. Bell & Howell Company. Micro Photo Division.
A century of great theatre from London's famed Covent Garden. [Prompt books in microform] [Wooster, Ohio] n.d. folder
1., Type of microform: Microfilm.
2. Availability: Available on microfilm or in book form.
3. Orders: Microphoto Division, Bell & Howell, Old Mansfield Road, Wooster, Ohio 44691.
4. Provides a list of the titles (but not the authors) of thirty-seven Covent Garden prompt books from the Newberry Library.

179. Bell & Howell Company. Micro Photo Division.
Underground press collections of the underground press syndicate. (In its Newspapers on microfilm. Catalog and price list. 1971. 25th anniversary edition [Wooster, Ohio, 1971] p. 55)
1. Type of microform: Microfilm.
2. Availability: Available on an annual subscription basis. Backfiles of earlier years are also available. Individual titles are not available.
3. Orders: Micro Photo Division, Bell & Howell Company, Old Mansfield Road, Wooster, Ohio 44691.

4. *The Underground Press Collections of the Underground Press Syndicate* is, according to the publisher, an attempt to "fully preserve the sixties . . . a decade of great turmoil in which unrest and rebellion fostered the development of many conflicting social and political views . . . and to provide for an area of the collection and preservation obligations inherent to developing today's more comprehensive libraries. . . . Over 60 current underground newspapers and approximately 175 backfiles of [now] defunct publications are available."

The publisher supplies with each shipment of film a pamphlet showing the contents of each reel. The following index covers some, but not all, of the titles in the collection.

Alternative press index. v. 1 - July/Dec. 1969 -

[Northfield, Minn., Radical Research Center]

180. Bergquist, G. William.
Three centuries of English and American plays, a checklist. England: 1500-1800; United States: 1714-1830. New York, Hafner Pub. Co., 1963. 281 p.

    1. Type of microform: Microprint.

    2. Availability: Complete set of more than 5,000 plays may be purchased.

    3. Orders: Readex Microprint Corporation, 5 Union Square, New York, New York 10003.

    4. The Bergquist checklist was originally compiled to serve as an index to the contents of the microprint edition called *Three Centuries of Drama,* compiled by Henry W. Wells. The plays are arranged in the microprint boxes alphabetically within chronological periods. The checklist is arranged in one alphabet, each entry including the chronological period in which the play will be found in the microprint edition.

181. Binger, Norman.
A bibliography of German plays on microcards. Hamden, Conn., The Shoe String Press, 1970. 224 p.

    1. Type of microform: Microcard.

    2. Availability: In process. Approximately 600 titles a year.

    3. Orders: Falls City Microcards, 1432 Cherokee Road, Louisville, Kentucky 40204.

    4. The Binger *Bibliography* provides a catalog of the plays published on microcards by Falls City Microcards in the series *German Drama on Microcards.* The collection covers plays from the sixteenth to the twentieth century.

        Catalog cards are offered by: Erasmus Press, 225 Culpepper Street, Lexington, Kentucky 40502.

182. Blanck, Jacob Nathaniel.
Bibliography of American literature compiled for the Bibliographical Society of America. New Haven, Yale University Press, 1955-

In progress. v. 1-5, 1955-69

    1. Type of microform: Microprint.

2. Availability: To be issued as prepared. Shipments will be invoiced as shipped.

3. Orders: Readex Microprint Corporation, 5 Union Square, New York, New York 10003.

4. The project referred to both as *The Great Works of American Literature* and just *American Literature* is based on the bibliography cited above. Readex Microprint will publish all first editions and authors' later revisions listed in the *Bibliography*, which aims to present American works that, for any reason, were thought significant in American, though not necessarily in world, literature.

183. Books for college libraries; a selected list of approximately 53,400 titles based on the initial selection made for the University of California's New Campuses Program and selected with the assistance of college teachers, librarians, and other advisers. Prepared under the direction of Melvin J. Voigt and Joseph H. Treyz. Chicago, American Library Association, 1967. 1,056 p.

1. Type of microform: Positive or negative microfiche (4″ x 6″); microopaque cards (4″ x 6″).

2. Availability: Titles are being offered according to subject-oriented groups. On July 1, 1971, 7 such groups (705 titles and 1,013 volumes) were available, namely: History-Great Britain; American Literature; English Literature; History-United States; History-Europe; Education; and Political Science. "In addition, many multi-volume titles are being reprinted independent of the above groups." As of July 1, 1971, 30 titles were available, 23 of which appeared also on the subject lists: History-Great Britain and American Literature.

3. Orders: Microcard Editions, 901 Twenty-sixth Street, Washington, D.C. 20037.

4. A retrospective list of monographs published prior to 1964 "designed to support a college teaching program that depends heavily on the library." The arrangement is by Library of Congress classification with author and subject indexes. Microcard Editions intends in this extended project to make available a large percentage of the books cited in *Books for College Libraries.*

184. Bradford, Thomas Lindsley.
The bibliographer's manual of American history, containing an account of all state, territory, town and county histories relating to the United States of North America, with verbatim copies of their titles and useful bibliographical notes . . . Philadelphia, S. V. Henkels & Co., 1907-10. 5 v. (Reprinted by Gale, 1968)

1. Type of microform: Microfilm.

2. Availability: Not yet available.

3. Orders: General Microfilm Company, 100 Inman Street, Cambridge, Massachusetts 02139.

4. Since the several microform projects reproducing Americana include relatively few of the 6,000 titles described in Bradford's *Bibliographer's Manual of American History*, the publisher plans to microfilm those titles not found in Evans and Sabin. In addition, Bradford's bibliography will be supplemented by Americana from other standard bibliographies, but only

after all the titles in Bradford have been reproduced. The announced title of this new project is *Americana Not in Sabin*. It is estimated that the project will be spread over a period of ten to fifteen years. Catalog cards will be available.

185. Brewer, Earl D. C., and Douglas W. Johnson.
      An inventory of the Harlan Paul Douglass collection of religious research reports. New York, Department of Research, National Council of the Churches of Christ in the U.S.A. [c1970] 196 p.
      1. Type of microform: Microfiche.
      2. Availability: Complete collection and printed index available. Index also available separately.
      3. Orders: Research Publications, Box 3903, Amity Station, New Haven, Connecticut 06525.
      4. The Harlan Paul Douglass Collection consists of church-related field research studies collected over the years by the Department of Research of the National Council of the Churches of Christ in the U.S.A. The collection available on microfiche, *Social Problems and the Churches, the Harlan Paul Douglass Collection of Religious Research Projects*, consists of well over 2,000 items indexed by author, denomination, geographical location, organizational level, and subject in the computer-processed *Inventory* cited above.

186. British and continental rhetoric and elocution. Ann Arbor, Michigan, University Microfilms, 1953. [11] p.
      1. Type of microform: Microfilm.
      2. Availability: 16 reels of 35mm microfilm may be purchased.
      3. Orders: University Microfilms, 300 North Zeeb Road, Ann Arbor, Michigan 48106.
      4. Lists the source materials on British and continental rhetoric and elocution filmed in cooperation with the Microfilm and Microcards Committee of the Speech Association of America. Gives in order the number of the reel; number of the item corresponding to that assigned by the committee making the selection; author and title, indicating date and place of publication if known; symbol showing library owning the original; and remarks concerning the film item, e.g., "pages out of sequence," "Volumes 2, 1, 3 in that order," etc.

187. British Museum. Dept. of Printed Books.
      Short-title catalogue of books printed in France and of French books printed in other countries from 1470 to 1600 now in the British Museum. London, Printed by order of the Trustees, 1924. 491 p.
      1. Type of microform: Microfilm.
      2. Availability: In progress. About 50,000 pages a year made available. Catalog cards based on information in the *Short-title Catalogue* may be purchased.
      3. Orders: General Microfilm Company, 100 Inman Street, Cambridge, Massachusetts 02139.
      4. The selection for the microfilm series *French Books before 1601* is based on, but not restricted to, titles in the *Short-title Catalogue*.

188. British Museum. Dept. of Printed Books.

   Short-title catalogue of books printed in Italy, and of Italian books printed in other countries from 1465 to 1600 now in the British Museum. London, Trustees of the British Museum, 1958. 992 p.

   1. Type of microform: Microfilm.
   2. Availability: In progress. About 50,000 pages a year made available. Catalog cards based on information in the *Short-title Catalogue* may be purchased.
   3. Orders: General Microfilm Company, 100 Inman Street, Cambridge, Massachusetts 02139.
   4. The selection for the microfilm series *Italian Books before 1601* is based on, but not restricted to, titles in the *Short-title Catalogue.*

189. British Museum. Dept. of Printed Books.

   Short-title catalogue of books printed in the German-speaking countries and of German books printed in other countries from 1455 to 1600 now in the British Museum. London, Trustees of the British Museum, 1962. 1,224 p.

   1. Type of microform: Microfilm.
   2. Availability: In progress. About 50,000 pages a year made available. Catalog cards based on information in the *Short-title catalogue* may be purchased.
   3. Orders: General Microfilm Company, 100 Inman Street, Cambridge, Massachusetts 02139.
   4. The selection for the microfilm series *German Books before 1601* is based on, but not restricted to, titles in the *Short-title Catalogue.*

190. British Museum. Dept. of Printed Books.

   Short-title catalogue of books printed in the Netherlands and Belgium and of Dutch and Flemish books printed in other countries from 1470 to 1600 now in the British Museum. London, Trustees of the British Museum, 1965. 274 p.

   1. Type of microform: Microfilm.
   2. Availability: In progress. The project, begun in 1967, offers about 50,000 pages a year, and will take from twelve to fifteen years to complete. Catalog cards available.
   3. Orders: General Microfilm Company, 100 Inman Street, Cambridge, Massachusetts 02139.
   4. The *Short-title Catalogue* is the basis for selection of titles to be microfilmed in this project, *Books Printed in the Low Countries Before 1601,* but the project will not be restricted to titles listed.

191. British Museum. Dept. of Printed Books.

   A short-title catalogue of French books, 1601-1700, in the Library of the British Museum, by V. F. Goldsmith. London, Dawsons, 1969-   v.

   1. Type of microform: Microfilm.
   2. Availability: In progress. About 50,000 pages a year are made available. Catalog cards may be purchased.
   3. Orders: General Microfilm Company, 100 Inman Street, Cambridge, Massachusetts 02139.

4. This project, *French Books, 1601 to 1700,* is organized roughly on the same basis as General Microfilm Company's series of European books before 1601. The selection is based on, but not limited to, titles in the *Short-title Catalogue,* currently in progress.

192. British periodicals, 17th-19th century . . . General. A guide to the first through the fifth years of the microfilm collection. Reels 1-136. Ann Arbor, Mich., University Microfilms, n.d. 18 p.
 1. Type of microform: Microfilm.
 2. Availability: Available on annual subscription, which includes approximately 100,000 microfilmed pages each year. Individual reels and back editions of the collection may also be purchased.
 3. Orders: University Microfilms, 300 North Zeeb Road, Ann Arbor, Michigan 48106.
 4. *British Periodicals—General of the 17th-19th Centuries* is a collection of periodicals (newspapers are excluded) devoted to economics, philosophy, and the social scene in Great Britain from the Restoration to the end of the nineteenth century. Dr. Daniel Fader, University of Michigan, was the bibliographer for the collection. University Microfilms furnishes guides with each annual shipment, which not only show the contents of each reel but give helpful notes about each periodical title, including notations about pagination, indexes, etc. The guide cited above is a consolidation covering the production of five years. Credit is given to the library whose copy was used for filming.

193. British periodicals, 17th-19th century, a guide to the first year of the microfilm collection. Reels 1-35—Creative arts. Ann Arbor, Mich., University Microfilms, n.d. 8 p.
 1. Type of microform: Microfilm.
 2. Availability: Available on an annual subscription basis, which includes approximately 100,000 microfilmed pages each year. Individual reels and back editions of the collection may also be purchased.
 3. Orders: University Microfilms, 300 North Zeeb Road, Ann Arbor, Michigan 48106.
 4. Consists of seventy periodicals in the fields of music, art, architecture, archeology, and drama. Some of them achieved a long and popular life, while others lasted only a short time. However, all volumes issued will be microfilmed so that the collection will completely represent the period. University Microfilms furnishes guides with each annual shipment, which show not only the contents of each reel, but give useful background notes about each periodical title, including notations about pagination, indexes, etc. Credit is given to the library whose copy was used for filming.

194. British periodicals, 17th-19th centuries, a guide to the first year of the microfilm collection. Reels 1-31—Literary (BPL) Ann Arbor, Mich., University Microfilms [1969?] 8 p.
 1. Type of microform: Microfilm.
 2. Availability: Available on annual subscription, which includes approximately 100,000 microfilmed pages each year. Individual reels and back editions of the collection may also be purchased.

3. Orders: University Microfilms, 300 North Zeeb Road, Ann Arbor, Michigan 48106.

4. Essentially a collection of British literary review journals from the seventeenth through the nineteenth centuries. It augments the collection, *English Literary Periodicals of the 17th, 18th, and 19th Centuries.* University Microfilms furnishes guides with each annual shipment, which show not only the contents of each reel, but give useful background notes about each title, including notations about pagination, indexes, etc. Credit is given to the library whose copy was used for filming.

195. Brown University. Library.

List of Latin American imprints before 1800, selected from bibliographies of José Toribio Medina, microfilmed by Brown University. Providence, 1952. 140 p.

1. Type of microform: Microfilm.

2. Availability: Positive copies are available. The approximate cost of any title, based upon the prevailing rate for microfilm, may be figured by consulting either the Medina bibliography listing the item or the Library of Congress printed catalogs. Specific estimates will be furnished upon request.

3. Orders: Brown University Library, Providence, Rhode Island 02912.

4. Lists alphabetically by main entry 2,339 Latin American imprints before 1800 selected from six Medina bibliographies and microfilmed by Brown University Library. Since the *List* is primarily a finding-list the main entry is followed by a short title, the place of publication, the date of publication, the Brown University call number, an abbreviated citation to the Medina bibliography, and the LC printed catalog card number.

The Library of Congress holds positive microfilm copies of all titles which were presented by Brown University Library under an agreement that it would print cards for all items in the project. The filming, cataloging, and printing of catalog cards extended over the period from 1940 to 1952.

196. Caron, Pierre.

Manuel pratique pour l'étude de la révolution francaise. Nouvelle édition. Paris, Picard, 1947. 324 p.

Monglond, André.

La France révolutionaire et impériale: annales de bibliographie méthodique et description des livres illustrés. Grenoble, B. Arthaud, 1930-[63] 9 v.

Tourneux, Maurice.

Bibliographie de l'histoire de Paris pendant la révolution francaise. Paris, Imprimerie Nouvelle, 1890-1913, 5 v. (Ville de Paris. Publications relatives à la révolution francaise)

1. Type of microform: Microfilm.

2. Availability: A commercial publication.

3. Orders: General Microfilm Company, 100 Inman Street, Cambridge, Massachusetts 02139.

4. The microfilm series, *The French Revolution: Critical and Historical Sources,* is designed to supplement the microcard edition of *French Revolu-*

tionary Pamphlets. It reproduces items from the three titles noted above, selected by the late Professor David Dowd of the University of Kentucky. Catalog cards for titles in the series are available from Erasmus Press, 225 Culpepper Street, Lexington, Kentucky 40502.

197. Chicago. University. Library.
　　Microfilm collection of manuscripts on American Indian cultural anthropology (Formerly: Middle American cultural anthropology series). Chicago, Dept. of Photoduplication, University of Chicago Library, n.d. 9 p. [Annotated price list]
　　1. Type of microform: Microfilm.
　　2. Availability: Complete unit or individual series may be purchased.
　　3. Orders: Department of Photoduplication, Joseph Regenstein Library, B70, 1100 East 57th Street, Chicago, Illinois 60637.
　　4. This collection, which began in 1946 with a focus on Middle America, is now concerned with all the Americas and the world as a whole. It is open-ended with respect to area coverage, although it continues to limit itself to cultural anthropology, broadly interpreted. The price list covers the first series (June 1946) through the ninth series (November 1969). For each number of each series (sixty-four in all), the list gives author and title, and in some cases brief descriptive notes.
　　An up-to-date catalog is in preparation, which will include all recent additions (over 100 items) in fourteen more series.

198. Clark, Thomas Dionysius, ed.
　　Travels in the new South, a bibliography. [1st ed.] Norman, University of Oklahoma Press [1962] 2 v. (The American exploration and travel series, v. 36)
　　1. Type of microform: Microcard.
　　2. Availability: Complete set available for purchase.
　　3. Orders: Lost Cause Press, 1140-46 Starks Bldg., Louisville, Kentucky 40202.
　　4. This bibliography served as the basis for the microcard project, *Travels in the New South.* Catalog cards for titles in the series are available from Erasmus Press, 225 Culpepper Street, Lexington, Kentucky 40502.

199. Clark, Thomas Dionysius.
　　Travels in the Old South, a bibliography. Norman, University of Oklahoma Press [1956-59] 3 v. (The American exploration and travel series, no. 19)
　　1. Type of microform: Microcard.
　　2. Availability: Complete set available for purchase.
　　3. Orders: Lost Cause Press, 1140-46 Starks Bldg., Louisville, Kentucky 40202.
　　4. The microcard edition of volumes from Clark's *Travels in the Old South,* covering the years 1527-1860, is complete except for items which have not been located for photographing. Lost Cause Press continues to search for such items. Catalog cards for titles in the series are available from Erasmus Press, 225 Culpepper Street, Lexington, Kentucky 40502.

200. Coleman, John Winston.
　　A bibliography of Kentucky history. Lexington, University of Kentucky Press, 1949. 516 p.
　　1. Type of microform: Microcard.
　　2. Availability: In process; approximately 584 volumes available in 1971.
　　3. Orders: Lost Cause Press, 1140-46 Starks Bldg., Louisville, Kentucky 40202.
　　4. Selections have been made from the Coleman *Bibliography*, as well as from other sources, for the *Kentucky Culture Series*. The Lost Cause Press issues lists of titles included in each shipment. Catalog cards are offered by Erasmus Press, 225 Culpepper Street, Lexington, Kentucky 40502.

201　Concordia Historical Institute, St. Louis.
　　Microfilm index and bibliography of the Concordia Historical Institute, the Department of Archives and History, The Lutheran Church - Missouri Synod, St. Louis, Missouri, 1954-1963. Aug. R. Suelflow, director. St. Louis, Mo., Concordia Press, 1966. 182 p. (*Its* Report, 1)
　　1. Type of microform: Microfilm.
　　2. Availability: Films may be borrowed on interlibrary loan; there is a service charge on each roll of film borrowed. Copies of the films will be made if the Institute has dissemination rights.
　　3. Orders: August R. Suelflow, Director, Concordia Historical Institute, 801 DeMun Avenue, St. Louis, Missouri 63105.
　　4. The *Microfilm Index* was designed to serve as a guide to the contents of approximately 100,000 feet of microfilm which enhances the substantial collection of documents owned by the Concordia Historical Institute relating to the history of the American Lutheran Church. The *Index* lists books, pamphlets, manuscripts, periodicals, and names of persons on whom some information is documented on film in one alphabetical list. It includes the titles of all printed and manuscript materials. For every item there is given: general title or name of an individual; date of publication; and type of publication, e.g., pamphlet, book, thesis, periodical, etc. There are numerous cross-references and notations indicating that a negative microfilm is owned by the Institute. If the microfilm is positive, the Institute's files indicate where the original is deposited and what the literary rights are. Finally, the *Index* gives the individual film number and the approximate location of an item on a given roll.

202. Coulter, Ellis Merton.
　　Travels in the Confederate States, a bibliography. Norman, University of Oklahoma Press, 1948. 289 p. (American exploration and travel [1])
　　1. Type of microform: Microcard.
　　2. Availability: Complete set available for purchase.
　　3. Orders: Lost Cause Press, 1140-46 Starks Bldg., Louisville, Kentucky 40202.
　　4. The microcard edition reproduces all items listed in the Coulter bibliography. The material included was written by "soldiers, journalists, foreigners, visitors and innocent victims" during the Civil War period. [LCP catalogue,

1967-68] Catalog cards for titles in the series are available from Erasmus Press, 225 Culpepper Street, Lexington, Kentucky 40502.

203. Crandall, Marjorie Lyle.
Confederate imprints; a check list based principally on the collection of the Boston Athenaeum. With an introduction by Walter Muir Whitehall. [Boston] Boston Athenaeum, 1955. 2 v. (Robert Charles Billings Fund publications, no. 11)

Harwell, Richard Barksdale.
More Confederate imprints. Richmond, Virginia State Library, 1957. 2 v. (Virginia State Library, Richmond. Publications, no. 4-5.)

1. Type of microform: Microfilm.
2. Availability: According to the publisher, this project will soon be completed.
3. Orders: Research Publications, Inc., Box 3903, Amity Station, New Haven, Connecticut 06525.
4. The microfilm project, *Confederate Imprints, 1861-1865,* is based on the two bibliographies cited above. Each item will appear with the number and in the order assigned to it by Crandall and Harwell. Professionally prepared cards for each item, including series title and microfilm reel location, will be available.

204. DeGroot, Alfred Thomas.
Evangelical academies and lay training centers of Europe and Great Britain. Historical sketches, conference programs, announcement bulletins, study guides, and other representative publications of these centers in Finland, France, Germany, Great Britain, Netherlands, Norway, Sweden, Switzerland. Estes Park, Colorado [197-?] 14 p.
1. Type of microform: Microfilm.
2. Availability: Normally sold as a single set of eleven rolls.
3. Orders: Dr. A. T. DeGroot, Director, Ecumenism Research Agency, P.O. Box 761, Estes Park, Colorado 80517.
4. Lists the publications of each center alphabetically by country and chronologically under each country, giving publication dates and pagination of the originals.

205. DeGroot, Alfred Thomas.
Library of American church records (personnel, statistics, development) in microfilm. [Fort Worth, Texas, 1966-   ]
1. Type of microform: Microfilm.
2. Availability: Series I and II normally sold as units, but it is possible to obtain the material for a single denomination.
3. Orders: Dr. A. T. DeGroot, Director, Ecumenism Research Agency, P.O. Box 761, Estes Park, Colorado 80517.
4. Lists by year of publication minutes, reports, lists of ministers and missionaries, yearbooks, etc., under each denomination, and gives pagination of the originals. Series I (1966) includes Assemblies of God, Christian Church (Disciples), Churches of Christ, Congregational Church, and Cumberland

Presbyterian Church, covering years from 1810 to 1965. Series II (1971) includes Associate Reformed Presbyterian Church, Brethren in Christ, Seventh-Day Adventists, and American Baptist Convention, covering years from 1803 to 1970.

206. DeGroot, Alfred Thomas, comp.
   Library of church unity periodicals in microfilm. [Series I - III. Fort Worth, Tex., 1969?] Unpaged.
   —————————— Series IV. [n.p.] Winter 1969. Unpaged.
   —————————— Series V. [n.p.] Spring 1971. Unpaged.
   1. Type of microform: Microfilm.
   2. Availability: Sold normally as complete sets, but selection of whole journals may be made.
   3. Orders: Dr. A. T. DeGroot, Director, Ecumenism Research Agency, Box 761, Estes Park, Colorado 80517.
   4. An "assault upon the widespread lack of authoritative information about the origins and development of the current church unity movement." Gives a short introduction to each periodical.

207. Dissertation abstracts international. v. 1-   1938-   Ann Arbor, Mich., University Microfilms, 1938-
   1. Type of microform: Microfilm.
   2. Availability and Price: Positive microfilm copies or Xerographic reproductions available at prices stated.
   3. Orders: University Microfilms, 300 North Zeeb Road, Ann Arbor, Michigan 48106.
      Payment should not accompany order; invoice including handling and shipping charges is sent at time of shipment.
   4. As *Microfilm Abstracts*, 1938-1951, this serial publication abstracted a limited number of doctoral dissertations and other monographs available on microfilm. In 1952 the title changed to *Dissertation Abstracts* to reflect an enlarged program of listing and abstracting the doctoral dissertations of most of the major universities of the United States. The present title adopted in July 1969 reflects another projected enlargement to include dissertations from European universities. Since July 1966 (v. 27), appears in two separately bound sections monthly: (A) the humanities and social sciences, (B) the sciences and engineering. Author and subject indexes (monthly with annual cumulations) were published for vols. 12 - 29, (1952-1968/69). Beginning with v. 29, no. 7 (January 1969), each monthly issue is accompanied by a keyword title and author index, and beginning with v. 30 the keyword title indexes, as well as the author indexes, will be cumulated annually.

208. English literary periodicals, 17th, 18th, and 19th centuries.
   Ann Arbor, Mich., University Microfilms [1951-   (loose-leaf)
   1. Type of microform: Microfilm.
   2. Availability: Available on an annual subscription basis (approximately 100,000 pages each year), or complete runs of individual titles may be purchased.

3. Orders: University Microfilms, 300 North Zeeb Road, Ann Arbor, Michigan 48106.

4. Aims to reproduce on microfilm about 200 selected literary periodicals from the British Isles. "Titles . . . were selected not only for their importance but for their scarcity—many of those chosen for filming were not available in more than two or three American libraries." Richmond P. Bond drew up a preliminary list which, after suggestions from scholars, was published as "English Literary Periodicals to Form New Microfilm Series," *Library Journal* 76 (Jan. 15, 1951), pp. 125-128. Begun in 1951, the project was finished in 1970. It is augmented by another project, *British Periodicals, 17th-19th Centuries—Literary*. With each shipment, the publisher furnishes separate leaves for each title, which give a general description of the titles included and the contents of each reel.

209. Evans, Charles.

American bibliography. A chronological dictionary of all books, pamphlets and periodical publications printed in the United States of America from the genesis of printing down to and including the year 1820. Chicago, Priv. print., 1903-59. 14 v.

1. Type of microform: Microprint.

2. Availability: Complete set available. Catalog information cards may be purchased.

3. Orders: Readex Microprint Corporation, 5 Union Square, New York, New York 10003.

4. The microprint series, *Early American Imprints, 1639-1800*, is based on an extensive revision of Charles Evans' *American Bibliography*. It attempts to include every existent book, pamphlet, and broadside (approximately 42,000 titles) printed in the United States between 1639 and 1800. The items are filed in the microprint boxes in the numerical sequence established in Evans.

An excellent guide to the microprint edition is Clifford Shipton's *National Index of American Imprints through 1800: The Short-title Evans*, published in 1969 by the American Antiquarian Society. It is a short-title list of both Evans' and additional items in one alphabetical order. This series is continued by Ralph R. Shaw's *American Bibliography*, 1801-1819.

210. Facts on film. Index. Prepared by Southern Education Reporting Service. Nashville [1958] 172 p.

———— ———— Supplement[s] July 1958 - June 1968. Nashville [1960?-1968?] 10 v.

1. Type of microform: Microfilm.

2. Availability: Commercially published.

3. Orders: Tennessee Microfilms, P.O. Box 1096, Nashville, Tennessee 37202.

4. The "Southern Education Reporting Service is an objective, fact-finding agency established by Southern newspaper editors and educators 'with the aim of providing accurate, unbiased information to school administrators, public officials and interested lay citizens on developments in educa-

tion arising from the U. S. Supreme Court opinion of 1954 declaring compulsory segregation in the public schools unconstitutional.' " *Facts on Film* makes available the unique collection of materials assembled by the SERS. Included in the collection are newspaper clippings, magazine articles, pamphlets, texts of court decisions, hearings, editorials, etc. The *Index* and its *Supplements* explain how to locate information in *Facts on Film* by using the *Index* as a general guide to the materials and the card catalog, which is included in the film as a means of getting at specific information.

211. Field, Thomas Warren.
An essay towards an Indian bibliography, being a catalogue of books, relating to the history, antiquities, languages, customs, religion, wars, literature, and origin of the American Indians, in the library of Thomas W. Field. With bibliographical and historical notes, and synopses of the contents of some of the works least known. New York, Scribner, 1873. 430 p.
   1. Type of microform: Microfilm.
   2. Availability: In progress. About 50,000 pages published annually. Catalog cards may be purchased.
   3. Orders: General Microfilm Company, 100 Inman Street, Cambridge, Massachusetts 02139.
   4. This collection, *The Literature of the American Indian,* is based on Field's *Essay,* a list of 1,708 volumes.

212. General Microfilm Company.
African documents. 35 mm microfilm edition. (In its Publications on microfilm: catalog and price lists. Cambridge, Mass. [1970?] Section 1)
   1. Type of microform: Microfilm.
   2. Availability: Fifteen groups immediately available. Groups may be purchased separately at prices listed.
   3. Orders: General Microfilm Company, 100 Inman Street, Cambridge, Massachusetts 02139.
   4. The initial phase of this project includes documents starting in 1957 through current documents. It is planned to copy all available documents as well as quasi-official documents from both self-governing and non-self-governing countries and islands normally associated with Africa. Catalog cards may be purchased.

213. General Microfilm Company.
Canadiana. Group I: Travel literature. 35 mm microfilm edition. (In its Publications on microfilm: catalog and price lists. Cambridge, Mass. [1970?] Section 9)
   1. Type of microform: Microfilm.
   2. Availability: Available at current prices.
   3. Orders: General Microfilm Company, 100 Inman Street, Cambridge, Massachusetts 02139.
   4. The collection of travel literature offered here covers the period from discovery and exploration to the twentieth century and includes accounts of travel within the present boundaries of Canada regardless of the nationality

of the author or place of publication. The project of reproducing Canadian literature, begun in 1967, is expected to be completed in six to eight years. Following Group I, Groups II and III will cover Canadian biography and history respectively. Catalog cards are available.

214. General Microfilm Company.

Chinese culture series. 35 mm microfilm edition. (In its Publications on microfilm: catalog and price lists. Cambridge, Mass. [1970?] Section 2)

1. Type of microform: Microfilm.

2. Availability: The first group of eleven rolls is available.

3. Orders: General Microfilm Company, 100 Inman Street, Cambridge, Massachusetts 02139.

4. This new series consists of microfilm copies of rare editions of Chinese classical literature. The first group includes editions of poetry and other works dating from the third to the fifteenth century. The company plans to deliver two or three similar groups each year for the next ten years. Catalog cards are not available at present.

215. General Microfilm Company.

Eighteenth century English literature and history. (In its Publications on microfilm: catalog and price lists. Cambridge, Mass. [1970?] Section 3)

1. Type of microform: Microfilm.

2. Availability: Prepublication announcement.

3. Orders: General Microfilm Company, 100 Inman Street, Cambridge, Massachusetts 02139.

4. This project will be in three parts. Part I, eighteenth-century English fiction, will run for about ten years, at about 50,000 pages a year. The initial selections are based on Andrew Block's *The English Novel, 1740-1850.* Part II, eighteenth-century English philosophy, theology and science, will furnish material closely related to literary and historical studies and will also run for about ten years. For the first six to eight years, the titles will be selected from the *Cambridge Bibliography of English Literature* and *Bibliography of British History: The Eighteenth Century, 1714-1789,* by Pargellis and Medley. Part III, eighteenth-century English history, is also based on Pargellis and Medley, and is expected to run fifteen to twenty years.

No specific order will be followed in filming the various titles, but they will be identified clearly on short-title lists which will accompany each shipment. Catalog cards may be purchased for each title.

216. General Microfilm Company.

Eighteenth century French fiction. 35 mm microfilm edition. (In its Publications on microfilm: catalog and price lists. Cambridge, Mass. [1970?] Section 3)

1. Type of microform: Microfilm.

2. Availability: Published in two groups. The entire project may be purchased; each group is also available separately.

3. Orders: General Microfilm Company, 100 Inman Street, Cambridge, Massachusetts 02139.

4. This is a continuation of a project initiated by the Fincastle Press (and

carried on briefly by the Erasmus Press). It is planned to include about 600 titles in the series, at the rate of about 75 per year for seven to nine years. A partial listing of the titles in the first two groups is given. Catalog cards may be purchased.

217. General Microfilm Company.

Eighteenth century French poetry. 35mm microfilm edition. (In its Publications on microfilm: catalog and price lists. Cambridge, Mass. [1970?] Section 3)

1. Type of microform: Microfilm.
2. Availability: Series I consisting of twenty-four titles is available.
3. Orders: General Microfilm Company, 100 Inman Street, Cambridge, Massachusetts 02139.
4. The first of two groups of French poetry. Catalog cards may be purchased.

218. General Microfilm Company.

Italian drama. 35mm microfilm edition. (In its Publications on microfilm: catalog and price lists. Cambridge, Mass. [1970?] Section 7)

1. Type of microform: Microfilm.
2. Availability: Available at current prices.
3. Orders: General Microfilm Company, 100 Inman Street, Cambridge, Massachusetts 02139.
4. Offers a comprehensive collection of Italian drama from the Middle Ages to the twentieth century, including all genres: marionette plays, opera libretti, conventional comedy and tragedy, pageants, radio, and cinema scripts. The selection is based on standard Italian literary histories and bibliographies of literature and the theatre. Fifty thousand pages a year are made available. The project is expected to continue for twelve to fifteen years. Catalog cards are available.

219. General Microfilm Company.

Latin American documents. 35mm edition. (In its Publications on microfilm: Catalog and price lists. Cambridge, Mass. [1970?] Section 9)

1. Type of microform: Microfilm.
2. Availability: Available at prices listed.
3. Orders: General Microfilm Company, 100 Inman Street, Cambridge, Massachusetts 02139.
4. This project, as begun in 1960, was selective in nature, furnishing opaque microfacsimiles of documents chosen from the "Recent Books" section of the *Inter-American Review of Bibliography*. Later, the project was expanded to include material reported currently in the *National Union Catalog*. Project A is the designation used for the material selected from the *Inter-American Review*, while Project B is the designation used for the expanded and more comprehensive program, which includes not only the titles from the *Inter-American Review of Bibliography* but also titles from the *National Union Catalog*. Around 1969 the publisher changed from opaque microfacsimiles to microfilm. Catalog cards may be purchased.

220. General Microfilm Company.
    Lincolniana. Famous Americans: Scarce printed materials and ephemera. 35 mm edition. (In its Publications on microfilm: catalog and price lists. Cambridge, Mass. [1070?] Section 9)
    1. Type of microform: Microfilm.
    2. Availability: Available at price listed.
    3. Orders: General Microfilm Company, 100 Inman Street, Cambridge, Massachusetts 02139.
    4. "The 742 items in this collection were selected from the distinguished special collection of Lincoln Memorial University." Printed books generally found in research libraries are excluded. On request, the publisher will supply a handlist of the collection in microform. Catalog cards are available.

221. General Microfilm Company.
    Literature of the American Revolution. Source material and critical and historical works. 35mm edition. (In its Publications on microfilm: catalog and price lists. Cambridge, Mass. [1970?] Section 9)
    1. Type of microform: Microfilm.
    2. Availability: Prepublication subscriptions ended December 31, 1970.
    3. Orders: General Microfilm Company, 100 Inman Street, Cambridge, Massachusetts 02139.
    4. The publisher in this prepublication announcement proposes a project to publish on microfilm out-of-print source materials on the American Revolution. The first group will be based on William Spohn Baker's *Bibliotheca Washingtoniana* (Philadelphia: R. M. Lindsay, 1889; reprinted by Gale, 1967) and a supplement, which is in preparation. Subsequent groups will be based on bibliographies in other biographical studies and on the Revolutionary sections in local, state, and regional bibliographies. A general outline of the series is given, several sources which will be used are enumerated, and scholars who will assist in selecting material are mentioned. Catalog cards for each title in the series will be available.

222. General Microfilm Company.
    Scandinavian culture series. 35mm edition. (In its Publications on microfilm: catalog and price lists. Cambridge, Mass. [1970?] Section 11)
    1. Type of microform: Microfilm.
    2. Availability: Available at price listed.
    3. Orders: General Microfilm Company, 100 Inman Street, Cambridge, Massachusetts 02139.
    4. This series will cover early Scandinavian imprints to 1700. Selection will be based on:

    Brun, Christian Walther.
      Bibliotheca danica. Systematisk Fortegnelse over den danske Litteratur fra 1482 til 1830 . . . København, Gyldendal, 1877-1931. 4 v., Suppl. and index.

    Nielsen, Lauritz.
      Dansk bibliografi, 1482-1500, 1551-1600, med saerligt hensyn til

dansk bogtrykkerkunsts historie. København, Gyldendal, 1919-35. 2 v. and Register.

Pettersen, Hjalmar.
Bibliotheca norvegica. Christiana, Cammeyer, 1899-1924. 4 v. in 5. v. 1. Norsk boglexikon, 1643-1813.

Sveriges bibliografi intill ar 1600, av Isak Collijn. Uppsala, Svenska Litteratursällskapet, 1927-38. 3v.

———— 1600-talet Bidrag till en bibliografisk förteckning av Isak Collijn. Uppsala, Almquist, 1942-46. 2 v.

Microfilm of books from Collijn is delivered as it becomes available from the Uppsala University Library and the Royal Library in Stockholm. Catalog cards based on bibliographical sources such as Collijn and Nielsen will be made available.

223. General Microfilm Company.
Travel in Mexico and the Caribbean area. Mexican. 35 mm microfilm edition. (In its Publications on microfilm: catalog and price lists. Cambridge, Mass. [1970?] Section 9)
1. Type of microform: Microfilm.
2. Availability: Available at current prices.
3. Orders: General Microfilm Company, 100 Inman Street, Cambridge, Massachusetts 02139.
4. Virtually all titles listed in the Library of Congress general card catalog under the subject "Mexico—Description and travel," up through 1914 imprints, are included in the present collection. The project, begun in 1964 and continuing, offers a catalog card showing the number of the roll on which each item appears. A short-title list is available on request.

224. Government reports index, Feb. 15, 1967-   Springfield, Va., National Technical Information Service. *Semi-monthly.*
1. Type of microform: Microfiche, microfilm.
2. Availability: Many of the reports indexed are made available in microfiche or microfilm, as well as in paper copy, magnetic tape, or punched cards. Specific information regarding form in which a report is available and prices are given in the Accession/Report Number index.
3. Orders: National Technical Information Service, Springfield, Virginia 22151.
4. This index, originally entitled *Government-wide Index to Federal Research and Development Reports,* changed its name in March 1971 to reflect the broader mission of the new National Information Service.
"The Clearinghouse for Federal Scientific and Technical Information which previously published this index, was largely limited in its activities to announcing and distributing research and development reports." The NTIS, in addition to making available research and development reports, will also

announce and disseminate technical publications of the Department of Commerce that are not research and development reports.

The index provides five approaches to reports: corporate author, subject, personal author, contract number, and accession report number.

225. Great Britain. House of Commons. Sessional Papers.
  I. Eighteenth Century (1731-1800)
  II. Nineteenth Century (1801-1900)
  III. Twentieth Century (1901-   )
  1. Type of microform: Microprint.
  2. Availability: Available as three collections: eighteenth century (1731-1800), nineteenth century (1801-1900), and twentieth century (1901-   ).
  3. Orders: Readex Microprint Corporation, 5 Union Square, New York, New York 10003.
  4. The microprint edition of the *Sessional Papers* of the eighteenth century, sponsored by the American Historical Association and edited by Edgar L. Erickson of the University of Illinois, makes available for the first time a practically complete collection of the *Papers* of the eighteenth century, based on the Abbott Collection. An interesting account of Erickson's task of collating, checking records, and searching libraries is found in his article, "The Sessional Papers; Last Phase," *College and Research Libraries* 21 (Sept. 1960): 343-356. Equally interesting is John Weatherford, "The Sessional Paper. An Epilogue," *Library Journal* 88 (April 15, 1963): 1630-1631, in which the author lists about fifty *Papers* of the eighteenth century not in the Abbott Collection, and as a result, not reproduced.

The *Sessional Papers* of the nineteenth century were also edited by Erickson, but again no complete collection existed anywhere, and there were many problems of locating, collating, reassembling, and editing.

The *Sessional Papers* of the twentieth century are being edited by F. W. Torrington. Despite the importance of the *Papers*, there are few research libraries in Great Britain or the United States which can boast of having complete sets, for Her Majesty's Stationery Office has never issued complete bound sets of the *Papers*. So again there is the problem of locating and organizing materials for reproduction. The publisher has only priced the *Papers* through 1920 according to the 1969-70 catalog.

Useful indexes for the eighteenth and nineteenth century *Papers* are:
  Gt. Brit. Parliament. House of Commons.
  Catalogue of papers printed by order of the House of Commons ... 1731-1800. London, 1807.
  ────── Hansard's catalogue and breviate of Parliamentary papers, 1691-1834. Reprinted in facsimile ... Oxford, Blackwell, 1953.

In addition to the above *Catalogue and Breviate*, Hansard printed 136 special, annual, and cumulative indexes covering the years from 1696 to 1900. All these 137 indexes appear in the microprint edition and are also available as a separate unit. Sessional index volumes and consolidated indexes for 1900-1948/49 and 1950-1958/59 will be included in the Readex Microprint edition of the twentieth century *Papers*.

226. Greenwood Publishing Corporation. Microform Division.
Black journals: periodical resources for Afro-American and African studies. Westport, Conn., [197?] 1 1.
   1. Type of microform: Microfiche.
   2. Availability: Complete collection or individual titles may be purchased.
   3. Orders: Microform Division, Greenwood Publishing Corporation, 51 Riverside Avenue, Westport, Connecticut 06880.
   4. An alphabetical list of the thirty-five periodical titles included in the project, thirty-three of which are no longer being published. Nineteen titles are being offered on film for the first time. Sixteen of the titles in this project are also offered in the project, *Reprints of Negro Periodicals: Series I.*

227. Greenwood Publishing Corporation. Microform Division.
Radical periodicals in the United States, 1890-1960: Series I. Radical periodicals of Great Britain. Period I: Protest literature of the industrial revolution (1794-1867). Reprints of negro periodicals: Series I. Westport, Conn., [1969?] [8] p.
   1. Type of microform: Microfiche, microfilm.
   2. Availability: Collections and also individual titles available for purchase.
   3. Orders: Microform Division, Greenwood Publishing Corporation, 51 Riverside Avenue, Westport, Connecticut 06880.
   4. Alphabetical listing of titles already available or well into production. This first group, *Radical Periodicals in the United States, 1890-1960*, is composed of serial titles that have previously been reprinted by other Greenwood companies. All the titles in the group, *Reprints of Negro Periodicals: Series I* are also included in the thirty-five titles which comprise the project, *Black Journals: Periodical Resources for Afro-American and African Studies.*

228. Greenwood Publishing Corporation. Microform Division.
Sources for the history of social welfare in America. [Westport, Conn., 197?] [2] p.
   1. Type of microform: Microfiche.
   2. Availability: Available as a project; each of the five titles also available separately.
   3. Orders: Microform Division, Greenwood Publishing Corporation, 51 Riverside Avenue, Westport, Connecticut 06880.
   4. The collection is composed of three groups of material: (1) 96 volumes of the *Official Proceedings* of the Social Welfare Forum of the National Conference on Social Welfare covering the years, 1874-1969; (2) unpublished manuscripts of the *Proceedings of the Annual Conference* of the National Child Labor Committee, New York, covering the years 1905-1929, and the *Minutes* of the Committee's Board of Trustees, covering the years 1904-1955; (3) complete sets of six of the most important social welfare journals.

229. Greenwood Publishing Corporation. Microform Division.

State constitutional conventions from Independence to the completion of the present union, 1776-1959. Westport, Conn., 1971. [4] p.

1. Type of microform: Microfiche.

2. Availability: Series I (the original states) now available. States are individually priced also.

3. Orders: Microform Division, Greenwood Publishing Corporation, 51 Riverside Avenue, Westport, Connecticut 06880.

4. This microfiche collection will be published in three stages. The first series will contain all the official convention material of the thirteen original states. The second series, to be published in early 1972, will contain the convention records of the twenty states which joined the Union prior to 1861. The third series, available late in 1972, will include the remaining seventeen states which joined the Union after the Civil War.

A full-size printed bibliography will accompany sets of microfiche for each state and is included in the price of the microfiche. The preliminary sample of a bibliography for one state, Massachusetts, which appears in Greenwood's advertising brochure is well done.

230. Hawkins, William.

Bulletins de presse, Petrograd-Moscou, 1917-1918, édition sur microfilm. Index alphabétique des noms [par William Hawkins] Paris, Service International de Microfilms, 1963. 75 p.

1. Type of microform: Microfilm.

2. Availability: Available in two groups at listed prices: *Indexed Microfilm* (Bulletins de presse, Petrograd, 27 April 1917-16 March 1918 and Bulletins de presse, Moscow, 18 March 1918-31 July 1918); *Non-Indexed Microfilm* (Bulletins de presse, Moscow, 14 June 1917-15 March 1918 and Bulletins de presse, Petrograd, 18 March 1918-21 January 1919).

3. Orders: Service International de Microfilms, 9, Rue du Commandant-Rivière, Paris VIIIᵉ, France.

4. This *Index alphabétique des noms* does not cover all the issues of the *Bulletins de presse*, Petrograd-Moscow, which are available on microfilm, the indexing being limited to those bulletins published in the city which was the seat of the Central Government (see note on availability above). The *Index* indicates both reel number and page number. A table of dates and pages enables the reader to approximate the date of a page reference.

The introduction to the *Index* provides historical background information on the *Bulletins de presse*, which were published in Petrograd and Moscow by official French agencies corresponding to what we today call "Bureaux de Presse" in our embassies. They were intended for the French colony and other foreign colonies in Russia.

231. Health, physical education and recreation microcard bulletin. v. 1-   1963-
————— Eugene, Microcard Publications, School of Health, Physical Education and Recreation, University of Oregon, 1963-

1. Type of microform: Microcard.

2. Availability: The publications are available on an annual subscription

plan. All titles announced at a particular time may be purchased as a group; individual titles are also available.

3. Orders: Microcard Publications, School of Health, Physical Education and Recreation, University of Oregon, Eugene, Oregon 97403.

4. *Microcard Publications* is a nonprofit project of the School of Health, Physical Education and Recreation of the University of Oregon. The materials offered are primarily research materials, especially doctoral dissertations, masters' theses, and scholarly out-of-print books. The October 1963 *Microcard Bulletin* superseded all former bulletins. Part I lists new titles and Part II lists all former titles. *Microcard Bulletin,* v. 2, is a cumulation covering March 1965 through October 1968. New titles are regularly listed in a fall *Bulletin* and a spring supplement. Titles are listed under five headings: physical education; physiology of exercise; recreation and camping; health education; psychology. The arrangement in each group is alphabetical by author; full bibliographic information is provided.

232. Hitchcock, Henry Russell.
American architectural books; a list of books, portfolios, and pamphlets on architecture and related subjects published in America before 1895. Minneapolis, University of Minnesota Press [1962] *Reprint of 3d revised edition, 1946.*

Park, Helen. List of architectural books available in America before the Revolution. *Journal* of the Society of Architectural Historians. v. 20, p. 115-30. October 1961.

1. Type of microform: Microfilm; most individual items can also be furnished in full-size Xerox reproduction.

2. Availability: Completion and delivery is scheduled for early 1972.

3. Orders: Research Publications, Inc., Box 3903, Amity Station, New Haven, Connecticut 06525.

4. The project, *American Architectural Books,* is based on the two bibliographies noted above. The publisher plans to film all titles which can be located. In most cases, however, only one edition of each title will be filmed, usually the first edition. "Later editions will be included only if the earlier one is not available or in instances when later editions are sufficiently revised or expanded to warrant inclusion." The microfilm follows the sequence in the Hitchcock and Park bibliographies, with the number used in these bibliographies appearing before each title. There will be a printed reel index, and professionally prepared catalog cards, which include series title and microfilm reel location, may be purchased.

233. Human Relations Area Files. [Microform edition]
1. Type of Microform: Microfilm, microfiche. The first ten years of the HRAF are on microfilm, cut into 5 inch lengths and inserted into 3 x 5 inch acetate jackets which are identified with the proper category and file numbers. Beginning with the eleventh year, microfiche has been used.

2. Availability: The microfilm-microfiche version of the Human Relations Area Files is furnished for associate members. "While the application for a subscription must be approved by HRAF, University Microfilms . . . is in charge of production and distribution."

3. Orders: Human Relations Area Files, 755 Prospect Street, New Haven, Connecticut 06511 *OR* University Microfilms, 300 North Zeeb Road, Ann Arbor, Michigan 48106.

4. The following quotation from the pamphlet, Human Relations Area Files, *Function and Scope* (New Haven, n.d.) indicates the reason for making HRAF files available in microform: "The Human Relations Area Files (HRAF) is a non profit research corporation sponsored and controlled by twenty-three major universities and research institutions. Broadly stated, the function of HRAF is to contribute to an understanding of man and the cultures he has produced. More specifically HRAF seeks to promote research on man and his ways of life by organizing and making widely available primary source material and by instigating comparative and interdisciplinary research on human behavior, social life and culture. . . . In 1958 HRAF made available a version of the files to which many institutions, both domestic and foreign, have subscribed as associate members of HRAF. . . . The selection of full members has been made in terms of the optimum geographic distribution of the files for their maximum potential use. . . . The problem of the rapidly growing number of users of the files coupled with the limitations on full membership was partially solved by the development of a microfilm version, to which any qualified institution may subscribe as an associate member."

The Human Relations Area Files, a continually expanding collection of primary source materials, basically ethnographic in content, covering the cultures of the world, is coded for rapid retrieval of information either on a particular culture or on a topic within a cross-cultural sample. The *Outline of World Cultures* and the *Outline of Cultural Materials* (cited below) provide the codes for the political or ethnic unit and topics (or subjects), respectively.

Consultation of the following titles is needed for an understanding and use of the files:

Behavior science notes. v. 1, 1966- [New Haven, Human Relations Area Files]

Murdock, George Peter. Ethnographic atlas. [Pittsburgh] University of Pittsburgh Press [1967] 128 p.

———— Outline of world cultures. 3d ed., rev. New Haven, Human Relations Area Files, 1963. 222 p. (Behavior science outlines [3])

Human Relations Area Files, Inc. HRAF research guide. New Haven, Human Relations Area Files, n.d. 43 p.

———— HRAF source bibliography. [Prepared by Joan Steffens and Timothy J. O'Leary. Rev. ed.] New Haven, Conn., Human Relations Area Files, 1969- 1 v. (loose-leaf)

Yale University. Institute of Human Relations. Outline of cultural materials [by] George P. Murdock [and others] 4th rev. ed. New Haven, Human Relations Area Files, 1961. 164 p. (Behavior science outlines, v. 1)

234. Kaminkow, Marion J.
    A new bibliography of British genealogy, with notes. Baltimore, Magna Charta Book Co., 1965. 170 p.

1. Type of microform: Microfilm.
2. Availability: In process. Catalog cards may be purchased.
3. Orders: General Microfilm Company, 100 Inman Street, Cambridge, Massachusetts 02139.
4. General Microfilm Company offers a series, *Genealogical Source Material on Microfilm*, a comprehensive collection of English, American, and European genealogical works on microfilm. The initial selection is English and Scottish works, based on the Kaminkow *Bibliography*. Subsequently, other standard bibliographies will be used.

235. Katalog mikrofilmów muzycznych. 1-   Warszawa, 1956-
    Issued by Stacja Mikrofilmowa and by Zaklad Muzyczny of the Biblioteca Narodowa.
    v. 2 has series note: Biblioteka Narodowa. Katalog mikrofilmów nr. 2.
    1. Type of microform: Microfilm.
    2. Availability: Positive prints and enlargements available. Microfilms may be examined in the reading room of the Microfilm Center of the National Library in Warsaw (Stacja Mikrofilmowa Biblioteki Narodowej w Warszawie); positive microfilms may also be borrowed by other libraries for a month.
    3. Orders: Stacja Mikrofilmowa, Biblioteca Narodowa, Palac Rzeczypospolitej, Plac Krasińskich 3/5, Warsaw, Poland.
    4. Lists the valuable musical manuscripts, scores, books, and related materials microfilmed by the National Microfilm Centre in order to bring together historical sources of Polish music. Volume I (1956) enumerates musical sources of the nineteenth and twentieth centuries microfilmed from 1950 to 1956, while Volume II (1962) enumerates musical sources belonging to state and ecclesiastical collections in Poland, as well as from some foreign collections, microfilmed from 1957 to 1961. Included in Volume II are medieval manuscripts (since the twelfth century), manuscripts and rare prints of the Renaissance and of the twelfth and thirteenth centuries. The introduction of the *Katalog* notes that the microfilming of historical sources of Polish music is not yet finished. Apparently, additional volumes of the *Katalog* will be published.

236. Kimball, Stanley Buchholz.
    Sources of Mormon history in Illinois, 1839-48, an annotated catalog of the microfilm collection at Southern Illinois University. 2d ed., rev. and enl., 1966. Carbondale, Library, Southern Illinois University [1966] 104 p. (Illinois. Southern Illinois University, Carbondale. Libraries. Bibliographical contributions, no. 1.)
    1. Type of microform: Microfilm (any other type of photographic copy is noted).
    2. Availability: Collection open to all qualified students and scholars. Prospective users should contact the Assistant Librarian for Readers' Services of the Lovejoy Library, Southern Illinois University, Edwardsville, where collection is housed. Southern Illinois University does not have the right to reproduce any of the documents. Permission to reproduce must be secured from the holders of the original documents who are designated.
    3. Annotated catalog of primary source materials, almost exclusively unpublished, relating to Mormon history in Illinois from 1839 to 1848. The

catalog is divided into eight parts: (1) letters and documents; (2) newspapers and periodicals; (3) theses; (4) indexes (the four indexes listed are typescript indexes to newspapers and collections represented in the collection); (5) appendices; (6) new materials for second edition (letters and documents, newspapers and periodicals, theses and miscellaneous items); (7) materials on order, unavailable or omitted (8) name index. Each item is cataloged in the same order as it appears on the microfilm.

237. Leavitt, Sturgis Elleno.

Revistas hispanoamericanas: indice bibliográfico, 1843-1935. Recopilado por Sturgis E. Leavitt con la colaboracion de Madaline W. Nichols y Jefferson Rea Spell. Santiago de Chile, Fondo Histórico y Bibliográfico José Toribio Medina, 1960. 589 p. (Homenaje al sesquicentenario de la Independencia Nacional, 1810-1960, 1)

1. Type of microform: Microfilm.
2. Availability: Available on 35 mm microfilm.
3. Orders: General Microfilm Company, 100 Inman Street, Cambridge, Massachusetts 02139.
4. All titles indexed by Leavitt in his *Revistas hispanoamericanas* are reproduced in this microfilm edition. General Microfilm Company proposes, in addition, to offer other selected titles of Latin American serials in Spanish, Portuguese, French, and English.

238. Lhéritier, Andrée.

Les physiologies, 1840-1845. Edition sur microfilm. Bibliographie descriptive. Introduction par W. Hawkins. Paris, Service International de Microfilms, 1966. [69] p.

1. Type of microform: Microfilm.
2. Availability: Copies of the microfilm are available.
3. Orders: Service International de Microfilms, 9, rue du Commandant-Rivière, Paris VIIIe, France.
4. This brochure includes an introduction by the editor, William Hawkins, and a reprint of Mlle. Lhéritier's bibliography *Les Physiologies*, including the introduction and indexes, which originally appeared in *Etudes de presse*. n.s. 9, no. 17 (1957). Not every title in the bibliography was filmed, but each title which was filmed is clearly indicated both in the body of the bibliography and in the indexes. Mr. Hawkins in his introduction provides interesting background material and explanations about the microfilm project. Mlle. Lhéritier in her introduction to the bibliography defines and describes "Les physiologies" (little illustrated romantic works), discussing both authors and artists.

239. Lost Cause Press.

British culture: a selection of books relating to eighteenth century English culture. (In its Microcard catalog. 1962-   )

1. Type of microform: Microcard.
2. Availability: 848 volumes available on microcards.

3. Orders: Lost Cause Press, 1140-46 Starks Bldg., Louisville, Kentucky 40202.

4. The Lost Cause Press issues lists of titles included in each shipment.

Catalog cards are offered by Erasmus Press, 225 Culpepper Street, Lexington, Kentucky 40502.

240. Lost Cause Press.
    19th century American literature. (In its Microcard catalog, 1962-   )
    1. Type of microform: Microcard.
    2. Availability: In process.
    3. Orders: Lost Cause Press, 1140-46 Starks Bldg., Louisville, Kentucky 40202.
    4. Lost Cause Press issues a list of titles to accompany each group as it is published. Catalog cards are offered by Erasmus Press, 225 Culpepper Street, Lexington, Kentucky 40502.

241. Medina, José Toribio.
    Biblioteca hispano-americana (1493-1810) Santiago de Chile, Impreso y grabado en casa del autor, 1898-1907. 7 v.
    1. Type of microform: Microfilm.
    2. Availability: In production. About 50,000 pages will be offered each year.
    3. Orders: General Microfilm Company, 100 Inman Street, Cambridge, Massachusetts 02139.
    4. All available works recorded by Medina in his *Biblioteca Hispano-americana* are to be microfilmed over a period of about twenty years. The more than 8,000 titles represent a vast source of material on the history of the Spanish-speaking peoples of the western hemisphere. Catalog cards will be available.
    University Microfilms produced a photocopy edition of the *Biblioteca* in 1958, and N. Israel of Amsterdam included it in the reprint series of José Toribio Medina's bibliographic works in 1968.

242. Meisel, Max.
    A bibliography of American natural history; the pioneer century, 1769-1865; the role played by the scientific societies; scientific journals, natural history museums and botanic gardens; state geological and natural history surveys; federal exploring expeditions in the rise and progress of American botany, geology, mineralogy and zoology. Brooklyn, N. Y., The Premier Publishing Co., 1924-29. 3 v.
    1. Type of microform: Microfilm.
    2. Availability: Work on this project is scheduled to start soon according to a letter from the publisher dated June 30, 1971.
    3. Orders: Research Publications, Inc., Box 3903, Amity Station, New Haven, Connecticut 06525.
    4. The microfilm project, *American Natural History, 1769-1865,* will include the periodical literature indexed by Meisel in his *Bibliography of*

American Natural History. According to the publisher, this bibliography will serve as an index to the collection.

243. Microcard Editions.

Jeffersonian Americana from the University of Virginia Library. Washington, D.C., n.d. [1] p.

1. Type of microform: Microfiche.
2. Availability: Complete set available for purchase.
3. Orders: NCR/Microcard Editions, 365 South Oak Street, West Salem, Wisconsin 54669.
4. This series was originally issued on microcards in 1955 by the Louisville Public Library. It consists of 708 scarce volumes relating to the Jeffersonian era, all of which are listed in Sabin's *Dictionary of Books Relating to America.* The editorial work was done by William H. Runge, Curator of Rare Books and of McGregor Library at the University of Virginia. Printed catalog cards are available for each item from Microcard Editions.

244. Microcard Editions.

Slavery source materials. (In its Catalog 12, 1971-1972, p. 48)

1. Type of microform: Microcard, microfiche.
2. Availability: Available for purchase as a collection.
3. Orders: NCR/Microcard Editions, 901 26th Street, N.W., Washington, D.C. 20037.
4. Comprises books and pamphlets (441 titles) which were written by and about the Negro and about slavery and antislavery before the Civil War. The material to be filmed was selected by the staff of the Amistad Research Center at Dillard University, New Orleans, supervised by Dr. Clifford H. Johnson, the Director of the Center. An annotated list of the titles in the collection, prepared by Dr. Carroll G. Barber, is available but was not seen by the compiler.

245. Microfilming Corporation of America.

The history of the black worker as found in the President's Committee on Fair Employment Practice (FEPC) 1941-46. Glen Rock, N.J. [1971?] [1] p.

1. Type of microform: Microfilm.
2. Availability: The entire collection or certain designated portions may be purchased.
3. Orders: Microfilming Corporation of America, 21 Harristown Road, Glen Rock, New Jersey 07452.
4. The records of government provide a wealth of primary source material for the researcher. The voluminous records of the Fair Employment Practices Committee will be of special interest to researchers interested in black studies, labor, the controls of a wartime economy, etc. The FEPC records microfilmed for this project are in the custody of the National Archives. Their arrangement and general description may be found in the pamphlet *Preliminary Inventory of the Records of the Committee of Fair Employment Practice,* by Charles Zaid of the National Archives staff. This pamphlet was adapted to provide a means of locating readily on the film the desired material as described in the inventory and completely incorporated into the

guide prepared for the collection. (Only the foreword and introduction to the guide were seen by the compiler.)

246. National Micropublishing Corporation.
     Complete collection of presidential press conferences from Wilson through Truman (1913-1953) published on microfilm. July 1971. [1] p.
     1. Type of microform: Microfilm.
     2. Availability: Available as a complete program.
     3. Orders: National Micropublishing Corporation, 31 Center Street, Wilton, Connecticut 06897.
     4. This publisher's announcement indicates that this "collection includes more than 1,000 fully indexed press conferences of Franklin D. Roosevelt; all known press conferences of Woodrow Wilson as assembled by Prof. Arthur S. Link, editor, *The Papers of Woodrow Wilson;* eighteen volumes of Calvin Coolidge's press conferences; and more than 3,000 pages of President Truman's press conferences as gathered by Dr. Philip Brooks, Director, Harry S. Truman Library." A 6,700 entry index accompanies the film. There is no indication as to whether it is a part of the film or in hard-cover.

247. National Micropublishing Corporation.
     Executive documents. (In its New microform collections. [Wilton, Conn., 1971?])
     1. Type of microform: Microfiche.
     2. Availability: Available at prices listed.
     3. Orders: National Micropublishing Corporation, 31 Center Street, Wilton, Connecticut 06897.
     4. This collection, *Executive Documents,* contains one multivolumed government publication and three of a serial nature: (1) U.S. President. *A Compilation of the Messages and Papers of the Presidents, 1789-1922,* 22 v.; (2) *Code of Federal Regulations of the United States of America Having General Applicability and Legal Effect in Force June 1, 1938,* 17 v.; (3) U. S. Comptroller of the Treasury, *A Digest of the Decisions in the Office of the Second Comptroller,* v. 1-4, 1817-1894; U.S. Comptroller of the Treasury, *Decisions . . . ,* v. 1-27, 1894-1921, and U.S. General Accounting Office, *Decisions of the Comptroller General of the United States,* v. 1-48, 1921-1969; (4) U.S. Dept. of Justice, *Official Opinions of the Attorneys General of the United States,* 1st-40th, 1791-1948.

248. National Micropublishing Corporation.
     The presidency. (In its New microform collections. [Wilton, Conn., 1971?])
     1. Type of microform: Microfilm, microfiche.
     2. Availability: Commercially published. Entire collection or individual titles may be purchased.
     3. Orders: National Micropublishing Corporation, 31 Center Street, Wilton, Connecticut 06897.
     4. Includes four titles: (1) Democratic Party, National Convention, *Official Proceedings,* 1st-35th, 1832-1968; (2) *Democratic Campaign Book,* 1st-17th, 1876-1940 (all published); (3) Republican Party, National Convention, *Official Proceedings,* 1st-29th, 1856-1968; and (4) *Republican Cam-*

paign Text-book, 1st-16th, 1880-1940 (all published). A hard-bound copyflo index accompanies the microfilm edition of the proceedings of each political party. It is a copy of the title pages and tables of contents of each collection of proceedings.

249. National Micropublishing Corporation.
> Violence in America—twentieth century. (In its New microform collections [Wilton, Conn., 1971?])
> 1. Type of microform: Microfilm, microfiche.
> 2. Availability: Series I available in its entirety or publications of a single commission may be purchased. Series II-IV will be available later in 1971 and 1972.
> 3. Orders: National Micropublishing Corporation, 31 Center Street, Wilton, Connecticut 06897
> 4. The basic source documents included in Series I provide the scholar with the reports and fourteen monographs published in 1931 by the U. S. National Commission on Law Observance and Enforcement (Wickersham Commission) and the original testimony given before two more recent investigative groups, namely, California, Governor's Commission on the Los Angeles Riots (McCone Commission) and the Fact-Finding Commission on Columbia Disturbances (Cox Commission). The proceedings of the McCone Commission were published in 1966 in eighteen volumes and those of the Cox Commission in 1968 in twenty-three volumes. The publisher states that with this series there will be both a microfilm and paperbound index.

250. New York. Public Library.
> French revolutionary pamphlets, a checklist of the Talleyrand & other collections. Compiled by Horace E. Hayden under the direction of Charles F. McCombs. New York, 1945. 152 p.
> 1. Type of microform: Microfilm, microfiche, micro-opaque cards.
> 2. Availability: The complete collection may be purchased. It is divided into six groups (500 pamphlets per group), each of which may be separately purchased.
> 3. Orders: NCR/Microcard Editions, 901 26th Street, N.W., Washington, D.C. 20037, *OR* World Microfilms, Distribution Division, 62 Queen's Grove, London, N.W. 8, England.
> 4. The pamphlets included in the microform publication, *French Revolutionary Pamphlets*, were selected primarily from the *Checklist* cited above. It lists the pamphlets in the Talleyrand collection in three groups: (1) list of pamphlets arranged alphabetically by author or by title, if anonymous; (2) official publications of civil, ecclesiastical, and other bodies; (3) periodical publications. There is a supplement which lists in the same fashion pamphlets from other collections in the New York Public Library. There are personal author and subject indexes.

251. Newberry Library, Chicago.
> A checklist of French political pamphlets, 1560-1644, in the Newberry Library, compiled by Doris Varner Welsh. Chicago, 1950. 204 p.
> ————————— A second checklist of French political pamphlets, 1560-1653,

in the Newberry Library, compiled by Doris Varner Welsh. Chicago, 1955. 190 p.

    1. Type of microform: Microfilm.

    2. Availability: May be purchased from Bell & Howell.

    3. Orders: Micro Photo Division, Bell & Howell Co., Old Mansfield Road, Wooster, Ohio 44691.

    4. A reprint of the index of *A Second Checklist of French Political Pamphlets* is furnished with the microfilm edition. It is a composite index, listing by author and title the entries in both the original checklist and the second list.

252. Oberlin College. Library.

    Anti-slavery propaganda in the Oberlin College Library, November 1968. Louisville, Kentucky, Lost Cause Press, 1968. 101 p.

    1. Type of microform: Microcard.

    2. Availability: Complete set, approximately 2,500 pamphlets, available for purchase. A set of catalog cards is included.

    3. Orders: Lost Cause Press, 1140-46 Starks Bldg., Louisville, Kentucky 40202.

    4. The Lost Cause Press has published on microcards pamphlets from the Hubbard *Classified Catalogue of the Collection of Anti-Slavery Propaganda in the Oberlin College Library* (Oberlin, 1932), and pamphlets added to the collection since 1932, and has issued an alphabetical catalog to accompany the set.

253. Pennsylvania. University. Library.

    The Maclure collection of French Revolutionary materials. Edited by James D. Hardy, Jr., John H. Jensen, and Martin Wolfe. (Philadelphia: University of Pennsylvania Press [1966]), 456 p.

    1. Type of microform: Microfilm.

    2. Availability: The announcement anticipates shipment over three fiscal years: one-third in June 1970, one-third in October 1970, with completion scheduled for July 1971.

    3. Orders: Research Publications, Inc., Box 2903 Amity Station, New Haven, Connecticut 06525.

    4. The collection of some 25,000 items is one of the greatest of its kind; it includes privately printed tracts, newspapers, legislative proceedings, important speeches, reports of committees and of deputies on mission, petitions, administrative decrees and laws, remonstrances, and almanacs. Almost two-thirds of the volumes have been bound by topic, and the material is filmed in the same order as listed in the catalog-index by Hardy, Jensen, and Wolfe; each item is identified on the film by the number assigned to it by the index. The catalog-index also contains an index of deputies, an index of authors (not deputies), and an index of committees and commissions. A copy of this work is included with each complete order for the Maclure Collection on microfilm.

254. Pollard, Alfred William.

    A short-title catalogue of books printed in England, Scotland, and Ireland

and of English books printed abroad, 1475-1640. Compiled by A. W. Pollard and G. R. Redgrave. London, The Bibliographical Society, 1926. 609 p.

1. Type of microform: Microfilm.
2. Availability: In process; completion expected in 1973.
3. Orders: University Microfilms, Inc., 300 N. Zeeb Road, Ann Arbor, Michigan 48106.
4. This microfilm series, called *Early English Books before 1640*, aims to reproduce all the books listed in Pollard & Redgrave's *Short-title Catalogue*, and many variants not listed. Each reel contains several books arranged according to the STC number. Access is obtained through the cross-indexes supplied by University Microfilms. This series is continued by *Early English Books, 1641-1700*, based on Donald Wing's *Short-title Catalogue*.

255. [Pride, Armistead Scott]
Negro newspapers on microfilm; a selected list. Washington, Library of Congress, Photoduplication Service, 1953. 8 p.

1. Type of microform: Microfilm.
2. Availability: Positive copies of the microfilms may be purchased.
3. Orders: Photoduplication Service, Library of Congress, Washington, D.C. 20540.
4. This list of selected Negro newspapers on microfilm is the result of a project to microfilm Negro newspapers sponsored by the Committee on Negro Studies of the American Council of Learned Societies. The Library of Congress agreed to serve as a depository and to make positive copies of the film available.

Bibliographic information appearing in the *Union List of Newspapers* was omitted from this list; also omitted was the detailed record of holdings for those titles represented by scattered issues, if these issues correspond to those reported in the *Union List of Newspapers*.

256. Readex Microprint Corporation.
English and American plays of the nineteenth century. American plays 1831-1900; English plays 1801-1900. New York, 1969-

1. Type of microform: Microprint.
2. Availability: In process; issued as prepared over the next seven to eight years.
3. Orders: Readex Microprint Corporation, 5 Union Square, New York, New York 10003.
4. This project follows as a logical extension of the *Three Centuries of English and American Plays*. The *Handlist of Plays* in volumes 4 and 5 of Allardyce Nicolls' *A History of English Drama, 1660-1900* (1952-1959) serves as the basic reference authority in the Readex collection for the plays published and produced in the British Isles. For American titles, the basic authorities are Arthur Hobson Quinn's *A History of the American Drama to the Beginning of the Civil War* (2d ed., 1951) and his *A History of the American Drama from the Civil War to the Present Day* (1936) supplemented by Robert Roden's *Later American Plays, 1831-1900* (1900) and Albert von Chorba's *Check List of American Drama . . . in the Possession of the Library*

of the University of Pennsylvania (1951). Eventually other collections will be searched for obscure titles and editions.

257. Readex Microprint Corporation.

    Landmarks of science, a comprehensive collection of the source materials in the history of science, comprising the significant contributions to the advancement of science and technology. Editors: Duane Roller [and] Sir Harold Hartley. (In its Publications, 1969-70. pp. 128-129)

    1. Type of microform: Microprint.

    2. Availability: In process; monthly installments over ten years.

    3. Orders: Readex Microprint Corporation, 5 Union Square, New York, New York 10003.

    4. This collection will include outstanding works of more than three thousand scientists, as well as the collected scientific writings of more than three hundred scientists.

258. Readex Microprint Corporation.

    Russian historical sources, first-second series, 1954-   (In Readex Microprint publications, 1969-70. p. 130-136)

    1. Type of microform: Microprint.

    2. Availability: First series complete; second series in process.

    3. Orders: Readex Microprint Corporation, 5 Union Square, New York, New York 10003.

    4. A collection on microprint of important research sources, chosen by Fred S. Rodkey with the collaboration of other eminent Russian scholars. Titles included are listed, with annotations, in *Readex Microprint Publications,* 1969-1970.

259. Research in education. v. [1]-   Nov. 1966-   Washington, 1966-

    1. Type of microform: Microfiche, hard cover.

    2. Availability: All the documents cited, except as noted, are available from the ERIC Document Reproduction Service.

    3. Orders: ERIC Document Reproduction Service, Leasco Information Products, Inc., 4827 Rugby Avenue, Bethesda, Maryland 20014.

    4. A monthly publication of the Educational Research Information Center "to make possible the early identification and acquisition of reports of interest to the educational community." The main part of each issue consists of "Document Résumés" followed by a subject index, an author index, and an institution index, plus other notes helpful to the user.

260. Research Publications, Inc.

    California county and regional histories. (In its County histories of the "Old Northwest," Series I: Wisconsin. 1971. p. 6-7)

    1. Type of microform: Microfilm.

    2. Availability: The complete California collection, including printed reel index, available. Individual titles may be ordered but only complete reels will be furnished. A set of three catalog cards for each title may be purchased.

3. Orders: Research Publications, Inc., Box 3903, Amity Station, New Haven, Connecticut 06525.

4. An alphabetical listing of the ninety-seven titles in the California series drawn from *California Local History; A Centennial Bibliography*, compiled by the California Library Association, Committee on Local History, edited by Ethel Bluman and Mabel W. Thomas (Stanford: Stanford University Press, 1950).

261. Research Publications, Inc.
County histories of the "Old Northwest." Series I: Wisconsin. [New Haven, 1971] 7 p.
1. Type of microform: Microfilm.
2. Availability: Completion of Series I is scheduled for Fall 1971. A printed author, short-title reel index is included with each complete set of film. Catalog cards, a set of three cards for each title, may be purchased.
3. Orders: Research Publications, Inc., Box 3903, Amity Station, New Haven, Connecticut 06525.
4. This brochure lists 158 Wisconsin histories and related materials, drawn from Margaret Gleason's *Printed Resources for Genealogical Searching in Wisconsin: A Selective Bibliography* (Detroit: Detroit Society for Genealogical Research, 1964). The publisher hopes to complete the filming of the other four states of the Old Northwest—Ohio, Indiana, Illinois, and Michigan—by late 1973.

262. Research Publications, Inc.
The Harold S. Jantz collection of German Baroque literature. New Haven, Conn., [197?] 1 1.
1. Type of microform: Microfilm.
2. Availability: In preparation.
3. Orders: Research Publications, Inc., Box 3903, Amity Station, New Haven, Connecticut 06525.
4. The filming of the Jantz Collection of German Baroque books owned by Professor Harold Jantz of Johns Hopkins University will provide a fitting companion and supplement to the microfilm edition of the Faber du Faur Collection of Yale University, since the Jantz Collection contains 3,000 titles not found in the Faber du Faur Collection. A bibliography listing the titles in the collection is in preparation and will be included in an order for the project. It will also be available separately.

263. Research Publications, Inc.
History of the Pacific Northwest and Canadian Northwest available on microfilm and Xerox Duopage. New Haven, Conn., 196? 20 p.
1. Type of microform: Microfilm; also available in Xerox Duopage form.
2. Availability: Complete set of 511 titles (326 titles on history of Pacific Northwest, 185 on history of Canadian Northwest) and individual titles available.
3. Orders: Research Publications, Inc., Box 3903, Amity Station, New Haven, Connecticut 06525.
4. In the preface, Archibald Hanna, Jr., Curator of the Yale Collection of

Western Americana states: "The following list of materials relating to the Pacific Northwest and the Canadian Northwest has been chosen to make available as large a group as possible of the printed sources for the early history of these two great regions.

"As far as possible titles which are still in print or easily procurable in the antiquarian book trade have been excluded. Most of those listed are scarce, and many of them extremely rare or unprocurable."

The materials included in the collection are listed alphabetically by author in two sections, the first dealing with the Pacific Northwest and the other with the Canadian Northwest.

264. Research Publications, Inc.
League of Nations: Documents and publications, 1919-1947. New Haven, Conn. [197?] 6 p.
  1. Type of microform: Microfilm.
  2. Availability: Scheduled for completion in 1971 or early 1972. The portion, *League of Nations Serial Publications,* completed summer of 1971. Individual series or parts of the collection may be purchased.
  3. Orders: Research Publications, Inc., Box 3903, Amity Station, New Haven, Connecticut 06525.
  4. This project will include many publications never before generally available, e.g., committee documentation circulated only to members of commissions, committees, and other subsidiary bodies of the League.

A printed calendar listing the documents by broad subjects and in number order is being prepared. Use is being made of the official numbers assigned to the majority of League documents at the time of publication. These official numbers are explained in Marie Carroll's *Key to League of Nations Documents Placed on Public Sale, 1920-1929* (Boston, Mass.: World Peace Foundation, 1930). In addition to the calendar of documents, a reel index guide will also be furnished.

The primary source for the documents comprising this project is the collection of League material in the Dag Hammarskjöld Library at United Nations Headquarters in New York, supplemented by the collection at the United Nations Library in Geneva.

Editor of the project is Harry N. M. Winton, formerly Chief of the Documents Reference Section of the United Nations Library in New York; consultant is Norman S. Field, Associate Chief Librarian of the United Nations Library in Geneva.

265. Research Publications, Inc.
Microfilm publication of published colonial records of the American colonies. New Haven, Conn. [1969] 7 p.
  1. Type of microform: Microfilm.
  2. Availability: Complete set, including a set of catalog cards for each title available.
  3. Orders: Research Publications, Inc., Box 3903, Amity Station, New Haven, Connecticut 06525.
  4. Included are the most important published series of colonial and state records of the original thirteen colonies, plus Maine and Vermont, from the

earliest available records to approximately 1800. The collection includes 68 titles and approximately 300,000 pages.

266. Research Publications, Inc.
Periodicals of the 17th and 18th centuries. New Haven, Conn., 197? 1 1.
1. Type of microform: Microfilm.
2. Availability: In preparation.
3. Orders: Research Publications, Inc., Box 3903, Amity Station, New Haven, Connecticut 06525.
4. The publisher states that this project will be based on the best and most recent bibliographies, including Fielding H. Garrison's exhaustive list, *Scientific and Medical Periodicals of the 17th and 18th Centuries.* The list for the first segment of the project is nearing completion, and the publisher hopes to distribute it in the fall of 1971.

267. Research Publications, Inc.
Spanish drama of the golden age, a collection of printed plays of the golden age at the University of Pennsylvania. New Haven, Conn., 197? 1 1.
1. Type of microform: Microfilm.
2. Availability: In preparation.
3. Orders: Research Publications, Inc., Box 3903, Amity Station, New Haven, Connecticut 06525.
4. The usefulness of this collection will be increased by a bibliography now in preparation. It "will consist of catalog cards reproduced in book form, which include the assigned reference number, the series title and the film location. In addition, author and title indexes will be included."

268. Research Publications, Inc.
Utah and the Mormons, a collection available on microfilm. New Haven, Conn., 196? 14 p.
1. Type of microform: Microfilm; most titles also available in Xerox Duopage format.
2. Availability: Orders are accepted for the complete collection as well as for either of the two parts of the collection: (1) periodical and serial collection; (2) book and pamphlet collection. Individual periodical titles may also be purchased.
3. Orders: Research Publications, Inc., Box 3903, Amity Station, New Haven, Connecticut 06525.
4. Archibald Hanna, Jr., Curator of the Yale Collection of Western Americana and editor of this project, states in his introductory note to this catalog: "The following list of sources for the history of Utah and the Mormons does not pretend to be complete. Rather it is an attempt to make available to the scholar as many as possible of those sources which are no longer in print and difficult or impossible to procure in the antiquarian book market." The materials included in the project are given in two parts. First comes the alphabetical listing of the 29 periodicals and serials, followed by an alphabetical listing of 196 books and pamphlets. Filming order follows that of the listings; indexing is according to MOR index numbers which appear in the listings.

269. Sabin, Joseph.
Bibliotheca Americana; a dictionary of books relating to America from its discovery to the present time. New York, Bibliographical Society of America, 1868-1936. 29 v.
    1. Type of microform: Microcard, microfiche.
    2. Availability: In process.
    3. Orders: Lost Cause Press, 1140-46 Starks Bldg., Louisville, Kentucky 40202.
    4. "Lost Cause Press is publishing in microform volumes from Sabin's *Dictionary of books relating to America*. We publish volumes relating to the Americas, which are textually significant, with primary emphasis on North America. Thus many translations and subsequent editions are being omitted." The press issues checklists of publications included in each group of this series, which is called *Selected Americana from Sabin's Dictionary*. Catalog cards for each title may be purchased from Erasmus Press, 225 Culpepper Street, Lexington, Kentucky 40502.

270. Sadleir, Michael.
XIX century fiction, a bibliographical record based on his own collection. London, Constable [1951] 2 v.
    1. Type of microform: Microfilm.
    2. Availability: In progress. Starting in 1967, about 50,000 pages are made available each year. Catalog cards may be purchased.
    3. Orders: General Microfilm Company, 100 Inman Street, Cambridge, Massachusetts 02139.
    4. The selection of titles for this collection, *Victorian and Other Nineteenth Century Fiction*, on microfilm is based on, but not limited to, Michael Sadleir's *XIX Century Fiction*. The location on film of the various titles will be indicated on short-title lists which accompany each shipment.

271. Shaw, Ralph Robert.
American bibliography; a preliminary checklist for 1801-1819. Compiled by Ralph R. Shaw and Richard H. Shoemaker. New York, Scarecrow Press, 1958-66. 22 v.
    1. Type of microform: Microprint.
    2. Availability: In process; issued as prepared over the next eighteen to twenty years.
    3. Orders: Readex Microprint Corporation, 5 Union Square, New York, New York 10003.
    4. The Shaw-Shoemaker bibliography is a continuation of Charles Evans' *American Bibliography*. In the microprint series, the titles are arranged chronologically in the order of the entries in the bibliography using the numerical sequence established by Shaw-Shoemaker. A program is being developed to supply catalog cards.

272. Simón Díaz, José.
Bibliografía de la literatura hispánica. Dirección y prólogo de Joaquin de Entrambasaguas. Madrid, Consejo Superior de Investigaciones Científicas, Instituto "Miguel de Cervantes" de Filología Hispánica, 1950-   v.

———— ———— Adiciones a los tomos I, II y III. Madrid, Consejo Superior de Investigaciones Científicas, 1954. 104 p.

———— ———— 2. ed. corr. y aumentada. Madrid, Consejo Superior de Investigaciones Científicas, Instituto "Miguel de Cervantes" de Filología Hispánica, 1960-   v.

British Museum: Dept. of Printed Books.
Short-title catalogue of books printed in Spain and of Spanish books printed elsewhere in Europe before 1601, now in the British Museum, by Henry Thomas. [London] Printed by order of the Trustees, 1921. 101 p.
    1. Type of microform: Microfilm.
    2. Availability: Available on subscription basis. Groups for earlier years also available.
    3. Orders: General Microfilm Company, 100 Inman Street, Cambridge, Massachusetts 02139.
    4. The initial section of this project, *Hispanic Culture: Spanish, Portuguese and American Books before 1601,* is based on standard bibliographical sources such as Simón Díaz, *Bibliografía de la Literatura Hispánica* and the British Museum *Short-title catalog.* It will include both belletristic writings and critical and scientific works in all fields. Catalog cards based on the information in the bibliographical sources are available.

273. Southern Baptist Convention. Historical Commission.
Microfilm catalog; basic Baptist historical materials on film. 1969 edition. Nashville, 1969. 139 p. (Baptist history and heritage. v. 4, Special number, June 1969.)
    1. Type of microform: Microfilm.
    2. Availability: All listed publications available.
    3. Orders: Historical Commission, Southern Baptist Convention, 127 9th Avenue, North, Nashville, Tennessee 37203.
    4. This catalog lists materials available according to several categories, e.g., proceedings of the Southern Baptist Convention; proceedings of the various state conventions; Baptist paper files (by state); Baptist periodicals, books, and pamphlets; British Baptist materials; catalogs and college records; church music; church records (by state); theses.

274. Spear, Dorothea N.
Bibliography of American directories through 1860. Worcester, Massachusetts, American Antiquarian Society, 1961. 389 p.
    1. Type of microform: Microfiche, microfilm.
    2. Availability: A commercial publication.
    3. Orders: Research Publications, Inc., Box 3903, Amity Station, New Haven, Connecticut 06525.
    4. The first segment of the microform series, *City Directories of the United States,* provides copies of the directories listed in Spear's *Bibliography,* namely, those published through 1860. Each microfiche is given a reference number in the order given in the *Bibliography.* In addition, a copy of the *Bibliography,* annotated with these reference numbers, was placed on microfilm and is included as a part of the collection.

Segment 2, *City Directories of the U. S., 1861-1881*, will, according to the publisher, be made available on microfilm rather than microfiche. The publisher has announced the list of city directories to be filmed. Included are those of the fifty largest cities of the period plus sixteen others to ensure, representation of all sections of the United States.

Segments 3 and 4 will cover 1882-1901, but prices and schedules will not appear until Segment 2 is completed.

275. Stanford University. Hoover Institution on War, Revolution and Peace.

Menshevik Collection of newspapers, periodicals, pamphlets, and books related to the Menshevik movement. [Palo Alto, 196?] 29 p.

1. Type of microform: Microfilm.

2. Availability: Series available for purchase.

3. Orders: Publications Department (Microfilms), The Hoover Institution on War, Revolution and Peace, Stanford University, Stanford, California 94305.

4. This guide lists alphabetically the newspapers and periodicals and the pamphlets and books included in the collection, giving reel number for each title. Due to technical difficulties, thirty-seven items originally in the microfilm edition of the collection are no longer available.

276. Starr, Edward Caryl, ed.

A Baptist bibliography, being a register of printed materials by and about Baptists; including works written against the Baptists. Philadelphia, Pub. by the Judson Press for the Samuel Colgate Baptist Historical Collection, Colgate Univ., 1947-   v.-   (15 vols. published through 1970)

1. Type of microform: Microfilm.

2. Availability: In progress. The first three groups of titles to be offered are available. Single titles may be purchased.

3. Orders: Baptist History Press, c/o W. Wayne Price, 10 Milwood Drive, Winchester, Kentucky 40391.

4. For this project, *A Basic Library of Baptist History on Microfilm*, it is planned to film all of the major works in Starr's *A Baptist Bibliography* which are in the public domain (i.e., over fifty-six years old) within the next twelve to fifteen years. The Baptist History Press will accept requests for specific titles and will endeavor to supply them with the next group. Catalog cards for all titles may be purchased.

277. Svodnyi Katalog russkoi knigi grazhdanskoi pechat: XVIII veka 1725-1800.

Red. kollegia: I. P. Kondakov i dr. Moscow, Izdanie Gos. Biblioteki SSSR im Lenina, 1962-67. 5v.

1. Type of microform: Microfilm.

2. Availability: Entire collection or a single group may be purchased. Ten groups are ready for delivery.

3. Orders: General Microfilm Company, 100 Inman Street, Cambridge, Massachusetts 02139.

4. This series, *Eighteenth Century Russian Publications*, based on the *Svodnyi Katalog* cited above, includes as many titles as possible. Catalog cards with a Romanized main entry and the descriptive portion photographed from

the entry in the *Svodnyi Katalog* can be supplied. On request a list of the numbers of the *Svodnyi Katalog* which are available will be supplied.

278. Thompson, Lawrence Sidney.
    A bibliography of French plays on microcard. Hamden, Conn., The Shoe String Press, 1967. 689 p.
    1. Type of microform: Microcard.
    2. Availability: In process.
    3. Orders: Falls City Microcards, 1432 Cherokee Road, Louisville, Kentucky 40204.
    4. The Thompson *Bibliography* is "primarily a guide to the microcard editions of nearly 7000 French plays published by Falls City Microcards, Louisville, Kentucky." The comprehensive collection of French plays from the seventeenth through the nineteenth centuries on microcards is called *French drama series.* Catalog cards are offered by Erasmus Press, 225 Culpepper Street, Lexington, Kentucky 40502.

279. Thompson, Lawrence Sidney.
    A bibliography of Spanish plays on microcards. Hamden, Conn., The Shoe String Press, 1968, 490 p.
    1. Type of microform: Microcard.
    2. Availability: In process; approximately 600 titles a year.
    3. Orders: Falls City Microcards, 1432 Cherokee Road, Louisville, Kentucky 40204.
    4. The "bibliography records over 6000 Spanish, Catalonian, and Spanish-American plays from the sixteenth century to the present, all published in microcard editions by Falls City Microcards . . . from 1957 through 1966." The microcard series is cited as *Four Centuries of Spanish Drama* and as *Spanish Drama Series.* Catalogue cards for groups issued since 1966 are available from Erasmus Press, 225 Culpepper Street, Lexington, Kentucky 40502.

280. Thompson, Ralph.
    American literary annuals and gift books, 1825-1865. New York, H. W. Wilson Company, 1936. 183 p.
    1. Type of microform: Microfilm.
    2. Availability: A commercial publication.
    3. Orders: Research Publications, Inc., Box 3903, Amity Station, New Haven, Connecticut 06525.
    4. The Thompson bibliography serves as an index to this collection of 469 volumes on microfilm.

281. Thomson, Elizabeth J. Military journals on microfilm. *Library Journal.* v. 83, p. 36-37. January 1, 1958.
    1. Type of microform: Microfilm.
    2. Availability: Copies may be purchased.
    3. Orders: Air University Library, Maxwell Air Force Base, Alabama 36112.
    4. This article describes the Military Microfilms Project launched early in

1956 under the sponsorship of the Military Librarians Division of the Special Libraries Association and lists the master negative microfilms of journals filmed as of October 1957 and deposited in the Air University Library, which serves as a central depository and distribution center for military journals on film.

282. Toronto. Public Library.
A bibliography of Canadiana; being items in the Public Library of Toronto, relating to the early history and development of Canada, edited by Frances M. Staton and Marie Tremaine, with an introduction by George H. Locke. Toronto, the Public Library [c1935] 828 p.
———— ———— First supplement . . . Edited by Gertrude M. Boyle assisted by Marjorie Colbeck, with an introduction by Henry C. Campbell. Toronto, the Public Library, 1959. 333 p.
    1. Type of microform: Microfiche, micro-opaque cards.
    2. Availability: Commercially published.
    3. Orders: Microcard Editions, Inc., 901 26th Street, N.W., Washington, D.C. 20037.
    4. Both the *Bibliography of Canadiana* and the *Supplement* use a chronological arrangement, thus providing a record of the history of Canada from its discovery to the confederation of the provinces in 1867. Included are books, pamphlets, and broadsides. The index contains author, title, and subject references.

283. Tremaine, Marie.
A bibliography of Canadian imprints, 1751-1800. Toronto, University of Toronto Press, 1952. 705 p.
    1. Type of microform: Microfilm.
    2. Availability: Copies of the microfilm may be purchased.
    3. Orders: The Library, Public Archives of Canada, 395 Wellington Street, Ottawa, Ontario
    4. The project based on Tremaine's *Bibliography* is entitled *Canadian Imprints, 1751-1800.* In the *Bibliography* are listed 1,204 items, each of which is described in detail and accompanied by a meaningful annotation. The newspapers and magazines included in the *Bibliography* were not filmed.

284. 2-M Microfilm Service.
Eighteenth-century sources for the study of English literature and culture. Scottsville, Va. [1970?] [1] p.
    1. Type of microform: Microfilm.
    2. Availability: Available on annual subscription. Individual titles may also be purchased.
    3. Orders: 2-M Microfilm Service, Route no. 2, Box 82F, Scottsville, Virginia 24590.
    4. A selected collection of works published in England, including some translations from French, German, and other European languages, relevant to eighteenth-century art, literature, and culture. Titles in the initial groups were selected with the editorial advice of Professors Ralph Cohen and Irvin

Ehrenpreis of the University of Virginia. It is expected that 50,000 to 75,000 pages will be made available annually and that the project will last ten to fifteen years. The publisher has catalog cards available for each title. Each catalog card bears the microfilm roll number.

285. United Nations. Dag Hammarskjöld Library.
      United Nations documents index. v. 1-
      Jan. 1950-   New York [etc.]
      ―――― Checklist of United Nations documents [1946-49] New York, 1949-53. Pts. 2-8 issued in sections.
        1. Type of microform: Microfilm, microfiche, microprint.
        2. Availability: Microfilm and microfiche are available from the United Nations Archives; microprint is available from Readex Microprint Corporation.
        3. Orders: United Nations Archives (for microfilm and microfiche), United Nations Plaza, New York, New York 10017 *OR* Readex Microprint Corporation (for microprint), 5 Union Square, New York, New York 10003.
        4. A monthly publication composed of a checklist and a subject index. Since 1964 (v. 14) monthly issues are replaced and superseded by two separate annual publications: (1) a cumulative checklist and (2) cumulative (subject) index. The *Index* covers all United Nations publications—except restricted material and internal papers—and all printed publications of the International Court of Justice.

U. S. Atomic Energy Commission.
      Nuclear Science Abstracts. Semimonthly. Wash., Govt. Print. Off., 1948-   v. 1-
        1. Type of microform: Microcard and microfiche.
        2. Availability: In the sixty-five U.S. depositories for U.S. AEC reports, primarily university libraries, the reports are available for consultation, either in printed form or in microcard or microfiche. Since July 1, 1965, all reports have been in the form of negative microfiche.
        The National Technical Information Service can supply AEC reports in both hard copy and on microfiche. The commercial firm, NCR Microcard Editions, can supply microcard or microfiche. Printed copies of certain reports are available from the Government Printing Office.
        3. Order: National Technical Information Service, U.S. Dept. of Commerce, Springfield, Virginia 22151 *OR* Processing Department, NCR Microcard Editions, 365 South Oak Street, West Salem, Wisconsin 54669 *OR* Superintendent of Documents, U.S. Government Printing Office, Washington, D.C. 20402.
        4. This semi-monthly publication abstracts reports in the field of nuclear science, both those emanating from the U.S. Atomic Energy Commission and those emanating from the atomic energy establishments of numerous other countries. Cumulative subject, author, and report number indexes make for ease of use. Availability of each report abstracted is noted.

287. U.S. Bureau of the Census.
      Catalog of United States census publications, 1790-1945, prepared by Henry J. Dubester. Washington, U.S. Govt. Print. Off., 1950. 320 p.
        1. Type of microform: Microfiche.

2. Availability: Available November 1971.

3. Orders: Microform Division, Greenwood Publishing Corporation, 51 Riverside Avenue, Westport, Connecticut 06880.

4. This *Catalog* is composed of two sections. Part 1 lists decennial census publications, while part 2 lists other census publications, arranged by subject, e.g., agriculture, business, housing, industry, etc. Each title is annotated, and the index provides reference to subjects contained in both titles and annotations. The project *Non-decennial Census Reports, 1902-1945* reproduces the publications listed in part 2. The publisher will provide, both on microfiche and in full-size printed form, a copy of this *Catalog.*

288. U.S. Congress. Senate. Library.

Index of congressional committee hearings (not confidential in character) prior to January 3, 1935, in the United States Senate Library. Edwin A. Halsey, secretary of the Senate. Revised by James D. Preston, Robert L. Baldridge, Harold D. Hantz, Senate Library. Washington, U. S. Govt. Print. Off., 1935. 1,056 p.

1. Type of microform: Microfiche.

2. Availability: Complete set of all indexed hearings available.

3. Orders: Microform Division, Greenwood Publishing Corporation, 51 Riverside Avenue, Westport, Connecticut 06880.

4. "Congressional hearings, testimony before committees of the United States Congress, 41st Congress through 73rd Congress (1869-1934)" on microfiche is based on the 1935 *Index* and includes all indexed hearings. The *Index,* arranged alphabetically by subject before specific committee, and according to specific bill number, is included in both reprint and microform at no additional cost.

289. U.S. Government Printing Office.

Non-GPO Imprints received in the Library of Congress, July 1967 through December 1969; a selective checklist compiled by the Exchange and Gift Division, Processing Department. Washington, Library of Congress, 1970. 73 p.

1. Type of microform: Microfilm, electrostatic prints.

2. Availability: The Library of Congress can supply microfilm or electrostatic prints of publications listed. (If known, availability and price of a publication are noted.) "Written permission from the issuing agency must accompany all photoduplication orders for items bearing the note 'Controlled distribution' or other indications of restricted distribution."

3. Orders: Photoduplication Service, Dept. C-171, Library of Congress, Washington, D.C. 20540.

4. This checklist is an attempt to bring under bibliographical control those United States government publications which fall outside the scope of the *Monthly Catalog of United States Government Publications,* as well as the other main bibliographies of United States government and government-sponsored publications. The listing is selective, including only publications of a research or informational nature. Publications marked "limited distribution" are usually not available from the issuing body, while the notation "controlled distribution" indicates that the issuing agency retains control over the distribution. The checklist consists of two sections (monographs and periodicals) and is accompanied by a subject index.

290. U.S. Congress. American state papers, 1789-1838. 38 v.
U.S. Congress. Serial set (Congressional edition) 1817-
   1. Type of microform: Microprint, microfilm.
   2. Availability: *American State Papers* are available as a unit. The *Serial Set* is offered for sale in groups varying somewhat in size but averaging about sixty numbered volumes. The set will be continued to include congressional sessions to 1900 or later, if the demand warrants.
   3. Orders: Readex Microprint Corporation, 5 Union Square, New York, New York 10003.
   4. The *American State Papers* contain the most important publications of the first 14 Congresses. The "serial set" or "congressional edition" brings together all the House and Senate *Reports* and *Documents* (at times there have been other series), plus the journals of both houses.
   For the location of specific documents, the reader must consult the series of indexes to United States government publications issued by the Government Printing Office since 1885.
   Microfilm of the *American State Papers* is available from University Microfilms, 300 North Zeeb Road, Ann Arbor, Michigan, and also from Microfilming Corporation of America, 21 Harristown Road, Glen Rock, New Jersey 07452.

291. U.S. Joint Publications Research Service.
Reports.
   1. Type of microform: Microprint.
   2. Availability: The JPRS Reports are listed in the *Monthly Catalog of United States Government Publications* and are therefore included in the Readex Microprint collection of United States government publications (nondepository). The JPRS Reports are also available as a separate group from Readex Microprint on an annual basis.
   3. Orders: Readex Microprint Corporation, 5 Union Square, New York, New York 10003.
   4. A very useful index designed to help the reader locate the JPRS Reports in the Readex Microprint edition of United States government publications is:

   Poole, Mary Elizabeth.
      Index to Readex Microprint edition of JPRS reports (Joint Publications Research Service). New York, Readex Microprint Corporation [1964]

   ———— ———— 1964/66 -   Prepared by Louise J. Hawkins. New York, Readex Microprint Corporation [1967-

This index correlates JPRS numbers with entry numbers in the *Monthly Catalog of United States Government Publications,* which are essential for locating the microprint copies of the reports in the Readex Microprint edition of United States Government publications. A copy of the index is furnished to subscribers to the microprint edition of JPRS reports.

A useful bibliography of JPRS reports on contemporary China is:

Sorich, Richard, ed.
Contemporary China; a bibliography of reports on China published by the United States Joint Publications Research Service. Prepared by the Joint Committee on Contemporary China of the American Council of Learned Societies and the Social Science Research Council. New York [Readex Microprint Corp.] 1961.

With a few exceptions noted in the introduction, this bibliography in Part I lists "all the reports on China published by the JPRS from its inception in late 1957 through July 1960," providing both titles and contents of the reports. Part II provides an explanation of abbreviations for Chinese and non-Chinese serial publications referred to in Part I. Part III, the index, consists of a category list which contains all the subject headings and subheadings used in the subject index, which follows, plus all the necessary cross-references. The purpose of the category list is to give an overall view of how subjects are classified.

292. U.S. Joint Publications Research Service (JPRS) Translations.
1. Type of microform: Microfilm, microfiche.
2. Availability: The CCM Corporation makes available all JPRS translations on microfilm or microfiche on a monthly subscription basis. Microfilm may also be ordered by broad geographic area: China and Asia, East Europe, Soviet Union, and Africa-Latin America.
3. Orders: CCM Information Corporation, 866 Third Avenue, New York, New York 10022.
4. The two titles noted below serve the purpose of both bibliographies and indexes for JPRS translations.
Transdex; bibliography and index to the United States Joint Publications Research Service (JPRS) translations. v. 9- 1971- New York, CCM Information Corp. Monthly
The basic section of *Transdex* is "Bibliographic Listings" in which documents are listed by JPRS number. For each document, all pertinent bibliographic data are given. Several approaches to the basic section are provided: serial and ad hoc titles list; the country/title index; the subject index; and the author index.
Catalog cards in book form for United States Joint Publications Research Service translations. [1st- 1957/61- Annapolis, Md.
This semiannual compilation is similar to the monthly *Transdex*. As in *Transdex* the basic section lists bibliographic information for JPRS translations by JPRS number sequence. The type of indexes has varied somewhat since the first issue. The latest volume (v. 8, no. 2, 1969) has the following indexes: code for JPRS reports; sci/tech subject index; social science subject index; index to serialized titles; index to nonserialized titles; and a cross-reference index.

293. U.S. Library of Congress.
A guide to the microfilm collection of early state records, prepared by the Library of Congress in association with the University of North Carolina.

Collected and compiled under the direction of William Sumner Jenkins; edited by Lillian A. Hamrick. [Washington] Library of Congress Photoduplication Service, 1950. 1 v. (various paging)

—— —— Supplement. Prepared by the Library of Congress in association with the University of North Carolina. Collected, compiled and edited by William Sumner Jenkins. [Washington] Library of Congress Photoduplication Service, 1951. 130, xviii p.

    1. Type of microform: Microfilm.

    2. Availability: Positive copies are available in quantities of one or more reels at the currently published rates of the Photoduplication Service of the Library of Congress.

    3. Orders: Photoduplication Service, Library of Congress, Washington, D.C. 20540.

    4. The *Guide* lists the contents of 1,600 reels of film, while the *Supplement* indicates the contents of an additional 160 reels. They serve the dual purpose of (1) supplying the user with information as to the location (265 public and private collections) of the original of each document and its location on the reels and (2) providing a catalog from which orders for reproduction of portions of the collection may be made.

Records are listed by the following broad general classes: (A) legislative records; (B) statutory law; (C) constitutional records; (D) administrative records; (E) executive records; (F) court records. Each general class is further subdivided, e.g., (A.1) journals, minutes and proceedings; (A.2) legislative debates; (A.3) proceedings of extraordinary bodies; (A.4) Committee Reports, etc.

Special classes, which are listed in the *Supplement,* are: (L) local records—county and city; (M) records of American-Indian nations; (N) newspapers; (R) rudimentary states and courts; (X) miscellany.

294. U.S. Library of Congress. Jefferson Collection.

Catalogue of the library of Thomas Jefferson. Compiled by E. Millicent Sowerby. Washington, Library of Congress, 1952-59. 5 v.

    1. Type of microform: Microfiche, micro-opaque cards, microfilm.

    2. Availability: Available at listed price.

    3. Orders: Order Processing Department, NCR/Microcard Editions, 365 South Oak Street, West Salem, Wisconsin 54669.

    4. The microform publication, *The Library of Thomas Jefferson,* consists of 683 items selected from the *Catalogue* cited above by John Cook Wyllie, former librarian of the University of Virginia. Printed catalog cards are available.

295. U.S. Library of Congress. Photoduplication Service.

Chinese Communist newspapers; special microfilm collection: Index [Washington, Library of Congress Photoduplication Service, 1964] 1 v. (unpaged)

    1. Type of microform: Microfilm.

    2. Availability: Copies available.

    3. Orders: Photoduplication Service, Library of Congress, Washington, D.C. 20540.

4. Not a true index, but rather an alphabetical list of the newspapers showing dates filmed, keyed to reel number.

296. U.S. National Library of Medicine.
Early American medical imprints, a guide to works printed in the United States, 1668-1820, by Robert B. Austin. Washington, U. S. Dept. of Health, Education, and Welfare, Public Health Service, 1961. 240 p.
    1. Type of microform: Microfilm.
    2. Availability: Completion scheduled for late 1971.
    3. Orders: Research Publications, Inc., Box 3903, Amity Station, New Haven, Connecticut 06525.
    4. The microfilm edition of the books included in *Early American Medical Imprints,* numbering over 1,600 titles, follows the same sequence as the listing in the bibliography, a copy of which in book form will be included with each complete order. The bibliography will be annotated to serve also as the reel index. Catalog cards covering each title are available in sets of three cards per title.

297. U.S. Office of Scientific Research and Development. National Defense Research Committee.
Microfilm index; summary technical report of NDRC. Washington [Distributed by U.S. Dept. of Commerce, Office of Technical Services] 1946. 760 p.
    1. Type of microform: Microfilm.
    2. Availability: Copies may be purchased.
    3. Orders: Photoduplication Service, Library of Congress, Washington, D.C. 20540.
    4. The *Summary Technical Report* of the National Defense Research Committee is an attempt to summarize and evaluate its work and present it in a useful and permanent form. It consists of sixty-eight volumes broken into groups corresponding to the NDRC divisions, panels, and committees. The *Microfilm Index* indexes the technical laboratory and field reports and other types of reference material which appear in the bibliographies for the *Summary Technical Report* of NDRC. At the request of the services, all these materials were microfilmed and copies made available to them.
    This *Microfilm Index* is really a record of the numerous research projects conducted by OSRD and its contractors. It is divided into three parts: (1) a microfilm index and bibliographical listing of reports for each of the eighteen divisions; (2) a cross-reference index; (3) a microfilm reel catalog. The microfilm indexes are numerical, based on the Dewey decimal system of classification. After being classified, the reports were filed chronologically for filming. The cross-reference index provides a means of drawing together all reports on the same subject regardless of the divisions in which they were prepared. Finally, the microfilm reel catalog enables the user to locate readily the reel number for a specific report.

298. U.S. Superintendent of Documents.
Monthly catalog of United States government publications. no. [1]- Jan. 1895-

Wash., Govt. Print. Off.

1. Type of microform: Microprint.

2. Availability: Publications are available in two groups, depository and nondepository publications, each of which is available on an annual subscription basis.

3. Orders: Readex Microprint Corporation, 5 Union Square, New York, New York 10003.

4. Readex Microprint publishes the text of all publications listed in the *Monthly Catalog* cited above. This project dates from January 1956 for depository items and from January 1953 for nondepository items. The *Monthly Catalog* clearly indicates each depository item. Prior to 1959, releases were not included in the nondepository edition. From January 1959 to date, many releases have been included, with the exception of press releases which are not available. The *Monthly Catalog* serves as a location index to the microprint edition, since publications are arranged according to the item numbers in the *Catalog*.

299. U.S. Superintendent of Documents.

Reports of explorations printed in the documents of the U.S. government ⟨A contribution towards a bibliography⟩. Compiled by Adelaide R. Hasse. Office Superintendent of Documents, Government Printing Office. Washington, Govt. Print. Off., 1899. 90 p.

1. Type of microform: Microfilm.

2. Availability: Complete collection on microfilm including printed reel index available.

3. Orders: Research Publications, Inc., Box 3903, Amity Station, New Haven, Connecticut 06525.

4. The collection *Reports of Explorations Printed in the Documents of the United States Government* includes the 554 reports listed in the Hasse bibliography. The reports cover many subjects: topography, botany, zoology, geology, Indian linguistics, routes for railroads and wagon roads, anthropology, and hydrography. They were published in a variety of government documents, census bulletins, Geological Survey monographs, Senate or House documents, other bulletins, and even as appendixes to annual reports.

300. The United States Historical Documents Institute, Inc.

Canadian parliamentary proceedings and sessional papers, 1841-1970. Washington [1971?] 16″ x 20 3/4″ sheet folded twice.

1. Type of microform: Microfilm.

2. Availability: Scheduled for delivery in the next several months (letter from publisher dated June 22, 1971). Complete collection and various combinations of microfilm and/or indexes available.

3. Orders: The United States Historical Documents Institute, Inc., 1647 Wisconsin Avenue, N.W., Washington, D.C. 20015.

4. The collection consists of (1) *Parliamentary Proceedings* of the United Province of Canada (1841-1866), which include *Journals* of the Legislative Assembly, *Journals* of the Legislative Council, and *Sessional Papers;* (2) *Parliamentary Proceedings* of the Dominion of Canada (1867-1970), which include *Debates* of the House of Commons, *Journals* of the House of

Commons, *Debates* of the Senate, and *Journals* of the Senate; (3) *Sessional Papers* of the Dominion of Canada (1867-1925), a continuation of the *Sessional Papers* previous to confederation, which include reports of commissions, departments, and institutions. The reprinting of the 133 indexes of the *Parliamentary Proceedings* in book form will make the use of the microfilm both easier and more pleasurable.

301. The United States Historical Documents Institute.
  Proceedings of the U.S. Congress 1789-1964, including: The Annals of Congress (1789-1824), The Register of Debates (1824-1838), The Congressional Globe (1833-1873) and the Congressional Record (1873-1964) Available for the first time in one convenient dual-media reference set. Washington, D.C., 1970. 16 p.
  1. Type of microform: Microfilm.
  2. Availability: All microfilm sets available for immediate delivery. Available also in various combinations. Indexes in book format were announced to be available in January 1971.
  3. Orders: The United States Historical Documents Institute Inc., 3701 Leland Street, N.W., Washington, D.C. 20015.
  4. This catalog contains a detailed listing of 477 reels of 35mm microfilm (containing the complete texts of speeches, debates, trials, presidential messages, and appendixes) and of the 101 casebound volumes (containing 220 sessional indexes, indexes to the Appendixes, and reprints of the histories of bills and resolutions).

302. University Microfilms, Ann Arbor, Michigan.
  The Series programs author-title index, one-volume guide to microfilm collections of British and American publications from 1475 to 1910. Ann Arbor, 197?
  1. Type of microform: Microfilm.
  2. Availability: See Item numbers referred to below.
  3. Orders: University Microfilms, 300 North Zeeb Road, Ann Arbor, Michigan 48106.
  4. University Microfilms has announced the publication of this one-volume (over 700 pages) index to the following microfilm series:

American Culture Series, I-II	(Item 173)
American Prose Fiction	(Item 310)
American Periodical Series, I-II	(Item 172)
American Periodical Series - Civil War and Reconstruction	(Item 172 a)
Early English Books, I	(Item 254)
Early English Literary Periodicals	(Item 208)
British Periodicals - Literary	(Item 194)
British Periodicals - General	(Item 192)
British Periodicals - Creative Arts	(Item 193)

The volume will be divided into two sections, the first listing books and letters alphabetically by author, and the second listing periodicals, pamphlets, maps, and charts alphabetically by title, giving for each item the series title, series year, and reel number.

303. Wagner, Henry Raup.
The plains and the Rockies; a bibliography of original narratives of travel and adventure, 1800-1865, rev. by Charles L. Camp. 3d ed. Columbus, Ohio, Long's College Book Company, 1953. 601 p.
1. Type of microform: Microcard.
2. Availability: In process.
3. Orders: Lost Cause Press, 1140-46 Starks Bldg., Louisville, Kentucky 40202.
4. Lost Cause Press has published, on microcard, every item they have been able to find from the Wagner-Camp bibliography, *The Plains and the Rockies.* Also included are volumes from *Burs under the Saddle,* by Ramon F. Adams (Norman: University of Oklahoma Press, 1964). A list of those items included in the set to date is available from the publisher. Catalog cards are offered by Erasmus Press, 225 Culpepper Street, Lexington, Kentucky 40502.

304. Wing, Donald Goddard.
Short-title catalogue of books printed in England, Scotland, Ireland, Wales and British America, and of English books printed in other countries, 1641-1700. New York, The Index Society, 1945-51. 3 v.
1. Type of microform: Microfilm.
2. Availability: In process.
3. Orders: University Microfilms, Inc., 300 N. Zeeb Road, Ann Arbor, Michigan 48106.
4. The microfilm edition of books listed in the Wing *Short-title Catalogue,* called *Early English Books, 1641-1700,* continues the series *Early English Books before 1640* based on Pollard & Redgrave's *Short-title Catalogue.* The items listed in Wing have not been filmed consecutively; access is through the indexes issued by University Microfilms. Additional sources for books included in the series are the Christ Church supplement to Wing's *Short-title Catalogue* (1956) and Wing's *A Gallery of Ghosts* (1967).

305. World Microfilms.
British birth control ephemera in the late nineteenth and early twentieth centuries (The Collis Collection), an original micropublication. London, n.d. [1] p.
1. Type of microform: Microfilm.
2. Availability: Available at price listed. Full-sized Xerox copyflo reprints of individual items are also available. All purchasers will be supplied free of charge the catalog of the collection, compiled by Peter Fryer, with an introduction by Professor D. V. Glass.
3. Orders: World Microfilms, Distribution Division, 62 Queen's Grove, London, N. W. 8, England *OR* World Microfilms, EAV Inc., Pleasantville, New York 10570.
4. An invaluable source for study and research into the history of birth control. The ephemera included in the collection fall into five broad classes:

(1) the early pioneering tracts of men like Allbutt, Robert Dale Owen, etc.; (2) the pamphlets of the young and struggling birth control movement, such as those of the Malthusian League; (3) the advertising and instructional materials put out by manufacturers and retailers; (4) some early historical sketches, by Himes, Talbot, and others; (5) and a few examples of polemics against birth control.

306. World Microfilms.
British birth control material at the British Library of Political and Economic Sciences. (In its Sectional catalogue—political science. 1970-71 catalogue . . . [London, 1970?] p. 9.)
    1. Type of microform: Microfilm, microfiche.
    2. Availability: Designated "forthcoming publication" in the 1970-71 catalog.
    3. Orders: World Microfilms, Distribution Division, 62 Queen's Grove, London, N.W. 8, England *OR* World Microfilms, EAV Inc., Pleasantville, New York 10570.
    4. "This collection contains unique material (ephemera, books, pamphlets, journals, etc.) on the growth of the Birth Control movement."

307. World Microfilms.
Institute of Chartered Accountants in England and Wales: Microfilmed collection of rare books on accounting and related subjects, selected and arranged for the Institute, by Professor B. S. Yamey. (In its Sectional catalogue - economics, accountancy and commerce. 1970-71 catalogue . . . [London, 1970?] p. [2]) and "List of titles" on 2 page loose insert.
    1. Type of microform: Microfilm.
    2. Availability: Complete sets, partial sets, series, and individual titles may be purchased. Full-size Xerox copyflo reprints of individual titles also available. A pamphlet describing briefly the contents of each reel is supplied with each order.
    3. Orders: World Microfilms, Distribution Division, 62 Queen's Grove, London, N.W. 8, England *OR* World Microfilms, EAV Inc., Pleasantville, New York 10570.
    4. Books for this collection are being selected to illustrate the development of double-entry bookkeeping since 1494. The collection is divided into groups by language, and the groups are further broken down into sections according to time-span. For example, group A includes English-language books in the sixteenth through nineteenth centuries; group B includes Italian-language books in the fifteenth through eighteenth centuries, etc.

308. World Microfilms.
The London Trades Council. Minutes & papers, 1860-1953. (In its Sectional catalogue - political science. 1970-71 catalogue . . . [London, 1970?] p. 1)
    1. Type of microform: Microfilm.
    2. Availability: Available at price listed.
    3. Orders: World Microfilms, Distribution Division, 62 Queen's Grove,

London, N.W. 8, England *OR* World Microfilms, EAV Inc., Pleasantville, New York 10570.

4. "For over 90 years the London Trades Council was in the forefront of the struggle to improve working conditions. Its *Minutes* and *Annual Reports* are a vivid, continuous and detailed record of the progress from disorganised groups of disaffected workers to a fully organized labour movement." The *Minutes, Accounts* for the first few years, and *Annual Reports* are being published for the first time. They contain a vast amount of detail about the workings and opinions of the council, picture the change in workers' attitudes to employers and government and their increasing involvement in political affairs, and provide a great wealth of information about the personalities who were involved in the council.

309. World Microfilms.
Rare militant British nineteenth-century freethought books (The Collis Collection). (In its Sectional catalogue - religious studies. 1970-71 catalogue . . . [London, 1970?] p. [2]) and "Complete list of titles" -[3 pages distributed separately].
1. Type of microform: Microfilm.
2. Availability: Complete sets or individual titles may be purchased. Full-size copyflo reprints of individual titles are also available. A catalog of the collection is supplied free of charge.
3. Orders: World Microfilms, Distribution Division, 62 Queen's Grove, London, N.W. 8, England *OR* World Microfilms, EAV Inc., Pleasantville, New York 10570.
4. "While many pamphlets and other papers were published by the Militant Freethought Movement, there were very few full-length books." The Collis Collection contains almost all these books, many of which are quite rare. The complete list of titles includes a total of fifty-two books.

310. Wright, Lyle Henry.
American fiction, 1774-1850; a contribution toward a bibliography. 2d rev. ed. San Marino, Calif., 1969. 411 p. (Huntington Library publications.)
——— American fiction, 1851-1875 . . . San Marino, Calif., 1965. 438 p. (Huntington Library publications)
——— American fiction, 1876-1900 . . . San Marino, Calif., 1966. 683 p. (Huntington Library publications)
1. Type of microform: Microfilm, micro-opaque, microfiche.
2. Availability: Complete set on microfilm available from Research Publications, Inc. Also in process on microfilm by University Microfilms, and selected titles on micro-opaques or microfiche by the Lost Cause Press.
3. Orders: Research Publications, Inc., Box 3903, Amity Station, New Haven, Connecticut 06525 *OR* University Microfilms, Inc., 300 N. Zeeb Road, Ann Arbor, Michigan 48106 *OR* Lost Cause Press, 1140-46 Starks Bldg., Louisville, Kentucky 40202.
4. In the edition by Research Publications, the numbers assigned by Mr. Wright precede volumes on the film, and titles are in alphabetical order by author or title, making direct access possible. In the University Microfilms edition, the reels are numbered by University Microfilms as they appear. A

guide is issued with each annual cumulation and provides a cross-index from the Wright entry number to the microfilm reel number. The Lost Cause Press provides a full set of catalog cards for each title at no additional cost.

311. Yale University. Library. Yale Collection of German Literature.
German Baroque literature; a catalogue of the collection in the Yale University Library by Curt von Faber du Faur, curator of the German Literature Collection. New Haven, Yale University Press, 1958-69. 2 v. (Bibliographical series from the Yale University Library collections)
   1. Type of microform: Microfilm.
   2. Availability: Complete collection (about 2,400 titles) may be purchased. Catalog cards are available from the publisher.
   3. Orders: Research Publications, Inc., Box 3903, Amity Station, New Haven, Connecticut 06525.
   4. The collection represents the baroque period from its beginnings (about 1575) to its end (about 1740). The microfilm has been filmed in the same sequence as the listing in the bibliography upon which the set is based.

312. Yushodo Film Publications Ltd., Tokyo.
Imanishi collection of original texts on Korean history. Microfilm catalog OP no. 3 (August 1970) Tokyo, 1970. 22 p.
   1. Type of microform: Microfilm.
   2. Availability: Each item available at price listed.
   3. Orders: Yushodo Film Publications, Ltd., 29 Sanei-cho, Shinjuku-ku, Tokyo, Japan.
   4. Dr. Ryu Imanishi, scholar of Korean history, spent many years in Korea collecting Korean materials. This microfilm edition reproduces the materials on Korean history.

313. Yushodo Film Publications, Inc.
Nippon shakai rodo undoshi shiryo. Documents on a history of the Japanese socialist and labor movement, 1919-1943. In the custody of Kyochokai, Tokyo. (In Yushodo Film Publications, Inc. General catalog 1970-71)
   1. Type of microform: Microfilm.
   2. Availability: Complete set of 118 reels may be purchased.
   3. Orders: Yushodo Film Publications, Inc., 29 Sanei-cho, Shinjuku-ku, Tokyo, Japan.
   4. Kyochokai (The Society for Cooperation between Capital and Labour, Tokyo) was organized in 1919 as an investigative group and an organization for arbitration of labor trouble before World War II. Documents on a history of Japanese Socialist labor movement, 1919-1943, are collected by the society and classified under several heads: labor union; labor dispute; Musan Seito (the Proletarian party); press cuttings; and legal records. Almost all materials are composed of copied records and data.

III. MANUSCRIPT AND ARCHIVAL COLLECTIONS

314. Adams Manuscript Trust.
     Microfilms of the Adams Papers owned by the Adams Manuscript Trust and deposited in the Massachusetts Historical Society. Boston, Massachusetts Historical Society, 1954-1959. 4 pts.
     1. Type of microform: Microfilm.
     2. Availability: Available for purchase.
     3. Orders: Massachusetts Historical Society, 1154 Boylston Street, Boston, Massachusetts 02164.
     4. These four pamphlets give the contents of the microfilm of the Adams papers by reel number. The papers were filmed in order to make them more accessible to scholars. As far as research is concerned, there are no restrictions on the use of the microfilm. The literary rights, however, remain in the control of the Massachusetts Historical Society, to whom application must be made for permission to publish any of the material.

315. Allis, Frederick Scouller.
     Guide to the microfilm edition of the Artemas Ward papers. Frederick S. Allis, Jr., editor, R. Bruce Pruitt, associate editor. Boston, Massachusetts Historical Society, 1967. 30 p.
     1. Type of microform: Microfilm.
     2. Availability: Five reels plus printed guide may be purchased; guide may be purchased separately. No interlibrary loan copy available.
     3. Orders: Director, Massachusetts Historical Society, 1154 Boylston Street, Boston, Massachusetts 02215.
     4. The publication on microfilm of the Artemus Ward manuscript collection in the Massachusetts Historical Society was sponsored by the National Historical Publications Commission. The *Guide* provides a biographical sketch of Ward, a description of the collection by reels, and an alphabetical list of correspondents. Each correspondent's letters are listed chronologically, giving the reel in which each is to be found.

316. Allis, Frederick Scouller.
     Guide to the microfilm edition of the Benjamin Lincoln papers, Frederick S. Allis, Jr., editor, Wayne A. Frederick, associate editor. Boston, Mass., Massachusetts Historical Society, 1967. 70 p.
     1. Type of microform: Microfilm.
     2. Availability: Thirteen rolls and printed guide available. The guide may be purchased separately. No interlibrary loan copy available.
     3. Orders: Director, Massachusetts Historical Society, 1154 Boylston Street, Boston, Massachusetts 02215.
     4. The *Guide* provides a biographical sketch of General Lincoln, condensed from that by Clifford K. Shipton in *Sibley's Harvard Graduates*, a description of the collection by reels, and a list of correspondents giving dates of letters. The papers are arranged chronologically. The microfilm edition was published under the auspices of the National Historical Publications Commission.

317. Allis, Frederick Scouller.
     Guide to the microfilm edition of the Forbes papers, Frederick S. Allis, Jr.,

editor, Alexander W. Williams, associate editor. Boston, Mass., Massachusetts
Historical Society, 1969. 68 p.

    1. Type of microform: Microfilm.

    2. Availability: Forty-seven reels and printed guide available. The guide
may be purchased separately. No interlibrary loan copy available.

    3. Orders: Director, Massachusetts Historical Society, 1154 Boylston
Street, Boston, Massachusetts 02215.

    4. The *Guide* provides a brief account of the Forbes family and their
achievements in commerce and business, a description of the collection by
reels, and an index of proper names. Almost all the Forbes papers in this
microfilm edition, published by the Massachusetts Historical Society under
the sponsorship of the National Historical Publications Commission, are in
the collections of the Captain Robert Bennet Forbes House, Inc., Milton,
Massachusetts.

318. Allis, Frederick Scouller.

    Guide to the microfilm edition of the Lemuel Shaw papers. Frederick S.
Allis, Jr., editor, Alfred S. Konefsky, associate editor. Boston, Massachusetts
Historical Society, 1970. 39 p.

    1. Type of microform: Microfilm.

    2. Availability: Forty-six reels plus printed guide may be purchased.
Guide may be purchased separately. No interlibrary loan copy available.

    3. Orders: Director, Massachusetts Historical Society, 1154 Boylston
Street, Boston, Massachusetts 02215.

    4. The Shaw family papers in the Massachusetts Historical Society and the
purely legal papers in the Social Law Library are reunited in the microfilm
edition published by the society under the auspices of the National Historical
Publications Commission. The *Guide* provides a biographical sketch of Lem-
uel Shaw, prominent state jurist of the first half of the nineteenth century,
and descriptive notes on the collection according to frame number.

319. Allis, Frederick Scouller.

    Guide to the microfilm edition of the Timothy Pickering papers, Frederick
S. Allis, Jr., editor, Roy Bartolomei, associate editor. Boston, Mass., Massachusetts Historical Society, 1966. 46 p.

    1. Type of microform: Microfilm.

    2. Availability: Sixty-nine reels plus reissue of printed *Historical Index*
and printed guide may be purchased. Guide may be purchased separately. No
interlibrary loan copy available.

    3. Orders: Director, Massachusetts Historical Society, 1154 Boylston
Street, Boston, Massachusetts 02215.

    4. An offset copy of the *Historical Index to the Pickering Papers* (Massa-
chusetts Historical Society Collections, sixth series, volume VIII) accompanies the microfilm edition, and gives detailed access by author and subject
to volumes 5 through 62, which were in the society's possession when the
Index was made. The printed *Guide* therefore describes fully only those
volumes added later, the family correspondence forming the first four volumes of the papers, and the business and legal papers. The *Guide* also includes
a biographical sketch of Timothy Pickering and a list of correspondents not

included in the *Historical Index*. The microfilm edition was sponsored by the National Historical Publications Commission.

320.   Allis, Frederick Scouller.
　　　Guide to the microfilm edition of the Winthrop Sargent papers, Frederick S. Allis, Jr., editor, Roy Bartolomei, associate editor. Boston, Mass., Massachusetts Historical Society, 1965. 55 p.
　　　1.　Type of microform: Microfilm.
　　　2.　Availability: Seven reels and printed guide available. The guide may be purchased separately. No interlibrary loan copy available.
　　　3.　Orders: Director, Massachusetts Historical Society, 1154 Boylston Street, Boston, Massachusetts 02215.
　　　4.　The microfilm edition of the Sargent papers includes all the papers of Winthrop Sargent in the Massachusetts Historical Society, together with three Sargent diaries lent by the Ohio Historical Society and a manuscript thesis on Sargent by Benjamin Harrison Pershing. The National Historical Publications Commission sponsored the publication. The *Guide* provides a biographical sketch of Sargent, a short history of the papers, a reel-by-reel description of the collection, and a list of correspondents, giving dates of letters.

321.   American Historical Association. Committee for the Study of War Documents.
　　　A catalogue of files and microfilms of the German Foreign Ministry Archives, 1867-1920. [Washington] 1959. 1,290 columns.
　　　1.　Type of microform: Microfilm.
　　　2.　Availability: Positive copies available.
　　　3.　Orders: The large majority of the negatives are held by the Air Ministry, London, but a substantial number are held by the National Archives, Washington; the others are scattered among eight institutions in the United States and abroad. Since conditions and prices for the provision of positive copies of the film vary, requests for such copies and inquiries regarding the microfilms should be addressed to the institutions listed on pp. xl-xlii of the introduction to the *Catalogue*.
　　　4.　Designed to present a complete record of the Political Department of the German Foreign Ministry, 1867-1920, this *Catalogue* also provides details of the microfilming of these files done by the German War Documents Project of the American, British, and French governments, by other governments, by certain universities and other institutions, and by private individuals. Up to 1952, only official representatives of other governments were allowed access to the files, and all microfilming was done on their behalf. In 1952 the custodial governments decided that the pre-1920 files should be made generally accessible for microfilming provided that all films should be available for copying.

322.   American Historical Association. Committee for the Study of War Documents.
　　　Guides to German records microfilmed at Alexandria, Va. Washington, National Archives and Records Service, General Services Administration, 1958-　no. 1-

1. Type of microform: Microfilm.
2. Availability: The microfilm deposited in the National Archives by the American Historical Association may be consulted there. Copies of one or more rolls may be purchased at currently published rates.
3. Orders: Checks or money orders should be made payable to the General Services Administration and sent to: Cashier, National Archives and Records Service, Washington, D.C. 20408.
4. The *Guides* are finding aids describing the microfilms of seized German records deposited in the National Archives. (The original records were returned to the Federal Republic of Germany.) In addition to the necessary finding information, notes provide a general idea of the nature of the materials, although they do not purport to be complete descriptions. Records were filmed by groups, e.g., no. 1 covers records of the Reich Ministry of Economics; no. 2, Office of the Reich Commissioner for the Strengthening of Germandom; no. 3, Records of the National Socialist German Labor Party, etc. The nature of the records filmed makes it necessary for researchers to consult each guide as there are no indexes.

323. American Historical Association. Committee for the Study of War Documents.
   List of archival references to material in the German Foreign Ministry Archives filmed under grant from the Old Dominion Foundation. Buckinghamshire, Whaddon Hall, 1958. 49 1.
   1. Type of microform: Microfilm.
   2. Availability: Available for use at the National Archives. Positive copies of complete rolls available for purchase at currently published rates.
   3. Orders: Orders accompanied by check or money order made payable to the General Services Administration should be sent to: Cashier, National Archives and Records Service, Washington, D.C. 20408. Orders from outside the United States and its possessions should be accompanied by an international money order or check drawn in United States dollars on a bank in the United States and made payable to the General Services Administration and sent to the address noted above.
   4. This list serves as a finding aid for Microcopies T-209 and T-291 in the National Archives. These microcopies are a part of the German records filmed at Whaddon Hall and consist of the archives of the German Embassy at Washington and files of former members of the German foreign ministry.

324. Anderson, James L.
   Guide to the microfilm edition of the papers of R. M. T. Hunter, 1817-1887. James L. Anderson & Mary F. Crouch, editors. [Charlottesville, Va.] 1967. 44 p. (Microfilm publications, no. 6)
   1. Type of microform: Microfilm.
   2. Availability: Thirteen rolls and pamphlet guide available. Guide may be purchased separately. Film and guide also available on interlibrary loan.
   3. Orders: Curator of Manuscripts, University of Virginia Library, Charlottesville, Virginia 22901.
   4. The *Guide* includes a chronology of the life of R. M. T. Hunter, roll notes, and a list of correspondents, giving dates as a key to location on the

film. The microfilm edition was sponsored jointly by the University of Virginia Library and the National Historical Publications Commission.

325 Atiya, Aziz Suryal.
   The Arabic manuscripts of Mount Sinai; a hand-list of the Arabic manuscripts and scrolls microfilmed at the library of the Monastery of St. Catherine, Mount Sinai. Foreword by Wendell Phillips. Baltimore, Johns Hopkins Press [1955] 97 p. (Publications of the American Foundation for the Study of Man, v. 1)
   1. Type of microform: Microfilm.
   2. Availability: Positive copies may be purchased.
   3. Orders: Photoduplication Service, Library of Congress, Washington, D.C. 20540.
   4. Not a complete analytical catalog but rather a guide giving brief precise descriptions of the 306 selected Arabic codices and 1,742 Arabic and Turkish firmans microfilmed by the American Foundation Mt. Sinai Expedition.

326. Bakken, Douglas A.
   [Guide to the microfilm edition of the] J. Sterling Morton papers, 1849-1902. Editor: Douglas A. Bakken; manuscript curators: Duane J. Reed, Richard E. Booker; microfilm technician: Elizabeth M. Arnold. Lincoln, Nebraska State Historical Society, 1967. 40 p.
   1. Type of microform: Microfilm.
   2. Availability: Seventy-eight rolls with pamphlet guide available. Individual rolls and guide may be purchased separately.
   3. Orders: Archivist, Nebraska State Historical Society, 1500 R Street, Lincoln, Nebraska 68508.
   4. The microfilm was produced with the assistance of the National Historical Publications Commission. The *Guide* gives a brief biographical sketch, explanation of the arrangement, and roll notes.

327. Bakken, Douglas A.
   [Guide to the microfilm edition of the] Nebraska Farmers' Alliance papers, 1887-1901. Editor: Douglas A. Bakken; manuscript curator: Richard E. Booker; microfilm technician: Elizabeth M. Arnold. Lincoln, Nebraska State Historical Society, 1966. [10] p.
   1. Type of microform: Microfilm.
   2. Availability: Seven rolls with pamphlet guide available. Individual rolls and guide may be purchased separately.
   3. Orders: Archivist, Nebraska State Historical Society, 1500 R Street, Lincoln, Nebraska 68508.
   4. The microfilm was produced with the assistance of the National Historical Publications Commission. The *Guide* provides a historical note on the Alliance, roll notes, and list of correspondents.

328. Bakken, Douglas A.
   [Guide to the microfilm edition of the] Robert W. Furnas papers, 1844-1905. Editor: Douglas A. Bakken; manuscript curator: Richard E.

Booker; microfilm technician: Elizabeth M. Arnold. Lincoln, Nebraska State
Historical Society, 1966. [10] p.
1. Type of microform: Microfilm.
2. Availability: Thirteen rolls with pamphlet guide available. Individual
rolls and guide may be purchased separately.
3. Orders: Archivist, Nebraska State Historical Society, 1500 R Street,
Lincoln, Nebraska 68508.
4. The microfilm was produced with the assistance of the National Historical Publications Commission. The *Guide* includes a brief sketch of Furnas
and roll notes.

329. Bakken, Douglas A.
[Guide to the microfilm edition of the] Samuel M. Chapman papers,
1866-1906. Editor: Douglas A. Bakken; manuscript curator: Richard E.
Booker; microfilm technician: Elizabeth M. Arnold. Lincoln, Nebraska State
Historical Society, 1966. [7] p.
1. Type of microform: Microfilm.
2. Availability: Ten rolls with pamphlet guide available. Individual rolls
and guide may be purchased separately.
3. Orders: Archivist, Nebraska State Historical Society, 1500 R Street,
Lincoln, Nebraska 68508.
4. The microfilm was produced with the assistance of the National Historical Publications Commission. The *Guide* gives a brief biographical sketch
of Chapman, notes on the arrangement of the papers, and roll notes.

330. Bakken, Douglas A.
[Guide to the microfilm edition of the] Samuel Maxwell papers,
1853-1901. Editor: Douglas A. Bakken; manuscript curator: Richard E.
Booker; microfilm technician: Elizabeth M. Arnold. Lincoln, Nebraska State
Historical Society, 1966. [7] p.
1. Type of microform: Microfilm.
2. Availability: Eight rolls with pamphlet guide available. Individual rolls
and guide may be purchased separately.
3. Orders: Archivist, Nebraska State Historical Society, 1500 R Street,
Lincoln, Nebraska 68508.
4. The microfilm was produced with the assistance of the National Historical Publications Commission. The *Guide* gives a brief biographical sketch
of Samuel Maxwell and roll notes.

331. Berner, Richard C.
Callbreath, Grant and Cook, merchants, Wrangell, Alaska: Letterpress
books, 1878-1898, at the University of Washington Libraries. Project director: Richard C. Berner; preparation by Kari Inglis and Ruth Johnson. Seattle,
1965. [4] p.
1. Type of microform: Microfilm.
2. Availability: Two rolls with pamphlet guide available. The guide alone
is available without charge.

3. Orders: Curator of Manuscripts, University of Washington Libraries, Seattle, Washington 98105.

4. The publication of the pamphlet guide and microfilm was made possible by a grant from the National Historical Publications Commission. The pamphlet gives a brief historical note and contents of the microfilm rolls.

332. Berner, Richard C.
Isaac Ingalls Stevens papers, 1831-1862, at the University of Washington Libraries. Project director: Richard C. Berner; preparation by Kari Inglis and Ruth Johnson. Seattle, 1965. 7 p.
1. Type of microform: Microfilm.
2. Availability: Four rolls with pamphlet guide. The guide alone is available without charge.
3. Orders: Curator of Manuscripts, University of Washington Libraries, Seattle, Washington 98105.
4. The publication of the Guide and microfilm was made possible by a grant from the National Historical Publications Commission. The Guide gives a brief biographical sketch of Stevens, contents of the rolls, lists of correspondents, and a description of the papers as a whole, including items not filmed.

333. Berner, Richard C.
John J. McGilvra papers, 1861-1903, at the University of Washington Libraries. Project director: Richard C. Berner; preparation by Kari Inglis and Ruth Johnson. Seattle, 1965. 7 p.
1. Type of microform: Microfilm.
2. Availability: Four rolls with pamphlet guide available. The guide alone is available without charge.
3. Orders: Curator of Manuscripts, University of Washington Libraries, Seattle, Washington 98105.
4. The publication of the Guide and microfilm was made possible by a grant from the National Historical Publications Commission. The Guide gives a brief biographical sketch of McGilvra, an explanation of the arrangement of the papers, contents of the microfilm by rolls, a list of major correspondents with inclusive dates of letters, and description of the papers not filmed.

334. Berner, Richard C.
Manning Ferguson Force papers, 1835-1885, at the University of Washington Libraries. Project director: Richard C. Berner; preparation by Kari Inglis and Ruth Johnson. Seattle, 1965. 4 p.
1. Type of microform: Microfilm.
2. Availability: Five rolls with pamphlet guide available. The guide alone is available without charge.
3. Orders: Curator of Manuscripts, University of Washington Libraries, Seattle, Washington 98105.
4. The publication of the pamphlet guide and microfilm was made possible by a grant from the National Historical Publications Commission. The pamphlet gives a brief biographical sketch of Manning Force, contents of the rolls, and a list of authors of incoming letters, which are arranged alphabetically.

335. Berner, Richard C.
Oregon Improvement Company records, 1880-1896, in the University of Washington Libraries. Project director: Richard C. Berner; preparation by Kari Inglis and Ruth Johnson. Seattle, 1965. 18 p.
   1. Type of microform: Microfilm.
   2. Availability: Thirty-seven rolls with pamphlet guide available. The guide alone is available without charge.
   3. Orders: Curator of Manuscripts, University of Washington Libraries, Seattle, Washington 98105.
   4. The publication of the microfilm and pamphlet guide was made possible by a grant from the National Historical Publications Commission. The pamphlet lists contents of inventory, gives a historical sketch of the Oregon Improvement Company and its subsidiaries, contents of the microfilm by rolls, and contents of the entire manuscript group.

336. Berner, Richard C.
Richard A. Ballinger papers, 1907-1920, in the University of Washington Libraries. Project director: Richard C. Berner; preparation by Kari Inglis and Ruth Johnson. Seattle, 1965. 26 p.
   1. Type of microform: Microfilm.
   2. Availability: Thirteen rolls with pamphlet guide available. The guide alone is available without charge.
   3. Orders: Curator of Manuscripts, University of Washington Libraries, Seattle, Washington 98105.
   4. The publication of the Guide and microfilm was made possible by a grant from the National Historical Publications Commission. The Guide gives a brief biographical sketch of Ballinger, a description of the arrangement of the papers, and lists of correspondents. Contents of the microfilm publication by rolls is on a separate sheet laid in.

337. Berner, Richard C.
William H. Wallace papers, 1851-1878, at the University of Washington Libraries. Project director: Richard C. Berner; preparation by Kari Inglis and Ruth Johnson. Seattle, 1965. 6 p.
   1. Type of microform: Microfilm.
   2. Availability: One roll with pamphlet guide available. The guide alone is available without charge.
   3. Orders: Curator of Manuscripts, University of Washington Libraries, Seattle, Washington 98105.
   4. The publication of the Guide and microfilm was made possible by a grant from the National Historical Publications Commission. The Guide gives a brief biographical sketch of William Henson Wallace, a list of the series filmed, a list of correspondents with dates of letters, and a list of items within the Wallace papers that were not filmed.

338. Berner, Richard C.
Washington Mill Company papers, 1857-88, at the University of Washington Libraries. Project director: Richard C. Berner; preparation by Kari Inglis and Ruth Johnson. Seattle, 1965. 4 p.
   1. Type of microform: Microfilm.

2. Availability: Three rolls with pamphlet guide available. The guide alone is available without charge.

3. Orders: Curator of Manuscripts, University of Washington Libraries, Seattle, Washington 98105.

4. The publication of the microfilm and pamphlet guide was made possible by a grant from the National Historical Publications Commission. The guide gives contents of the microfilm by rolls, a historical sketch of the company, and arrangement of the papers as a whole.

339. Berner, Richard C.

Washington territorial government papers, 1853-1875, at the University of Washington Libraries. Project director: Richard C. Berner; preparation by Kari Inglis and Ruth Johnson. Seattle, 1965. [3] p.

1. Type of microform: Microfilm.

2. Availability: One roll with pamphlet guide available. The guide alone is available without charge.

3. Orders: Curator of Manuscripts, University of Washington Libraries, Seattle, Washington 98105.

4. The publication of the microfilm and pamphlet guide was made possible by a grant from the National Historical Publications Commission. The guide lists correspondence of the governor's and secretary's office which has been filmed, and also notes other territorial papers in the collection which were not included in the film.

340. Beyer, George R.

Guide to the microfilm of the Simon Cameron papers at the Historical Society of Dauphin County, Harrisburg, Pennsylvania. Harrisburg, Pennsylvania Historical and Museum Commission, 1971. 91 p.

1. Type of microform: Microfilm.

2. Availability: Ten rolls and printed guide available. The guide may be purchased separately.

3. Order: Pennsylvania Historical and Museum Commission, Box 232, Harrisburg, Pennsylvania 17108.

4. This microfilm publication reproduces the papers (1824-1892) of Simon Cameron, businessman, politician, and government official, located at the Historical Society of Dauphin County in Harrisburg. The collection consists primarily of incoming correspondence and business papers but also includes thirteen letters or drafts of letters by Cameron.

The *Guide* points out that these papers are distinct from the collection of Simon Cameron papers owned by the Library of Congress in which the bulk of the material falls in the period 1860-1880. The papers are listed in the order in which they appear on the microfilm. With few exceptions, they are arranged chronologically. Unless otherwise indicated, entries refer to letters, which are identified by name of recipient, name of writer, place of writing (when known), and date. If no recipient is given, the letter is addressed to Simon Cameron. The roll number appearing immediately above the first entry for each new roll and repeated at the top of each successive page makes the *Guide* easy to use.

341. California. University. Library.

An index of German Foreign Ministry archives, 1867-1920, microfilmed at Whaddon Hall for the General Library, University of California, Berkeley. Berkeley, 1957.

1 v. (various pagings)

1. Type of microform: Microfilm.

2. Availability: Positive copies of the archives, in units of one or more complete reels, may be purchased.

3. Orders: Photographic Service, University of California Library, Berkeley, California 94720.

4. The University of California Library filmed portions of the German Foreign Ministry Archives, which were moved to England during the Berlin blockade. Until they were returned to Germany, the archives were housed at Whaddon Hall near Bletchley, Buckinghamshire, England. Microfilming of the archives was done by the American, British, and French governments, by other governments, by several universities and institutions, and by private individuals.

The University of California Library's filming "centered around the Bismarck period, Anglo-German and German-American relations. The selections included important areas in German internal relations and in relations with other countries including Austria, Russia and Turkey for the period 1867-1914. In certain instances where these files ran over into the 1914-1919 period, those years were included in the Library's filming. Some filming was also done of the files relating to the Central American republics and Mexico and to some other countries, chiefly European."

The *Index* contains notes on the "Repertory of the Official Documents of the Political Section of the Ministry of Foreign Affairs," a list of the archives in the order in which they were filmed, and an index to the list of reels, which provides an approach by country.

342. Clark, Kenneth Willis, ed.

Checklist of manuscripts in St. Catherine's Monastery, Mount Sinai, microfilmed for the Library of Congress, 1950, prepared under the direction of Kenneth W. Clark, general editor of the Mount Sinai Expedition, 1949-50. Washington, Library of Congress Photoduplication Service, Library of Congress, 1952. 53 p.

1. Type of microform: Microfilm.

2. Availability: Positive copies may be purchased at current prices.

3. Orders: Photoduplication Service, Library of Congress, Washington, D.C. 20540.

4. Indexes with brief but precise identification the 1,687 manuscripts from the library of St. Catherine's Monastery, Mt. Sinai, selected for microfilming in 1950 under the auspices of the American School of Oriental Research with the support of the Library of Congress. Also listed are 1,284 miniatures taken from 113 manuscripts, which were copied on 4 x 5 inch photographic negatives, 671 Turkish firmans, 1,071 Arabic firmans, and other Arabic historical documents.

343. Clark, Kenneth Willis, ed.
   Checklist of manuscripts in the Libraries of the Greek and Armenian patriarchates in Jerusalem, microfilmed for the Library of Congress, 1949-50, prepared under the direction of Kenneth W. Clark, director and general editor of the Jerusalem Expedition, 1949-50. Washington, Library of Congress Photoduplication Service, 1953. 44 p.
   1. Type of microform: Microfilm.
   2. Availability: Positive copies are available at currently published rates.
   3. Orders: Photoduplication Service, Library of Congress, Washington, D.C. 20540.
   4. Indexes with economy of description but with precise identification of the 998 manuscripts from the library of the Greek Orthodox Patriarchate and the 32 from the library of the Armenian Patriarchate selected for microfilming in 1949-50 under the auspices of the American School of Oriental Research with the support of the Library of Congress. Also listed are the 1,187 miniatures (755 from the codices of the Greek Orthodox Patriarchate and 432 from the Codices of the Armenian Patriarchate) copied on 4 x 5 inch photographic negatives.

344. Cornell University. Libraries.
   The Wittgenstein papers, a catalogue. [Ithaca, N. Y., 1968] 10 1.
   1. Type of microform: Microfilm.
   2. Availability: Positive copies of the complete set only (twenty reels) may be purchased.
   3. Orders: Miss Elizabeth M. Murphy, Budget and Accounting Office, John M. Olin Library, Cornell University, Ithaca, New York 14850.
   4. The catalog lists the manuscripts, typescripts, and dictations contained on the film, with an additional listing in the order in which the items appear on the film, giving the corresponding volumes of the bound Xerox copies of the film, which are in the Cornell University Library.

345. Crick, Bernard R., ed.
   A guide to manuscripts relating to America in Great Britain and Ireland. Edited by B. R. Crick and Mildred Alman under the general supervision of H. L. Beals. [London] Published for the British Association for American Studies by the Oxford University Press, 1961. 667 p.
   1. Type of microform: Microfilm.
   2. Availability: Each item in the series may be purchased separately.
   3. Orders: Micro Methods Limited, 17 Denbigh Street, London, S.W. 1, England.
   4. The series, *British Records Relating to America,* includes both papers grouped according to subject, e.g., *The Rhodes House Anti-Slavery Papers; Material Relating to America from the Anti-Slavery Collection . . . 1839-1868* from Rhodes House, Oxford, and the collected papers of an individual firm, or association, e.g., *The American Journals of George Townsend Fox, 1831-1868* and *The Hobhouse Letters, 1722-55; Letters and other Papers of Isaac Hobhouse & Co., Bristol Merchants.*
   Crick's work served as a basis for this series and is useful for descriptions of

the collections filmed. However, the series is not necessarily limited to the material listed in Crick.

"On the advice of the general editor [W. E. Minchinton] appointed by the British Association for American Studies, Micro Methods Limited prepares for publication major collections of manuscripts and primary printed material (newspapers, pamphlets, guides, etc.) in British repositories, libraries and archives relating to the history of the United States and to the colonies in British North America before Independence. The selection of material relies not only on the standard guides but also on the lists of new acquisitions published by the National Register of Archives, the British Museum, county record offices and other national and local record repositories."

Each film is accompanied by a brief signed introduction setting out the archival nature of the papers and relating them to existing publications. The introduction to *The Hobhouse Letters, 1722-55*, by W. E. Minchinton is available in pamphlet form, and the publisher hopes to produce other introductions in the same form.

346. Davis, Jane Spector.
Guide to a microfilm edition of the Henry Hastings Sibley papers. St. Paul, Minnesota Historical Society, 1968. 27 p.
1. Type of microform: Microfilm.
2. Availability: Thirty-two rolls and printed guide may be purchased. Guide and individual rolls may be purchased separately.
3. Orders: Manuscripts Department, Minnesota Historical Society, 690 Cedar Street, St. Paul, Minnesota 55101.
4. The Sibley papers include the full collection in the possession of the society, manuscripts loaned by the Sibley House Association of the Minnesota Daughters of the American Revolution, and copies of manuscripts from the Burton Historical Collection of the Detroit Public Library. The microfilm edition and the *Guide* were made possible by a grant of funds from the National Historical Publications Commission to the Minnesota Historical Society. The *Guide* provides a biographical sketch, description of the papers, the contents of each roll, a selected list of authors, and a list of subjects covered. A complete list of all correspondents may be purchased as a separate item.

347. Diaz, Albert James.
A guide to the microfilm of papers relating to New Mexico land grants. Albuquerque, University of New Mexico Press, 1960. 102 p. (University of New Mexico publications. Library series, no. 1)
1. Type of microform: Microfilm.
2. Availability: Positive microfilm may be purchased.
3. Orders: Zimmerman Library, University of New Mexico, Albuquerque, New Mexico 87106.
4. The *Guide* is designed to assist the researcher in using the papers relating to New Mexico land grants from the United States Bureau of Land Management in Santa Fe, which were microfilmed by the University of New Mexico Library in 1955. The papers fall into four main categories: (1)

documents described in vol. I of Ralph E. Twitchell's *Spanish Archives of New Mexico* (Cedar Rapids, Iowa, 1914); (2) various indexes and record books kept prior to the establishment of the office of Surveyor General, including the index to Spanish and Mexican documents kept by Donaciano Vigil and the books in which land titles were recorded in accordance with the provisions of the Kearney Code; (3) records of the Surveyor General of New Mexico; (4) records of the Court of Private Land Claims. For filming, the papers were arranged in twenty-three sections and filmed in numerical sequence within sections using numbers previously assigned to the documents or records. The *Guide* is basically a finding device, giving little or no information about cases.

348. Dillard University, New Orleans. Amistad Research Center.
   Author and added entry catalog of the American Missionary Association archives, with reference to schools and mission stations . . . Introduction by Clifton H. Johnson. Westport, Conn., Greenwood Publishing Corporation, n.d. 3 v.
   1. Type of microform: Microfilm.
   2. Availability: Complete set or by state or country.
   3. Order: Microfilm Project, Amistad Research Center, Dillard University, New Orleans, Louisiana 70122.
   4. The American Missionary Archives contain approximately 350,000 manuscript pieces, the mass of which were written during the period 1839-1882. Although the papers include some account books, annual reports, minutes of executive committee meetings, letters make up the large majority of the papers. The archives provide source material for research on abolition, the Civil War and Reconstruction, and Negro education. The *Author and Added Entry Catalog* serves as a guide to the papers, but it covers only about 105,000 of the nearly 250,000 items that have been processed. However, it should be noted that catalogers selected what they considered the most valuable papers for cataloging. "The catalog entry, unless otherwise indicated, is for the author of the manuscript."

349. Feinstone, Sol.
   The Sol Feinstone Collection of the American Revolution. The American Revolution was a struggle of free men to remain free. Guide to the microfilm edition . . . Philadelphia, Rhistoric Publications, 1969. 44, 29 p.
   1. Type of microform: Microfilm.
   2. Availability: Available with guide. Guide alone may also be purchased.
   3. Orders: Rhistoric Publications, Inc., 302 North 13th Street, Philadelphia, Pennsylvania 19107.
   4. This private collection of more than 1,700 manuscripts, letters, and documents relating to the American Revolution and its leaders was assembled during the past forty years by Sol Feinstone of Washington Crossing, Pa. The *Guide to the Microfilm Edition* of the collection lists the material in an alphabetical arrangement, each item being assigned a number. These item numbers are used for reference in the twenty-nine page index.

350. Finch, Herbert.
   Andrew Dickson White papers at Cornell University, 1846-1919. Herbert

Finch, editor; Patricia H. Gaffney, assistant editor. Ithaca, N. Y., Collection of Regional History and University Archives, John M. Olin Library, 1970. 81 p.

1. Type of microform: Microfilm.
2. Availability: 149 rolls with pamphlet guide. Individual rolls and guide may be purchased separately.
3. Orders: Collection of Regional History and University Archives, John M. Olin Library, Cornell University, Ithaca, New York 14850.
4. The microfilm publication was produced with the assistance of the National Historical Publications Commission. The guide gives a biographical sketch of Andrew D. White, a description of the collection, reel notes, and an index to correspondence reels.

351. Finch, Herbert.
George Bancroft papers at Cornell University, 1811-1901. Ithaca, N. Y., 1965. [12] p.

1. Type of microform: Microfilm.
2. Availability: Seven rolls and printed guide available. Individual rolls and guide may be purchased separately. Also available on interlibrary loan.
3. Orders: Collection of Regional History and University Archives, John M. Olin Library, Cornell University, Ithaca, New York 14850.
4. The pamphlet guide gives a history of the collection, nature and contents of the collection, and notes on each reel. The microfilm was produced with the assistance of the National Historical Publications Commission.

352. France. Archives Nationales.
État des microfilms conservés aux Archives Nationales (Service Photographique, Section Outre-Mer et Dépot des Archives d'Outre-Mer) par Christian Gut et Ferréol de Ferry avec la collaboration de Serge Czarnecki. En appendice: Répertoire des microfilms de complément du Service Historique de la Marine, par J. P. Busson . . . Paris, S.E.V.P.E.N., 1968. 279 p.

1. Type of microform: Microfilm.
2. Availability: For consultation.
3. This catalog consists of two parts and an index. The first part, "Microfilms de Complément Conservés aux Archives Nationales (au 1er décembre 1967)" is divided into three sections. Section A lists the microfilms in the Service Photographique (258 entries). Section B is a "Table de concordance" between the classification numbers of the original documents and the classification numbers of the "microfilms de complément" of the Service Photographique. Section C is a list of the microfilms in the Section Outre-Mer des Archives Nationales. These microfilms are grouped under eight headings, e.g., inventories of archives, family archives, economic archives, etc. The second part, "Etat des microfilms de sécurité conservés aux Archives Nationales (Service Photographique)," under Section A lists documents from various sections of the Archives Nationales filmed for security reasons. Under Section B are listed microfilms of ministerial archives, and under Section C is the record of the inventories of 1937 and 1955. M. Busson's *Repertoire des Microfilms de Complément du Service Historique de la Marine* is a list of 29 microfilmed items which may be consulted only at the Service Historique on the authorization of the chief of the Service. The index of fourteen pages is a

general index covering the entire work. It is easy to use and seems quite adequate.

353. France. Direction des Archives.
    Catalogue des microfilms de sécurité et de complément conservés dans les archives des départements, par Michel Duchien, archiviste à la Direction des Archives de France. Avant-propos de Charles Braibant. Paris, Impr. nationale, 1955. 260 p.
    ——— ——— 1er Supplément (1955-1958) Avant-propos d'André Chamson. Paris, Impr. nationale, 1960. 410 p.
    ——— ———2ème Supplément (1959-1965) Par Alexandre Labat, Robert Favreau et Michel Quétin . . . sous la direction de Michel Duchein. Paris, S.E.V.P.E.N., 1968, 325 p.
    1. Type of microform: Microfilm.
    2. Availability: For consultation.
    3. In the introductory remarks, the point is made that this *Catalogue* is not to be considered a list of all the documents of French archives which have been microfilmed, since many institutions and libraries possess microfilm collections which are not recorded in the *Catalogue*. The Service Technique of the Direction des Archives de France, in line with information supplied by the chief archivists of the departments, set up the entries for the *Catalogue* and was also responsible for the "Table des Documents Microfilmés" and the "Table Alphabétique."
    The *Catalogue* is concerned with those microfilms which enable a depository to complete a series of documents and with those which provide security for the most valuable records. Part I of the *Catalogue*, "Catalogue des Microfilms," lists "microfilms de complément" and "microfilms de securité" in an alphabetical arrangement by department. Number of rolls or strips, place where original document is preserved, identifying class number, type of film, and date of execution of microfilm are given. In Part II, the "Table des Documents Microfilmés" lists by depository the documents enumerated in Part I. The "Table Alphabétique" provides an index of persons and places with references to page numbers.

354. Gabriel, Astrik Ladislas.
    A summary catalogue of microfilms of one thousand scientific manuscripts in the Ambrosiana Library, Milan. Notre Dame, Ind., Mediaeval Institute, University of Notre Dame, 1968. 439 p.
    1. Type of microform: Microfilm.
    2. Availability: This microfilm collection housed in the Mediaeval Institute in the Notre Dame Memorial Library is at the disposal of scholars. Positive films may be borrowed on interlibrary loan; they cannot be copied.
    3. Orders: Interlibrary Loan Service, Memorial Library, Notre Dame University, South Bend, Indiana 46556.
    4. This catalog provides a guide and checklist for the historian of science who needs to consult the comprehensive collection of film of the Ambrosiana manuscripts at Notre Dame. The manuscripts, described primarily on the basis of earlier catalogs, cover the entire range of science and technology. Arrangement is alphabetical according to the Ambrosiana catalog number. A

subject and name index and a bibliography of important reference works accompany the catalog.

355. Gaffney, Patricia H.
   Goldwin Smith papers at Cornell University, 1844-1915. Ithaca, N. Y., Collection of Regional History and University Archives, John M. Olin Library, 1971. 37 p.
   1. Type of microform: Microfilm.
   2. Availability: Twenty-eight reels and the printed guide available. Individual reels and guide may be purchased separately. Also available on interlibrary loan.
   3. Orders: Collection of Regional History and University Archives, John M. Olin Library, Cornell University, Ithaca, New York 14850.
   4. This microfilm publication, made possible by the generosity of an anonymous admirer of Goldwin Smith, is endorsed by the National Historical Publications Commission. The guide gives a biographical sketch of Goldwin Smith, a description of the collection, and notes on each reel.

356. Garrison, Curtis Wiswell.
   Guide to the microfilm edition of James Monroe papers in Virginia repositories. Curtis W. Garrison, editor, David L. Thomas, assistant editor. [Charlottesville, Va.] University of Virginia Library, 1969. 86 p. (Microfilm publications, no. 7)
   1. Type of microform: Microfilm.
   2. Availability: Thirteen rolls plus pamphlet guide available. The guide may be purchased separately. Film and guide also available on interlibrary loan.
   3. Orders: Curator of Manuscripts, University of Virginia Library, Charlottesville, Virginia 22901.
   4. The *Guide* provides a general introduction, a chronology of the life of James Monroe, filming plan, roll notes, and an index. The microfilm edition produced by the University of Virginia Library was made possible by a grant from the National Historical Publications Commission.
   Some eighty-five documents relating to James Monroe, but not appropriate for inclusion in the National Historical Publications Commission film, have been filmed separately by the University of Virginia Library. This film strip, *Film Supplement of Materials in Virginia Repositories Relating to James Monroe,* accompanied by a pamphlet guide, may be ordered from the Curator of Manuscripts, University of Virginia Library.

357. Gordon, Vesta Lee, ed.
   Guide to the microfilm edition of the Letter book, 1688-1761 of the Company for propagation of the gospel in New England. [Charlottesville, Va.] University of Virginia Library, 1969. 9 p. (Microfilm publications, no. 8)
   1. Type of microform: Microfilm.
   2. Availability: One roll of microfilm with pamphlet guide available. The guide may be purchased separately. Film and guide also available on interlibrary loan.

3. Orders: Curator of Manuscripts, University of Virginia Library, Charlottesville, Virginia 22901.

4. The introduction to the *Guide* comments briefly on the history of the "Society for Propagation of the Gospel in New England" and presents a short bibliography on its history. A description of the letter book and information relating to its provenance follow. The last nine pages are devoted to the index which "cites only personal names—correspondents, recipients signators, witnesses, and names on financial receipts." Names appearing within the text are not included in the index. Names indexed are keyed to pagination. Members of the company and commissioners are indicated, and the dates of their election or the year in which their names appear in the records are given. Under the heading "documents" are indexed charters, indentures, etc.

358. Gt. Brit. Admiralty.

A catalogue of the German naval archives microfilmed at the Admiralty, London, for the University of Cambridge and the University of Michigan; a filming program directed by F. H. Hinsley [and] H. M. Ehrmann. London, Admiralty, 1959. 41 1.

1. Type of microform: Microfilm.

2. Availability: "The catalogue shows, in the case of each reel, whether the negative film is held by the University of Cambridge or the University of Michigan. In addition, the Public Record Office has a positive copy of all 133 reels; Cambridge University has a positive copy of the 111 reels of the Cambridge-Michigan program; and the University of Michigan has a positive copy of all reels for which it holds the negative film." There is no indication as to whether the material is available on loan or whether it can be reproduced.

3. The German naval records listed in this *Catalogue* were selected and microfilmed for Cambridge University and the University of Michigan. The 111 reels of documents recorded on pp. 1-34 were selected from the Marine-Kabinett, the Admiralstab der Marine, Abteilung "A" and "B," mainly for the years 1889-1919, and are the result of a joint Cambridge University-University of Michigan project. The 22 reels of documents listed on pp. 35-40, a University of Michigan project, were drawn in part from the Admiralstab der Marine, "A" and "B," for the years 1900-1916, but are composed primarily of files relating to Italy and the Italian navy, between 1933 and 1945.

Mr. Hinsley of Cambridge selected for filming all files of political importance, however indirect. Only purely technical files or strictly administrative subjects were excluded. Professor Ehrmann of Michigan selected files which emphasized Italy's relations with her allies and the role of the Italian navy on the eve of and during World War I and World War II.

The *Catalogue* gives: (1) admiralty reference; (2) archival reference; (3) title; (4) volume number; (5) dates; (6) reel numbers; (7) frame numbers. It also shows, in the case of each reel, whether the negative is held by the University of Cambridge or the University of Michigan.

359. Gt. Brit. Historical Manuscripts Commission.

Report on American manuscripts in the Royal Institution of Great Britain.

London, Printed for H. M. Stationery Off., by Macie & Co., Ltd., 1904-1909. 4 v.

1. Type of microform: Microfilm.
2. Availability: Complete set, including calendar, is available.
3. Orders: Micro Photo Division, Bell & Howell, Wooster, Ohio 44691.
4. The *British Headquarters Papers*, or the *Sir Guy Carleton Papers, 1747 (1777)-1783*, were formerly owned by the Royal Institution of Great Britain and are now kept in the Public Record Office. A set of positive photostats of the *Papers* is in the possession of Colonial Williamsburg, Inc., and it was this set that was filmed. The *Papers* are primarily correspondence from British commanding officers in the Southern colonies to the Commander-in-Chief of the British armies, the last of whom was Sir Guy Carleton, Lord Dorchester. Also included are letters of many other important people, General Nathanael Green, John Hancock, General Henry Lee, George Washington, Lafayette, etc. The *Report on American Manuscripts* cited above is in fact a calendar of the American manuscripts in the Royal Institution and as such is very helpful in using this microfilm edition of the *British Headquarters Papers*.

360. Ham, F. Gerald.
The Morris Hillquit papers; guide to a microfilm edition. F. Gerald Ham, editor; Carole Sue Warmbrodt, associate editor. Madison, The State Historical Society of Wisconsin, 1969. 116 p. (Guides to historical sources)
1. Type of microform: Microfilm.
2. Availability: Ten rolls with printed guide available. Individual rolls and guide may be purchased separately. Available also on interlibrary loan.
3. Orders: Curator of Manuscripts, State Historical Society of Wisconsin, 816 State Street, Madison, Wisconsin 53706.
4. The printed *Guide* provides a biographical sketch of Morris Hillquit, a history and description of the collection, the contents of the microfilm by reels, and a list of correspondents giving dates as a key to location on the film. The microfilm edition was published under the sponsorship of the National Historical Publication Commission.

361. Ham, F. Gerald.
The papers of Henry Demarest Lloyd; guide to a microfilm edition. F. Gerald Ham, editor; Josephine L. Harper, Eleanor Niermann, and Carol Sue Warmbrodt, associate editors. Madison, The State Historical Society of Wisconsin, 1971. 27 p. (Guides to historical sources)
1. Type of microform: Microfilm.
2. Availability: Fifty-two reels with printed guide available. Individual reels and guide may be purchased separately. Available also on interlibrary loan.
3. Orders: Curator of Manuscripts, State Historical Society of Wisconsin, 816 State Street, Madison, Wisconsin 53706.
4. Produced under the sponsorship of the National Historical Publications Commission, the microfilm edition of the Lloyd papers makes accessible to researchers the correspondence, research notes, notebooks, drafts of speeches and articles, and book manuscripts of a journalist, lecturer, writer, and international reformer of America's Gilded Age. The *Guide* gives a biographi-

cal sketch of Lloyd followed by a description of the five groups in which the papers are arranged: (1) correspondence; (2) writings, (3) research materials; (4) scrapbooks and clippings; (5) miscellany. Finally, there is a listing of contents by reel number.

362. Ham, F. Gerald.
Records of the Socialist Labor Party of America; guide to a microfilm edition. F. Gerald Ham, editor; Carole Sue Warmbrodt and Josephine L. Harper, associate editors; Lee E. Steinberg, manuscripts preparator. Madison, The State Historical Society of Wisconsin, 1970. 28 p. (Guides to historical resources)
 1. Type of microform: Microfilm.
 2. Availability: Thirty-nine rolls with pamphlet guide. Individual rolls and guide may be purchased separately. Available also on interlibrary loan.
 3. Orders: Curator of Manuscripts, State Historical Society of Wisconsin, 816 State Street, Madison, Wisconsin 53706.
 4. The microfilm edition was published under the sponsorship of the National Historical Publications Commission. The *Guide* includes a brief history of the party, description of the collection, and contents by reels.

363. Hansen, Ralph Waldemar.
Guide to the microfilm edition of the David Starr Jordan papers, 1861-1964. Ralph W. Hansen, project director, Patricia J. Palmer, editor, Connie Stein, editorial assistant. A project of the Stanford University Archives in the Stanford University Libraries sponsored by the National Historical Publications Commission. [Stanford, Calif., 1969] 31 p.
 1. Type of microform: Microfilm.
 2. Availability: 184 rolls with printed guide available. The guide may be purchased separately.
 3. Orders: Stanford University Archives, Main Library, Stanford, California 94305.
 4. The *Guide* provides a biographical sketch of Jordan, a description of the collection, roll identification, a partial list of correspondents, and a partial list of other repositories of Jordan material.

364. Heinz, Grete.
NSDAP Hauptarchiv; guide to the Hoover Institution microfilm collection. Compiled by Grete Heinz and Agnes F. Peterson. [Stanford, Calif.] Hoover Institution on War, Revolution and Peace, Stanford University, 1964. 175 p. (Hoover Institution. Bibliographical Series, 17)
 1. Type of microform: Microfilm.
 2. Availability: Copies of one or more reels may be purchased. Only orders for complete reels are accepted.
 3. Orders: Publications Department, Hoover Institution, Stanford University, Stanford, California 94305.
 4. This detailed *Guide* provides access to a very complex collection of documents, the "Collection NSDAP Hauptarchiv" or the main archive of the National Socialist party (Nationalsozialistische Deutsche Arbeitpartei or NSDAP). The introduction provides a brief history of the NSDAP Archiv and

its organization. The *Guide* follows the scheme of the "Collection NSDAP Hauptarchiv" found in the Document Center in Berlin where the filming began in the autumn of 1958. Part 1 (folders 1-1421) is arranged into twenty-nine subject groups assigned by the Berlin Document Center, while Part 2 (folders 1426-1923) is "arranged by provenance, that is, by the agency heading indicated by the Berlin Document Center." Also included are selected materials from the Streicher and Himmler collections of the Berlin Document Center. The *Guide* cites reel number, folder number, number of frames per folder and "contents and observations." The index includes all persons and organizations mentioned in the *Guide* either in the German titles or the English comments.

365. Hillard, Denise.
Le Tite-Live de Charles V, manuscrit de la Bibliothèque Sainte-Geneviève. Edition sur microfilm. Notice de Denise Hillard. Paris, Service International de Microfilms, 1969. 10 p.
  1. Type of microform: Microfilm.
  2. Availability: A copy of the film and the brochure may be purchased.
  3. Orders: Service International de Microfilms, 9, rue du Commandant Rivière, Paris VIIe, France.
  4. The author of this brochure, which provides both background for and description of one of the most beautiful manuscripts of the Bibliothèque Sainte-Geneviève, is an archivist-paleographer and librarian at the Bibliothèque Sainte-Geneviève in Paris. Mlle. Hillard gives the historical background of the manuscript, discusses the translation from Latin to French by Pierre Bersuire, a translation executed on order of Charles V in the first years of his reign (between 1364 and 1373), and speaks of the quality of the thirty-nine miniatures, which are dispersed throughout the text, and the two very beautiful pages at the head of the first and third décade (fol. 7 and fol. 316). A description of the text is given and a list of the miniatures showing location and subject matter. A brief bibliography is appended.

366. Hoffman, Paul P.
Guide to the microfilm edition of John Henry Ingram's Poe Collection. Paul P. Hoffman, editor, Mary F. Crouch, assistant editor, Richard S. Pride, editorial assistant. [Charlottesville, Va.] University of Virginia Library, 1967. 31 p. (Microfilm publications, no. 4)
  1. Type of microform: Microfilm.
  2. Availability: Nine rolls with pamphlet guide available. The guide may be purchased separately. Film and guide also available on interlibrary loan.
  3. Orders: Curator of Manuscripts, University of Virginia Library, Charlottesville, Virginia 22901.
  4. Ingram's Poe Collection, consisting of magazine and newspaper articles, photographs, letters, documents, and other manuscripts, is now owned by the University of Virginia Library and has been published on microfilm, sponsored by the National Historical Publications Commission. The *Guide* includes a chronology of the life of Edgar Allan Poe, a biographical sketch of John Henry Ingram, roll notes, and a list of major correspondents.
In addition to the *Guide*, John Carl Miller's *John Henry Ingram's Poe*

Collection at the University of Virginia, a Calendar . . . (Charlottesville, Va., 1960) serves as a finding aid. It is offered for sale with the microfilm and is also reproduced on roll one.

367. Hoffman, Paul P.
Guide to the naval papers of Sir Andrew Snape Hamond, bart., 1766-1783, and Sir Graham Eden Hamond, bart., 1799-1825. Paul P. Hoffman, editor; Mary F. Crouch, assistant editor; John L. Molyneaux, assistant editor: Hamond papers. Charlottesville, Va., University of Virginia Library, 1966. 41 p. (Microfilm publications, no. 2)
1. Type of microform: Microfilm.
2. Availability: Three rolls and pamphlet guide available. The guide may be purchased separately. Film and guide also available on interlibrary loan.
3. Orders: Curator of Manuscripts, University of Virginia Library, Charlottesville, Virginia 22901.
4. This project was sponsored jointly by the University of Virginia Library and the National Historical Publications Commission. The *Guide* provides chronologies of the two Hamonds, descriptions of the papers by volume and by series, arrangement on the rolls, and a list of major correspondents.

368. Hoffman, Paul P.
Guide to the microfilm edition of the Carter family papers, 1659-1797, in the Sabine Hall Collection. Paul P. Hoffman, editor; Mary F. Crouch, assistant editor; Lindsay M. Gold, editorial assistant. [Charlottesville, Va.] University of Virginia Library, 1967. 26 p. (Microfilm publications, no. 3)
1. Type of microform: Microfilm.
2. Availability: Four rolls with pamphlet guide available. The guide may be purchased separately. Film and guide also available on interlibrary loan.
3. Orders: Curator of Manuscripts, University of Virginia Library, Charlottesville, Virginia 22901.
4. The microfilm edition of the Carter family papers, sponsored jointly by the University of Virginia Library and the National Historical Publications Commission, includes land documents, correspondence, and diaries of Landon Carter and his son Robert Wormeley Carter in the Sabine Hall Collection on deposit at the University of Virginia Library. Copies of papers in the Earl Gregg Swem Library of the College of William and Mary and the Virginia Historical Society are also included.
The *Guide* includes chronologies of the lives of Landon Carter and Robert Wormeley Carter, roll notes, and a list of correspondents. Walter Ray Wineman's *The Landon Carter Papers in the University of Virginia Library: A Calendar and Biographical Sketch* (1962) serves as a partial finding aid, containing entries for about two-thirds of the correspondence included in the microfilm publication.

369. Hoffman, Paul P.
Guide to the microfilm edition of the Lee family papers, 1742-1795. Paul P. Hoffman, editor; John L. Molyneaux, assistant editor. Charlottesville, Va., University of Virginia Library, 1966. 51 p. (Microfilm publications, no. 1)
1. Type of microform: Microfilm.

2. Availability: Eight rolls plus pamphlet guide are available. Guide may be purchased separately. Film and guide also available on interlibrary loan.

3. Orders: Curator of Manuscripts, University of Virginia Library, Charlottesville, Virginia 22901.

4. This project, sponsored jointly by the University of Virginia Library and the National Historical Publications Commission, brings together Lee family papers in the University of Virginia Library and copies of Lee holdings in the Harvard University Library, the American Philosophical Society, the Historical Society of Pennsylvania, Yale University Library, The Minnesota Historical Society, and the Library of Congress. Several finding aids have been included in the first roll of microfilm: Justin Winsor's *Calendar of the Arthur Lee Manuscripts in the Library of Harvard University* (Cambridge, Mass., 1882); *Calendar of the Correspondence relating to the American Revolution of . . . Hon. Richard Henry Lee, Hon. Arthur Lee . . . in the Library of the American Philosophical Society* (Philadelphia, 1900); an unpublished name index to the Lee family papers in the University of Virginia Library, and a key to the ciphers used during the war by the Lee brothers and others, prepared by Edmund C. Burnett. The *Guide* provides a sketch of the Lee family of Virginia before 1750, chronologies of Arthur Lee, Richard Henry Lee, and William Lee, a brief account of the Lee family papers, roll notes, and a list of major correspondents.

370. Hoffman, Paul P.
Guide to the microfilm edition of the Virginia Gazette daybooks, 1750-1752 & 1764-1766. [Charlottesville, Va.] University of Virginia Library, 1967. 55 p. (Microfilm publications, no. 5)

1. Type of microform: Microfilm.

2. Availability: One roll, with pamphlet guide, available. Guide may be purchased separately. Film and guide also available on interlibrary loan.

3. Orders: Curator of Manuscripts, University of Virginia Library, Charlottesville, Virginia 22901.

4. The two indexes forming the bulk of the *Guide* were prepared by the Research Department of Colonial Williamsburg, Inc. The microfilm edition was sponsored jointly by the University of Virginia Library, owner of the *Daybooks*, and the National Historical Publications Commission.

371. Hungary. Orszagos Levéltár. Filmtár.
Ausztriai levéltári anyagról készült mikrofilmek (1969. januar 1-én) Repertórium, összeállitotta: Borsa Iván. Budapest, A Müvelödesügyi Minisztérium Levéltári Igazgatóságának Megbizásából a Magyar Országos Levéltár, 1969. 209 p. (Levéltári leltárak, 46)
A list of microfilms of Austrian archival materials in the Film Library of the National Archives of Hungary as of January 1, 1969.

372. Hungary. Országos Levéltár. Filmtár.
Az ausztriai levéltári anyagról készült mikrofilmek az Országos Levéltár Filmtárában. (1960. január 1-én) Repertórium, összeállitotta: Borsa Iván. Budapest, Levéltárak Országos Központja, 1960. 225 p. (Levéltári leltárak, 11)

A list of microfilms of Austrian archival materials in the Film Library of the National Archives of Hungary as of January 1, 1960.

373. Hungary. Országos Levéltár. Filmtár.
Csehszlovákiai levéltári anyagról készült mikrofilmek az Országos Levéltár filmtárában. (1963 január 1-en) Összeállitotta: Borsa Iván. Budapest, Müvelödesügyi Minisztérium Levéltari Osztálya, Levéltárak Országos Központja, 1963. 231 p. (Levéltári leltárak, 19)
A list of microfilms of Czechoslovakian archival materials in the Film Library of the National Archives of Hungary as of January 1, 1963.

374. Hungary. Országos Levéltár. Filmtár.
Az esztergomi római katolikus föegyházmegye anyakönyveinek mikrofilmjei az Országos Levéltár Filmtárában. Tematikai konspektus, készitette: Mandl Sándorné. Budapest, Müvelödésügyi Minisztérium Levéltári Osztálya, Levéltárak Országos Központja, 1964. 98 p. (Levéltári leltárak, 30)
A list of microfilms of the registers of births, marriages, and deaths of the Roman Catholic Archdiocese of Esztergom in the Film Library of the National Archives of Hungary.

375. Hungary. Országos Levéltár. Filmtár.
Jugoszláviai levéltári anyagról készült mikrofilmek az Országos Levéltár Filmtárában. (1963. január 1-en) Osszeállitotta: Borsa Iván. Budapest, Müvelödésügyi Minisztérium Levéltári Osztálya, Levéltárak Országos Központja, 1963. 234 p. (Levéltári leltárak, 21)
A list of microfilms of Yugoslavian archival materials in the Film Library of the National Archives of Hungary as of January 1, 1963.

376. Hungary. Országos Levéltár. Filmtar.
Küföldi levéltári anyagról készült mikrofilmek az Orszagos Levéltár Filmtárában (1965. január 1-én) Ausztria, Csehszlovákia, Jugoszlávia és Roménia Kivételével. Osszeállitotta: Borsa Iván. Budapest, Müvelödesügyi Minisztérium Levéltári Osztálya, Levéltárak Országos Központja, 1965. 199 p. (Levéltári leltárak, 34)
A list of the microfilms of foreign archival materials with the exception of Austria, Czechoslovakia, Romania, and Yugoslavia in the Film Library of the National Archives of Hungary.

377. Hungary. Országos Levéltár. Filmtár.
Romániai levéltári anyagról készült mikrofilmek az Országos Levéltár Filmtárában (1964. január 1-en) Osszeállította: Borsa Iván. Budapest, Müvelödesügyi Minisztérium Levéltári Osztálya Levéltarak Országos Központja, 1964. 283 p. (Levéltári leltárak, 28)
A list of microfilms of Romanian archival materials in the Film Library of the National Archives of Hungary as of January 1, 1964.

378. Kadrmas, Constance J.
Guide to a microfilm edition of the James Wickes Taylor papers. St. Paul, Minnesota Historical Society, 1968. 16 p.

1. Type of microform: Microfilm.
2. Availability: Ten rolls and printed guide may be purchased. The guide and individual rolls may be purchased separately.
3. Orders: Manuscripts Department, Minnesota Historical Society, 690 Cedar Street, St. Paul, Minnesota 55101.
4. The *Guide* provides a biographical sketch of Taylor, a chronological description of the papers, the contents of the microfilm by rolls, a selected list of authors, and a list of subjects covered. The microfilm edition and the *Guide* were made possible by a grant of funds from the National Historical Publications Commission to the Minnesota Historical Society.

379. Kent, Donald H.
Guide to the microfilm of the Records of the Provincial Council, 1682-1776, in the Pennsylvania State Archives, a microfilm project sponsored by the National Historical Publications Commission. Donald H. Kent, project director; Martha L. Simonetti, assistant project director; George Dailey and George R. Beyer, editors. [Harrisburg] Pennsylvania Historical and Museum Commission, 1966. 130 p.
1. Type of microform: Microfilm.
2. Availability: Twenty-six rolls with pamphlet guide available. The guide may be purchased separately.
3. Orders: Pennsylvania Historical and Museum Commission, Box 232, Harrisburg, Pennsylvania 17108.
4. The *Guide* gives a brief account of the Provincial Council, finding aids for the Provincial Record, papers of the Provincial Council, colonial records, and a list of the papers of the Provincial Council by rolls.

380. Kevles, Daniel Jerome.
Guide to the microfilm edition of the George Ellery Hale papers, 1882-1937, at the Mount Wilson and Palomar Observatories Library, Pasadena, California. [Washington? D.C.] Carnegie Institution of Washington and the California Institute of Technology, 1968. 47 p.
1. Type of microform: Microfilm.
2. Availability: A hundred rolls and printed guide available. Single rolls may be purchased, and the guide alone is without charge.
3. Orders: Director, Mount Wilson and Palomar Observatories, 813 Santa Barbara St., Pasadena, California 91108.
4. The *Guide* provides an introduction to the collection and a roll index giving frame numbers. The microfilm edition was made possible by a grant of funds from the National Historical Publications Commission to the Carnegie Institution of Washington, owner of the collection which is housed in the Library of the Mount Wilson and Palomar Observatories.

381. Kielman, Chester Valls.
Guide to the microfilm edition of the Bexar Archives, 1717-1836. A University of Texas microfilm publication sponsored by the National Historical Publications Commission. Austin, Texas, 1967-1971. 3 pts.
1. Type of microform: Microfilm.

2. Availability: Thirty-one rolls with pamphlet guide available. The guide may be purchased separately.

3. Orders: Librarian, Main Bldg. 202, University of Texas at Austin, Austin, Texas 78712.

4. The *Guide* explains the arrangement of the Bexar Archives and describes in some detail the contents of each microfilm roll of these colonial archives of Texas which were produced during the Spanish and Mexican periods, 1717-1836. Both printed and manuscript material are included.

382. Lentz, Andrea Durham.
The Warren G. Harding papers: an inventory to the microfilm edition. Andrea D. Lentz, editor; Madalon M. Korodi, Sara S. Fuller, assistants. Columbus, Ohio, Archives and Manuscripts Division, Ohio Historical Society, 1970. 283 p.

1. Type of microform: Microfilm.

2. Availability: 263 rolls with printed guide. The guide and individual rolls may be purchased separately.

3. Orders: Order Department, Ohio Historical Society, Ohio Historical Center, I-71 & 17th Avenue, Columbus, Ohio 43211.

4. The microfilm edition was made possible by a National Historical Publications Commission grant. The *Guide* includes a biographical chronology of Warren Gamaliel Harding, a description of the series into which the papers are divided, roll notes, indexes, and a guide to related materials.

383. McAvoy, Thomas Timothy.
Guide to the microfilm edition of the Orestes Augustus Brownson papers. Thomas T. McAvoy, project director; Lawrence J. Bradley, manuscripts preparator. Notre Dame, Ind., University of Notre Dame Archives, 1966. 48 p.

1. Type of microform: Microfilm.

2. Availability: Nineteen rolls and printed guide available. Individual rolls and guide may be purchased separately.

3. Orders: Microfilm Publication Project, University of Notre Dame Archives, Memorial Library, Notre Dame, Indiana 46556.

4. This microfilm publication was sponsored by the National Historical Publications Commission. The *Guide* provides a biographical sketch of Orestes Brownson, a description of the collection by rolls, and a list of correspondents. A complete listing of all items microfilmed, in the order microfilmed, appears on roll one.

384. McAvoy, Thomas Timothy.
Guide to the microfilm edition of the records of the Diocese of Louisiana and the Floridas, 1576-1803. Thomas T. McAvoy, project director; Lawrence J. Bradley, manuscripts preparator. Notre Dame, Ind., University of Notre Dame Archives, 1967. 45 p.

1. Type of microform: Microfilm.

2. Availability: Twelve rolls with pamphlet guide available. Individual rolls and guide may be purchased separately.

3. Orders: Microfilm Publication Project, University of Notre Dame Archives, Memorial Library, Notre Dame, Indiana 46556..

4. The microfilm publication and the *Guide* were published under the sponsorship of the National Historical Publications Commission. The *Guide* gives a brief account of the Catholic Church in Louisiana and Florida, 1513-1815, a description of the collection by rolls, and an alphabetical list of persons and places.

385. McAvoy, Thomas Timothy.
   Guide to the microfilm edition of the Thomas Ewing, Sr., papers. Thomas T. McAvoy, project director; Lawrence J. Bradley, manuscripts preparator. Notre Dame, Ind., University of Notre Dame Archives, 1967. 25 p.
   1. Type of microform: Microfilm.
   2. Availability: Six rolls with pamphlet guide available. Individual rolls may be purchased separately. The guide alone is available without charge.
   3. Orders: Microfilm Publication Project, University of Notre Dame Archives, Memorial Library, Notre Dame, Indiana 46556.
   4. The microfilm edition was published by the University of Notre Dame Archives under the sponsorship of the National Historical Publications Commission. The *Guide* gives a biographical sketch of Ewing, a description of the collection by rolls, and a list of correspondents with dates of letters.

386. McAvoy, Thomas Timothy.
   Guide to the microfilm edition of the William Tecumseh Sherman family papers (1808-1891). Thomas T. McAvoy, project director; Lawrence J. Bradley, manuscripts preparator. Notre Dame, Ind., University of Notre Dame Archives, 1967. 24 p.
   1. Type of microform: Microfilm.
   2. Availability: Fifteen rolls and printed guide available. Individual rolls and guide may be purchased separately.
   3. Orders: Microfilm Publication Project, University of Notre Dame Archives, Memorial Library, Notre Dame, Indiana 46556.
   4. The microfilm publication and the *Guide* were produced with the assistance of the National Historical Publications Commission. The *Guide* provides a biographical sketch of General Sherman and a description of the collection by rolls.

387. Magyar Tudományos Akadémia, Budapest. Könyvtár.
   Microcard catalogue of the rare Hebrew codices, manuscripts, and ancient prints in the Kaufmann Collection reproduced on microcards. Introduced by a lecture of the late Prof. Ignácz Goldziher. [Editor: R. Gergely] Budapest, Pub. House of the Hungarian Academy of Sciences, 1959. 44 p. (Publications of the Oriental Library of the Hungarian Academy of Sciences, 4)
   1. Type of microform: Microcard, microfiche.
   2. Availability: Available for purchase. Prices given upon request.
   3. Orders: Requests and inquiries should be addressed to: Oriental Library, Hungarian Academy of Sciences, Akadémia utea 2, Budapest V, Hungary.
   4. Lists the most important items (Hebrew codices, manuscripts, and books) of the David Kaufmann collection. Also available on microcard or microfiche is a copy of the complete catalog of the collection, compiled and

published by Dr. Max Weiss, *Katalog der hebräischen Handschriften und Bücher in der Bibliothek des Professors Dr. David Kaufmann* (Frankfurt am Main: J. Kaufmann, 1906), 280 p.

388.   Manross, William Wilson, comp.
The Fulham papers in the Lambeth Palace Library; American colonial section calendar and indexes. Oxford, Clarendon Press, 1965. 524 p.
    1.   Type of microform: Microfilm.
    2.   Availability: Entire collection available. Materials of individual states and countries also available.
    3.   Orders: World Microfilms, 62 Queen's Grove, London, N.W. 8, England OR World Microfilms, EAV Inc., Pleasantville, New York 10570.
    4.   The Fulham papers include general correspondence and other papers such as missionary bonds, ordination papers, etc., addressed to the Bishop of London from Canada, the thirteen American colonies, and the West Indies during the late seventeenth and eighteenth centuries. Manross classifies and lists these papers under six headings: "General Correspondence," "Ordination Papers, 1748-1824," "Missionary Bonds," "Diocesan Book for the Plantations," "Entries for Clergy Licensed for the Plantations," and "Pamphlets." He provides excellent summaries for each item listed under General Correspondence (pp. 3-294) and two detailed indexes, "Names and Topics Referred to in the Summaries" and "Names Appearing in the Documents but not in the Summaries."

389.   Marks, Bayly Ellen.
Guide to the microfilm edition of the David Bailie Warden papers. Baltimore, Md., The Maryland Historical Society, 1970. 21 p.
    1.   Type of microform: Microfilm.
    2.   Availability: Eight rolls and pamphlet guide available. Individual rolls and guide may be purchased separately.
    3.   Orders: Maryland Historical Society, 201 West Monument Street, Baltimore, Maryland 21201.
    4.   This publication was sponsored by the National Historical Publications Commission. The *Guide* provides a description of the collection of Warden papers at the Maryland Historical Society (another large group, not filmed, is at the Library of Congress), a biographical sketch of Warden, and microfilm roll notes.

390.   Marks, Bayly Ellen.
Guide to the microfilm edition of the Robert Goodloe Harper family papers. Baltimore, Md., The Maryland Historical Society, 1970. 25 p.
    1.   Type of microform: Microfilm.
    2.   Availability: Five rolls and pamphlet guide available. Individual rolls and guide may be purchased separately.
    3.   Orders: Maryland Historical Society, 201 West Monument Street, Baltimore, Maryland 21201.
    4.   This microfilm was published under the sponsorship of the National Historical Publications Commission. The *Guide* provides a biographical sketch of Harper and microfilm roll notes.

391. Maryland Historical Society.
Guide to the microfilm edition of the papers of the Maryland State Colonization Society, a collection of the Maryland Historical Society. [Philadelphia, Pa., Rhistoric Publications, Inc.] 1970. 34 p.
   1. Type of microform: Microfilm.
   2. Availability: Thirty-one rolls and pamphlet guide available.
   3. Orders: Rhistoric Publications, Inc., 302 North 13th Street, Philadelphia, Pennsylvania 19107.
   4. The *Guide* provides a history of the Maryland State Colonization Society and a chronology, a description of the papers, and an index to the microfilm. The description of the papers is by William D. Hoyt, Jr., revised from his classification which appeared in the *Maryland Historical Magazine* (September 1937) 32: 247-271.

392. Meixner, Esther Chilstrom.
Guide to the microfilm edition of the John Ericsson papers. Philadelphia, Pa., American Swedish Historical Foundation, 1970. 30 p.
   1. Type of microform: Microfilm.
   2. Availability: Eight rolls and printed guide available. The guide may be purchased separately.
   3. Orders: Rhistoric Publications, Inc., 302 North 13th Street, Philadelphia, Pennsylvania 19107.
   4. The *Guide* provides a biographical sketch of John Ericsson, Swedish-born engineer and inventor, a description of the collection, and contents by rolls.

393. Michigan. University. Library.
A catalogue of German Foreign Ministry archives, 1867-1920, microfilmed at Whaddon Hall for the University of Michigan under the direction of Howard M. Ehrmann. [Ann Arbor] 1957. 73 1.
   1. Type of microform: Microfilm.
   2. Availability: Positive copies available for purchase; also available on loan through the usual interlibrary procedure.
   3. Order: Periodicals, Microforms, Newspapers Department, University of Michigan Library, Ann Arbor, Michigan 48104.
   4. Lists the contents of the University of Michigan collection of 150 reels of microfilm copies of captured German Foreign Ministry documents. This collection does not duplicate, and, in some cases, supplements or completes other filming programs such as those of the University of California, London University, the London School of Economics, Florida State University, St. Antony's College, Oxford, and the American Committee for the Study of War Documents. The documents included cover a variety of subjects: "Italy, the colonial possessions of Italy, Egypt, British territories in Africa, Ethiopia, Persia, Afghanistan, Serbia, Montenegro, Albania, German inter-state relations, German political parties, particularism in Germany, the German navy, the future of the Baltic provinces, Belgian neutrality, Spain, the colonial possessions of Spain, the Spanish-American War, Panama and Japan."

394. Microcard Editions.
    Slave narrative collection. (In its Catalog 12, 1971-1972, p. 47)
    1. Type of microform: Microfilm.
    2. Availability: Available as a unit at price given.
    3. Orders: Order Processing Department, NCR/Microcard Editions, 365 South Oak Street, West Salem, Wisconsin 54669.
    4. Consists of the microfilm edition of the original typewritten records of over 2,000 interviews with former slaves, conducted in seventeen states from 1936 through 1938, by researchers in the Federal Writers' Project. The narratives are arranged by state of origin and within a state, alphabetically by the name of the interviewee. The original typescripts are in the Rare Book Department of the Library of Congress.

395. Morristown National Historical Park.
    A guide to the manuscript collection, Morristown National Historical Park. Bruce W. Stewart, Park historian. Hans Mayer, Park librarian. [Morristown, N.J., 1967] 142 p.
    At head of cover title: National Historical Publications Commission. Microfilm Publication Program.
    1. Type of microform: Microfilm.
    2. Availability: Complete publication (sixty-nine reels) may be purchased; individual reels also available.
    3. Orders: Superintendent, Morristown National Historical Park, 230 Morris Street, Morristown, New Jersey 07960.
    4. Originating chiefly from the bequest of Lloyd W. Smith, but with many additions, this manuscript collection consists of nearly 17,500 manuscripts, journals, account books, letter books, and military orderly books, particularly strong for the period of the American Revolution. The *Guide* gives individual microfilm reel descriptions, list of correspondents (pp. 17-110), and a selected list of recipients. The arrangement is alphabetical.

396. Neubeck, Deborah K.
    Guide to a microfilm edition of the National Nonpartisan League papers. St. Paul, Minnesota Historical Society, 1970. 22 p.
    1. Type of microform: Microfilm.
    2. Availability: Eighteen rolls and printed guide are available. Individual rolls and guide may be purchased separately.
    3. Orders: Manuscripts Department, Minnesota Historical Society, 690 Cedar Street, St. Paul, Minnesota 55101.
    4. The *Guide* provides historical background of the League, origin of the collections, description of the papers, contents by rolls, a selected list of authors, and a list of subjects covered. The last four rolls of microfilm reproduce Henry G. Teigan's papers that undoubtedly were once part of the League's records. The *Guide* and microfilm edition were made possible by a grant of funds from the National Historical Publications Commission.

397. New Mexico. State Records Center. Archives Division.
    Guide to the microfilm of the Spanish Archives of New Mexico, 1621-1821, in the Archives Division of the State of New Mexico Records

Center. A microfilm project sponsored by the National Historical Publications Commission. Microfilmed by the State of New Mexico Records Center. Santa Fe, New Mexico, 1967. 23 p.

——————Calendar of the microfilm edition. Santa Fe, N.M., 1968. 182 p.

   1. Type of microform: Microfilm.

   2. Availability: Complete set available.

   3. Orders: Archives Division, State Records Center, 404 Montezuma, Santa Fe, New Mexico 87501.

   4. The twenty-two rolls of this microfilm reproduce the extant Spanish Archives of New Mexico in the custody of the Archives Division of the State of New Mexico Records Center concerning the administration of the region from the period of Spanish colonial sovereignty to the establishment of the Mexican national government in 1821. Included also are items in the custody of the Zimmerman Library of the University of New Mexico. Filming is chronological. The *Guide* includes notes on each roll.

398. New Mexico. State Records Center. Archives Division.

Guide to the microfilm edition of the Mexican Archives of New Mexico, 1821-1846, in the Archives Division of the State of New Mexico Records Center. A microfilm project sponsored by the National Historical Publications Commission. Microfilmed by the State of New Mexico Records Center, Santa Fe, New Mexico, 1969. 26 p.

—————— Calendar . . . by Mary Ellen Jenkins. Santa Fe, New Mexico, 1970. 144 p.

   1. Type of microform: Microfilm.

   2. Availability: Complete set available.

   3. Orders: Archives Division, State Records Center, 404 Montezuma, Santa Fe, New Mexico 87501.

   4. This microfilm edition (forty-two rolls) reproduces the extant official administrative records of New Mexico under the sovereignty of the Mexican national government, August 24, 1821-August 18, 1846. Most of the originals are in the custody of the Archives Division of the State Records Center. Official documents in the Zimmerman Library of the University of New Mexico and the administrative records in the custody of the Bureau of Land Management regional office of the Department of the Interior, housed in the Federal Building in Santa Fe, are included. Filming is chronological, with the archives for each year organized into several major record groups. The *Guide* includes notes on each roll.

399. Niermann, Eleanor, ed.

Papers of John L. Lewis; guide to a microfilm edition, edited by Eleanor Niermann. Madison, Wisconsin, State Historical Society of Wisconsin, 1970. 12 p. (Guides to historical resources)

   1. Type of microform: Microfilm.

   2. Availability: Four reels and guide available.

   3. Orders: State Historical Society of Wisconsin, 816 State Street, Madison, Wisconsin 53706.

   4. "The microfilm edition of the John L. Lewis papers is the result of a co-operative effort by Cornell University, Wayne State University, and the

State Historical Society of Wisconsin in which all three pooled their financial resources to prevent the dispersal of the Lewis papers at an auction on December 7, 1969."

Lewis deposited most of his papers in the archives of the United Mine Workers of America in Washington, D.C. This microfilm collection is made up of materials which Lewis considered of a personal nature. In addition to the items bought at auction by the three institutions, the collection contains copies of many letters bought by private collectors. The *Guide* lists the important dates in Lewis' life, gives a brief bibliography, a history and a description of the collection, and outlines the contents of four reels of microfilm.

400. Nussbaum, Frederick Louis.

A check list of film copies of archival material in the University of Wyoming Library from the Public Record Office, the India Office, the British Museum in London, the Archives Nationales in Paris. Collected and cataloged by F. L. Nussbaum. [Laramie] 1936. (University of Wyoming Publications. v. 2, no. 11, p. 213-43. December 1, 1936)

    1. Type of microform: Microfilm.

    2. Availability: Prints of the microfilm are not for sale, but the microfilms may be borrowed on interlibrary loan. Hard copy can be supplied at 10¢ per frame.

    3. Orders: Interlibrary Loan Service, William Robertson Coe Library, Box 334, University Station, Wyoming 82070.

    4. Lists microfilms of archival materials collected by Mr. Nussbaum when he was a professor of history at the University of Wyoming. The purpose of the collection was to provide "materials that would serve as a basis for the training of advanced undergraduate and beginning graduate students in history in the delights and difficulties of working with unpublished materials. Hence the collection includes items of very diverse character."

401. Parral, Mexico. Archivo.

Index to El Archivo de Hidalgo del Parral, 1631-1821. [Tucson, Arizona Silhouettes, 1961] 484 p.

Photocopy (positive) made by Micro Photo, Inc., Cleveland.

    1. Type of microform: Microfilm.

    2. Availability: Complete set, over 360,000 pages, plus bound index, available.

    3. Orders: Micro Photo Division, Bell & Howell Company, Old Mansfield Road, Wooster, Ohio 44691.

    4. The Archives contain much information on the Spanish colonial era in North and West Mexico and Southwestern United States. Each year is divided into five principal sections. The first, covering official day-to-day administration of the territory "Nueva Vizcaya," includes details of livestock controls and contracts for the supply of meat to communities, judgments on commercial controls and local currency, descriptions of Indian affairs, descriptions of public entertainments, military history complete with rosters of men, animals, and equipment, and territorial censuses. The second section deals with mining claims. The third section is a collection of manuscripts describing

the residences of government officials. The fourth section provides an exhaustive example of Roman law modified and interpreted for the place and the times. Wills listed in this section provide land transaction records and inventories of personal effects. The fifth section is comprised of documents relating to crime.

402. Patton, James Welch.
[Guide to the microfilm edition of] the Benjamin Cudworth Yancey papers in the Southern Historical Collection of the University of North Carolina Library. James W. Patton, project director; Clyde Edward Pitts, editor. Chapel Hill, 1967. 13 p.
   1. Type of microform: Microfilm.
   2. Availability: Sixteen rolls with pamphlet guide available. Single rolls may be purchased, and the guide alone is available without charge.
   3. Orders: Director, Southern Historical Collection, University of North Carolina Library, Chapel Hill, North Carolina 27514.
   4. The microfilm edition, produced by the University of North Carolina Library Photographic Service, was sponsored by the National Historical Publications Commission. The *Guide* gives a brief biographical sketch of Yancey, description of the papers, and roll notes.

403. Patton, James Welch.
[Guide to the microfilm edition of] The Benjamin Franklin Perry papers in the Southern Historical Collection of the University of North Carolina Library. James W. Patton, project director; Clyde Edward Pitts, editor. Chapel Hill, 1967. [11] p.
   1. Type of microform: Microfilm.
   2. Availability: Two rolls with pamphlet guide available. The guide alone available without charge.
   3. Orders: Director, Southern Historical Collection, University of North Carolina Library, Chapel Hill, North Carolina 27514.
   4. The microfilm edition, produced by the University of North Carolina Library Photographic Service, was sponsored by the National Historical Publications Commission. The *Guide* gives a brief biographical sketch of Perry, description of the papers, roll notes, and a list of correspondents with dates of letters.

404. Patton, James Welch.
[Guide to the microfilm edition of] The Christopher Gustavus Memminger papers in the Southern Historical Collection of the University of North Carolina Library. James W. Patton, project director; Clyde Edward Pitts, editor. Chapel Hill, 1966. 9 p.
   1. Type of microform: Microfilm.
   2. Availability: One roll with pamphlet guide available. The guide alone is available without charge.
   3. Orders: Director, Southern Historical Collection, University of North Carolina Library, Chapel Hill, North Carolina 27514.
   4. The microfilm edition, produced by the University of North Carolina Library Photographic Service, was sponsored by the National Historical

Publications Commission. The *Guide* gives a brief biographical sketch of Memminger and a description of the papers.

405. Patton, James Welch.
[Guide to the microfilm edition of] The Claude Kitchin papers in the Southern Historical Collection of the University of North Carolina Library. James W. Patton, project director; Margaret Lee Neustadt, editor. Chapel Hill, 1966. 29 p.
1. Type of microform: Microfilm.
2. Availability: Forty-two rolls with pamphlet guide available. Individual rolls may be purchased separately, and the guide alone is available without charge.
3. Orders: Director, Southern Historical Collection, University of North Carolina Library, Chapel Hill, North Carolina 27514.
4. The microfilm edition, produced by the University of North Carolina Library Photographic Service, was sponsored by the National Historical Publications Commission. The *Guide* gives a description of the papers, roll notes, and a partial list of correspondents with dates of letters.

406. Patton, James Welch.
[Guide to the microfilm edition of] The David Outlaw papers in the Southern Historical Collection of the University of North Carolina Library. James W. Patton, project director; Margaret Lee Neustadt, editor. Chapel Hill, 1966. 10 p.
1. Type of microform: Microfilm.
2. Availability: One roll with pamphlet guide. The guide alone is available without charge.
3. Orders: Director, Southern Historical Collection, University of North Carolina Library, Chapel Hill, North Carolina 27514.
4. The microfilm edition, produced by the University of North Carolina Library Photographic Service, was sponsored by the National Historical Publications Commission. The *Guide* describes the papers, which are principally letters written by Outlaw to his wife when he was a member of Congress in Washington.

407. Patton, James Welch.
[Guide to the microfilm edition of] the Duff Green papers in the Southern Historical Collection of the University of North Carolina Library. James W. Patton, project director; Ritchie O. Watson, editor. Chapel Hill, 1967. 26 p.
1. Type of microform: Microfilm.
2. Availability: Twenty-five rolls with pamphlet guide available. Individual rolls may be purchased separately, and the guide alone is available without charge.
3. Orders: Director, Southern Historical Collection, University of North Carolina Library, Chapel Hill, North Carolina 27514.
4. The microfilm edition, produced by the University of North Carolina Library Photographic Service, was sponsored by the National Historical Publications Commission. The *Guide* includes a brief biographical sketch of Duff Green, description of the collection, roll notes, and a partial list of correspondents with dates of the correspondence.

408. Patton, James Welch.
    [Guide to the microfilm edition of] the Edgar Gardner Murphy papers in the Southern Historical Collection of the University of North Carolina Library. James W. Patton, project director; Margaret Lee Neustadt, editor. Chapel Hill, 1966. 10 p.
    2. Availability: One roll with pamphlet guide. The guide alone is available without charge.
    3. Orders: Director, Southern Historical Collection, University of North Carolina Library, Chapel Hill, North Carolina 27514.
    4. The microfilm edition, produced by the University of North Carolina Library Photographic Service, was sponsored by the National Historical Publications Commission. The *Guide* gives a brief biographical sketch of Murphy and a description of the papers.

409. Patton, James Welch.
    [Guide to the microfilm edition of] the Edward Dromgoole papers in the Southern Historical Collection of the University of North Carolina Library. James W. Patton, project director; Clyde Edward Pitts, editor. Chapel Hill, 1966. 13 p.
    1. Type of Microform: Microfilm.
    2. Availability: Four rolls with pamphlet guide available. Single rolls may be purchased, and the guide alone is without charge.
    3. Orders: Director, Southern Historical Collection, University of North Carolina Library, Chapel Hill, North Carolina 27514.
    4. The microfilm, produced by the University of North Carolina Library Photographic Service, was sponsored by the National Historical Publications Commission. The *Guide* gives a description of the collection, a list of correspondents, and roll notes.

410. Patton, James Welch.
    [Guide to the microfilm edition of] The Ethelbert Stewart papers in the Southern Historical Collection of the University of North Carolina Library. James W. Patton, project director; Margaret Lee Neustadt, editor. Chapel Hill, 1966. 10 p.
    1. Type of microform: Microfilm.
    2. Availability: Two rolls with pamphlet guide available. The guide alone is available without charge.
    3. Orders: Director, Southern Historical Collection, University of North Carolina Library, Chapel Hill, North Carolina 27514.
    4. The microfilm edition, produced by the University of North Carolina Library Photographic Service, was sponsored by the National Historical Publications Commission. The *Guide* includes a description of the papers and roll notes.

411. Patton, James Welch.
    [Guide to the microfilm edition of] the Henry Clay Warmoth papers in the Southern Historical Collection of the University of North Carolina Library. James W. Patton, project director; Margaret Lee Neustadt, editor. Chapel Hill, 1967. 21 p.
    1. Type of microform: Microfilm.

2. Availability: Twenty-two rolls with pamphlet guide available. Single rolls may be purchased, and the guide alone is available without charge.

3. Orders: Director, Southern Historical Collection, University of North Carolina Library, Chapel Hill, North Carolina 27514.

4. The microfilm edition, produced by the University of North Carolina Library Photographic Service, was sponsored by the National Historical Publications Commission. The *Guide* gives a brief biographical sketch of Henry Clay Warmoth, a description of the papers, roll notes, and a partial list of correspondents with dates of letters.

412. Patton, James Welch.

[Guide to the microfilm edition of] the Hilary Abner Herbert papers in the Southern Historical Collection of the University of North Carolina Library. James W. Patton, project director; Margaret Lee Neustadt, editor. Chapel Hill, 1966. 13 p.

1. Type of microform: Microfilm.

2. Availability: Two rolls with pamphlet guide available. The guide alone is available without charge.

3. Orders: Director, Southern Historical Collection, University of North Carolina Library, Chapel Hill, North Carolina 27514.

4. The microfilm edition, produced by the University of North Carolina Library Photographic Service, was sponsored by the National Historical Publications Commission. The *Guide* gives a brief sketch of Hilary Herbert and roll notes.

413. Patton, James Welch.

[Guide to the microfilm edition of] the John MacPherson Berrien papers in the Southern Historical Collection of the University of North Carolina Library. James W. Patton, project director; Margaret Lee Neustadt, editor. Chapel Hill, 1967. 14 p.

1. Type of microform: Microfilm.

2. Availability: Three rolls with pamphlet guide available. Individual rolls may be purchased separately, and the guide alone is available without charge.

3. Orders: Director, Southern Historical Collection, University of North Carolina Library, Chapel Hill, North Carolina 27514.

4. The microfilm, produced by the University of North Carolina Library Photographic Service, was sponsored by the National Historical Publications Commission. The *Guide* describes the papers, and gives roll notes and a list of correspondents with dates of letters.

414. Patton, James Welch.

[Guide to the microfilm edition of] the John Rutledge papers in the Southern Historical Collection of the University of North Carolina Library. James W. Patton, project director; Clyde Edward Pitts, editor. Chapel Hill, 1967. 12 p.

1. Type of microform: Microfilm.

2. Availability: Two rolls with pamphlet guide available. The guide alone is available without charge.

3. Orders: Director, Southern Historical Collection, University of North Carolina Library, Chapel Hill, North Carolina 27514.

4. The microfilm edition, produced by the University of North Carolina Library Photographic Service, was sponsored by the National Historical Publications Commission. The *Guide* gives biographical information about the Rutledge family of South Carolina, a description of the papers, roll notes, and a list of correspondents with dates of letters.

415. Patton, James Welch.
[Guide to the microfilm edition of the] Thomas Bragg diary, 1861-1862, in the Southern Historical Collection of the University of North Carolina Library. James W. Patton, project director; Clyde Edward Pitts, editor. Chapel Hill, 1966. 10 p.
1. Type of microform: Microfilm.
2. Availability: One roll with pamphlet guide available. The guide alone is available without charge.
3. Orders: Director, Southern Historical Collection, University of North Carolina Library, Chapel Hill, North Carolina 27514.
4. The microfilm, produced by the University of North Carolina Library Photographic Service, was sponsored by the National Historical Publications Commission. The *Guide* describes the diary which Thomas Bragg kept from January 3, 1861, to November 7, 1862, and gives a partial list of persons mentioned.

416. Patton, James Welch.
[Guide to the microfilm edition of] the Thomas Burke papers in the Southern Historical Collection of the University of North Carolina Library. James W. Patton, project director; Clyde Edward Pitts, editor. Chapel Hill, 1967. 11 p.
1. Type of microform: Microfilm.
2. Availability: Five rolls with pamphlet guide available. Single rolls may be purchased, and the guide alone is without charge.
3. Orders: Director, Southern Historical Collection, University of North Carolina Library, Chapel Hill, North Carolina 27514.
4. The microfilm, produced by the University of North Carolina Library Photographic Service, was sponsored by the National Historical Publications Commission. The Thomas Burke papers in the State Department of Archives and History in Raleigh are reproduced, as well as those in the Southern Historical Collection. The *Guide* gives a brief account of the papers and roll notes.

417. Patton, James Welch.
[Guide to the microfilm edition of] the William Gaston papers in the Southern Historical Collection of the University of North Carolina Library. James W. Patton, project director; Clyde Edward Pitts, editor. Chapel Hill, 1966. 13 p.
1. Type of microform: Microfilm.
2. Availability: Eight rolls with pamphlet guide available. Individual rolls

may be purchased separately, and the guide alone is available without charge.

3. Orders: Director, Southern Historical Collection, University of North Carolina Library, Chapel Hill, North Carolina 27514.

4. The microfilm edition, produced by the University of North Carolina Library Photographic Service, was sponsored by the National Historical Publications Commission. The *Guide* includes a description of the papers, a list of correspondents, and roll notes.

418. Patton, James Welch.
[Guide to the microfilm edition of] the William Lowndes papers in the Southern Historical Collection of the University of North Carolina Library. James W. Patton, project director, Clyde Edward Pitts, editor. Chapel Hill, 1967. 13 p.

1. Type of microform: Microfilm.

2. Availability: Two rolls with pamphlet guide available. The guide alone is available without charge.

3. Orders: Director, Southern Historical Collection, University of North Carolina Library, Chapel Hill, North Carolina 27514.

4. The microfilm edition, produced by the University of North Carolina Library Photographic Service, was sponsored by the National Historical Publications Commission. The *Guide* gives a description of the papers, roll notes, and a partial list of correspondents with dates of letters.

419. Pennsylvania. Historical and Museum Commission.
Guide to the microfilm of the Baynton, Wharton, and Morgan papers in the Pennsylvania state archives (Manuscript group 19). A microfilm project sponsored by the National Historical Publications Commission. Donald H. Kent, project director. Harrisburg, Pa., 1967. 29 p.

1. Type of microform: Microfilm.

2. Availability: Ten rolls and printed guide available. The guide may be purchased separately.

3. Orders: Pennsylvania Historical and Museum Commission, Box 232, Harrisburg, Pennsylvania 17108.

4. The microfilm edition includes the more important parts of the Baynton, Wharton, and Morgan papers, 1757-1787, which came into the possession of the Commonwealth by sequestration in legal proceedings to settle the accounts and land transactions of Peter Baynton, State Treasurer, 1797-1801. The *Guide* provides an inventory of the entire body of the sequestered papers, with careful notation of materials omitted from the microfilm. The papers are presented in the film in the order indicated in the inventory, with roll number and frames designated.

420. Pennsylvania. Historical and Museum Commission.
Guide to the microfilm of the John Nicholson papers in the Pennsylvania state archives (Manuscript group 96) . . . A microfilm project sponsored by the National Historical Publications Commission. Donald H. Kent, project director; Martha L. Simonetti, assistant project director; George R. Beyer, editor of microfilm. Harrisburg, 1967. 52 p.

1. Type of microform: Microfilm.

2. Availability: Twenty-one rolls and printed guide available. The guide may be purchased separately.

3. Orders: Pennsylvania Historical and Museum Commission, Box 232, Harrisburg, Pennsylvania 17108.

4. The microfilm includes only Nicholson's correspondence, 1778-1816, but the descriptive guide covers the entire collection which is arranged in the following groups: (1) general correspondence, 1772-1819; (2) legal papers, 1765-1800; (3) general business accounts, 1776-1800; (4) individual business accounts; (5) impeachment papers, 1783-1852. "The descriptive inventory is followed by an alphabetical list of correspondents in the General correspondence, giving name of correspondent, place, date, and frame number." The roll numbers stand out clearly, since they appear in capitals and are surrounded by sufficient white space.

421. Pfaller, Louis.
Guide to the microfilm edition of the Major James McLaughlin papers. Richardton, North Dakota, Assumption College, 1969. 23 p.

1. Type of microform: Microfilm.

2. Availability: Thirty-nine rolls and printed guide are available. Individual rolls and printed guide may be purchased separately.

3. Orders: Assumption Abbey Archives, Richardton, North Dakota 58652.

4. The *Guide* provides a brief biographical sketch of McLaughlin, a history of the collection, description of the papers, and roll notes. Rolls 31-37 consist of National Archives documents. Rolls 38-39 are index rolls containing 15,675 cross-reference cards, which give exact frame numbers on the rolls. The microfilm edition was sponsored by the Louis W. and Maud Hill Family Foundation and meets the standards expected by the National Historical Publications Commission.

422. Phillips, Venia Laota (Tarris).
Guide to the microfilm publication of the minutes and correspondence of the Academy of Natural Sciences of Philadelphia, 1812-1924. Prepared by the Academy's archivist, Venia T. Phillips; edited by Maurice E. Phillips. [Philadelphia], 1967. 92 p. (Academy of Natural Sciences of Philadelphia. Special publication no. 7)

1. Type of microform: Microfilm.

2. Availability: Thirty-eight rolls and printed guide may be purchased. Individual rolls and guide may be purchased separately. Also available on interlibrary loan.

3. Orders: Academy of Natural Sciences of Philadelphia, 19th and The Parkway, Philadelphia, Pennsylvania 19103.

4. The microfilm was produced with the assistance of the National Historical Publications Commission. The *Guide* provides a short history of the academy, contents of each roll in detail, and a list of signers of correspondence.

423. Prince, Carl E.
Guide to the microfilm edition of the papers of Albert Gallatin [by] Carl

E. Prince. Sponsored by New York University [and] The National Historical Publications Commission. Microfilm publication by Rhistoric Publications. [New York?] 1970. 29 p.

    1. Type of microform: Microfilm.

    2. Availability: Forty-six rolls; printed guide and index available. The guide, index roll, and index (copyflo) may be purchased separately. Also available through interlibrary loan from New York University Library.

    3. Orders: Rhistoric Publications, 302 North 13th Street, Philadelphia, Pennsylvania 19107.

    4. The letters and documents reproduced in the microfilm edition come from ninety archives and collections, including the extensive collections in the New York Historical Society, the National Archives, and the Library of Congress. The *Guide* provides a brief biographical sketch of Gallatin, a description of the collection, glossaries of target abbreviations, target references to published works and archival abbreviations, target symbol identifications, and roll notes.

424. Research Publications, Inc.

    Records of the Moravian Mission among the Indians of North America, filmed from the Collection of the Archives of the Moravian Church at Bethlehem, Pennsylvania. New Haven, Conn., 197? [3] p.

    1. Type of microform: Microfilm.

    2. Availability: Records and index noted below are available; index also available separately.

    3. Orders: Research Publications, Inc., Box 3903, Amity Station, New Haven, Connecticut 06525.

    4. These Indian missionary records are an important source of information for scholars in many fields. Carl John Fliegel, Research Assistant at the Archives of the Moravian Church, Bethlehem, Pennsylvania, from 1952 until his death in 1961, arranged the records in three categories: "Personalia," "Generalia," and "Indian Languages," numbering each box and each folder within a box; normally, he also identified each item within a folder. Material added since his death has been filed according to Fliegel's system of arrangement, but no additions have been made to his card index, containing approximately 135,000 entries.

    This card index, reproduced in book form, is included as part of the project. All items in the collection are identified by number and listed in a table of contents, also in book form.

425. Rhistoric Publications, Inc.

    African missionary archives of the United Society for the Propagation of the Gospel. (In its Catalog - Fall 1970. Philadelphia, 1970. p. 15) No guide available. Information from publisher, 27 July 1971.

    1. Type of microform: Microfilm.

    2. Availability: In preparation Fall 1970.

    3. Orders: Rhistoric Publications, Inc., 302 North 13th Street, Philadelphia, Pennsylvania 19107.

    4. The missionary records of the SPG (since 1965 the United Society) for South Africa include letters and papers from 1819 to 1900: correspondence

from the Bishop of the Diocese, letters from missionaries and missions' annual reports, grants, stipends, etc. All manuscripts are filed by their diocese (chronologically within each diocese). The microfilms will cover the three earliest South African dioceses of Capetown, Grahamstown, and Natal, followed about 1870 by St. John's (Kaffraria) and Zululand. The publisher states that the microfilm will be fully indexed.

426. Rhistoric Publications, Inc.
    The Archives of the Marquess of Bath at Longleat. (In its Catalog - Fall 1970. Philadelphia, 1970. p. 22) No guide available. Information from publisher, 27 July 1971.
    1. Type of microform: Microfilm.
    2. Availability: The entire collection may be purchased. The following groups of papers may be purchased separately: Devereux papers; Dudley papers; Whitlocke papers; order books of the Council of State of the Protector, Richard Cromwell; Seymour papers. Filming of the Seymour papers was incomplete at the time the catalog was printed.
    3. Orders: Rhistoric Publications, Inc., 302 North 13th Street, Philadelphia, Pennsylvania 19107.
    4. The papers of the Devereux family relate mainly to the period 1573 to 1647 and consist of the correspondence and other documents relating to Walter Devereux and his son Robert, 2d Earl of Essex. The papers of the 2d Earl are mainly concerned with his expedition to Cadiz in 1596.
    The Dudley papers in the main cover the period 1559 to 1590 and consist of personal correspondence, household and wardrobe inventories, together with miscellaneous papers of Robert Dudley, Earl of Leicester.
    The Whitlocke papers are those of Bulstrode Whitlocke, member of Parliament for Marlow in the Long Parliament, Commissioner of the Great Seal, Ambassador to Sweden, and Commissioner of the Treasury during the period of the Commonwealth.
    The fourth item is the order books of the Council of State of the Protector, Richard Cromwell (1658-1659) and certain early printed books from the library at Longleat.
    The Seymour papers consist of correspondence and accounts of the Seymour family, Earls of Hertford and later Dukes of Somerset, covering the period 1532-1686.

427. Rhistoric Publications, Inc.
    The Forster collection in the Victoria and Albert Museum. (In its Catalog - Fall 1970. Philadelphia, 1970. p. 23) No guide available. Information from publisher, 27 July 1971.
    1. Type of microform: Microfilm.
    2. Availability: Available at prices listed.
    3. Orders: Rhistoric Publications, Inc., 302 North 13th Street, Philadelphia, Pennsylvania 19107.
    4. The manuscripts and autograph letters in the Forster collection are cataloged in South Kensington Museum, London, Forster Collection, *Forster Collection: A Catalogue of the Paintings, Manuscripts, Autograph Letters, Pamphlets, etc. . . .* (London, 1893). The microfilms presently available, made

by Micro Methods, Ltd., and distributed in the United States by Rhistoric Publications, cover the major holdings in the collection. Included are the majority of the manuscripts and annotated proofs of Charles Dickens, correspondence of the 1st and 2d Dukes of Ormonde, the 1st Earl of Orrery, Robert Southey, and David Garrick. Not included in the microfilm edition are single letters or isolated manuscript pages. The Dickens manuscripts and proofs are not at the present time distributed by Rhistoric Publications or listed in their catalog.

428. Rhistoric Publications, Inc.
Indian mission archives of the Society for the Propagation of the Gospel. Introduction by Isobel Pridmore, archivist to the U.S.P.G. (In its Catalog - Fall 1970. Philadelphia, 1970. p. 17) No guide available. Information from publisher, 27 July 1971.
    1. Type of microform: Microfilm.
    2. Availability: The complete series or individual series may be purchased: Series E 1856-1900, Missionary reports; Series E/PRE 1840-1861, Ceylon/ Madras/Calcutta; Series C/IND/GEN ca. 1770-184, Missionary records, Boxes 1-7; Calendars only 1815-1859, Calcutta/Madras/Bombay and Rev. Christian David: Letterbook Vol. 3 (1818-24).
    3. Orders: Rhistoric Publications, Inc., 302 North 13th Street, Philadelphia, Pennsylvania 19107.
    4. The earliest archives cover the period before the SPG was at work in India. The Danish mission was founded by Frederick IV of Denmark, who sent two missionaries to South India in 1705. It was partly funded by the Society for Promoting Christian Knowledge, which became responsible for the English mission in 1726. In 1825 the SPG assumed responsibility for the whole area, by now a British possession. With the creation of the See of Calcutta in 1814, SPG was free to begin work in India and from that date has its own archives.
    The microfilm was reproduced from the originals in the possession of the United Society for the Propagation of the Gospel, successor to the SPG.

429. Rhistoric Publications, Inc.
Indian Rights Association. [Letters sent and received, 1883-1901] (In its Catalog - Fall 1970. Philadelphia, 1970. p. 16) No guide available. Information from publisher, 27 July 1971.
    1. Type of microform: Microfilm.
    2. Availability: Available at listed price.
    3. Orders: Rhistoric Publications, Inc., 302 North 13th Street, Philadelphia, Pennsylvania 19107.
    4. "The microfilm includes Letters Sent and Letters Received for the years 1883 through 1901. The letters are of a wide variety, from Presidents, Secretaries of the Interior, Commissioners of Indian Affairs and leading reformers of the period, as well as a wide sampling of grass-roots letters. Also included is the Welsh Collection which comprises Mr. Welsh's [Corresponding Secretary of the Association] correspondence, editorial works and other comments he considered pertinent." The originals are in the manuscript collections of the Historical Society of Pennsylvania.

430. Rhistoric Publications, Inc.
The papers of the Pennsylvania Abolitionist Society. (In its Catalog - Fall 1970. Philadelphia, 1970. p. 11) No guide available. Information from publisher, 27 July 1971.
    1. Type of microform: Microfilm.
    2. Availability: Available at listed price.
    3. Orders: Rhistoric Publications, Inc., 302 North 13th Street, Philadelphia, Pennsylvania 19107.
    4, "This collection, owned by the Historical Society of Pennsylvania, commences with minutes and manuscripts of the Susan Parrish Wharton Collection compiled by 'The Society for the Relief of Free Negroes Unlawfully kept in Bondage' which was organized in 1775. . . . Temporarily suspended during war years it was vigorously reactivated in 1787 and adopted the title of 'The Pennsylvania Society for Promoting the Abolition of Slavery and the Relief of Free Negroes Unlawfully held in Bondage.' . . . Minutes from 1787 to 1916 are a part of this set and are followed by an unusually extensive manuscript collection (1787 through 1868). . . . The collection is summarized and analyzed in a history of the Society by William J. Buck which is in manuscript form and never before published."

431. Rhistoric Publications, Inc.
The Socialist party of the United States. The personal papers of Darlington Hoopes. (In its Catalog - Fall 1970. Philadelphia, 1970. p. 8). No guide available. Information from publisher, 27 July 1971.
    1. Type of microform: Microfilm.
    2. Availability: Available at listed price.
    3. Orders: Rhistoric Publications, Inc., 302 North 13th Street, Philadelphia, Pennsylvania 19107.
    4. Darlington Hoopes served as state secretary of the Pennsylvania Socialist party from 1923 to 1927, socialist member of the Pennsylvania General Assembly from 1930 to 1936, National Chairman of the Socialist party of the United States from 1946 to 1968, and presidential candidate of the Socialist Party in the elections of 1952 and 1956. The collection consists of three main groupings: material pertaining to the Socialist party of the United States from 1917 to 1968; Pennsylvania Socialist party material from 1921 to 1952; and records of the Reading, Pa., Socialist party from 1915 to 1960.

432. Robin, Richard Shale.
Annotated catalogue of the papers of Charles S. Peirce. [Amherst] University of Massachusetts Press, 1967. 268 p.
    1. Type of microform: Microfilm.
    2. Availability: Thirty-two rolls available for purchase. Individual rolls may also be purchased.
    3. Orders: Photographic Division, Widener Library, Harvard University, Cambridge, Massachusetts 02138.
    4. The *Catalogue* provides a key to the contents of Peirce's papers, both the original papers which are housed in the Houghton Library, Harvard University, and the microfilm edition.

433. Rylance, Daniel.
    Guide to the microfilm edition of the Dakota territorial records. Grand
Forks, Orin G. Libby Manuscript Collection, University of North Dakota,
1969. 44 p.
    1. Type of microform: Microfilm.
    2. Availability: Eighty-six rolls and printed guide available. Guide may be
purchased separately.
    3. Orders: Curator of the Libby Manuscript Collection, Chester Fritz
Library, University of North Dakota, Grand Forks, North Dakota 58201.
    4. The *Guide* gives an explanation of the territorial system, a history of
the Territory of Dakota (1861-1889), a bibliography, and the contents of the
microfilm by rolls. The microfilm edition was produced with the assistance of
the National Historical Publications Commission.

434. St. Louis University. Libraries.
    A checklist of Vatican manuscript codices available for consultation at the
Knights of Columbus Vatican Film Library. (In *Manuscripta*. vol. 1 (1957)
pp. 27-44, 104-16, 139-74; vol. 2 (1958) pp. 41-49, 84-99, 167-81; vol. 3
(1959) pp. 38-46, 89-99; vol. 12 (1968) pp. 176-78. Appendix.)
    1. Type of microform: Microfilm.
    2. Availability: Scholars interested in Vatican manuscripts are welcome to
use them in the Pius XII Memorial Library of St. Louis University. Reels of
microfilm are not available on interlibrary loan, but reproductions of individual manuscripts may be ordered through the St. Louis University Library
from the Vatican Library in Rome.
    3. Orders: Inquiries should be addressed to: Charles J. Ermatinger, Li-
brarian, Knights of Columbus Vatican Film Library, Pius XII Memorial
Library, St. Louis University, 3655 West Pine Boulevard, St. Louis, Missouri
63108.
    4. The *Checklist* consists of the codex numbers of Vatican Library manu-
scripts microfilmed over a period of years for the Knights of Columbus
Vatican Film Library. In *Manuscripta* 12 (1968): 170-75, Charles J.
Ermatinger discusses several related projects in his article "Projects and
Acquisitions in the Vatican Film Library."

435. Saint John's University, Collegeville, Minn.
    Checklist of manuscripts microfilmed for the Monastic Manuscript Micro-
film Library, Saint John's University, Collegeville, Minnesota. Compiled by
Julian G. Plante, curator. Volume 1: Austrian monasteries. Part 1. Collegeville, Minn., 1967.
    1. Type of microform: Microfilm.
    2. Availability: Films cannot be reproduced without the explicit written
permission of the library owning the original document.
    3. Orders: Inquiries regarding visits to St. John's and permission for
obtaining copies should be directed to: Professor Julian G. Plante, Curator,
Monastic Manuscript Microfilm Library, St. John's University, Collegeville,
Minnesota 56321.
    4. The Monastic Manuscript Microfilm Library began in 1964 a project to
microfilm all medieval manuscripts dating before the year 1600 belonging to

European monastic libraries. The codex numbers constituting the checklist are the officially accepted ones by which the individual codices are identified and cited. Each microfilmed manuscript is on a separate reel and each reel is assigned a project number which is also supplied in this list. A list of the forty-three Austrian collections photographed is included. Part 1 includes sixteen of the forty-three. Each collection is headed by a note giving the number of manuscripts filmed and where a catalog of the collection may be found.

436. Schwändt, Ernst.
Index of microfilmed records of the German foreign ministry and the Reich's Chancellery covering the Weimar Period. Washington, National Archives, 1958. 95 p.
  1. Type of microform: Microfilm.
  2. Availability: May be purchased whole or in part.
  3. Orders: Checks or money orders should be made payable to the General Services Administration, and sent to: Cashier, National Archives and Records Service, Washington, D.C. 20408.
  4. "The microfilm described in this list is part of National Archives Record group 242, World War II Collection of Seized Enemy Records." The *Index* was prepared under the direction of the Committee on War Documents of the American Historical Association. For each file on film, the *Index* gives the provenance, title, volume number, date, serial number, container number, and frame numbers. Each serial is covered by a data sheet included in the film.

437. Service International de Microfilm.
Epistolae Haereticorum. Le célèbre recueil conservé à Paris est entièrement reproduit dans cette édition sur microfilm . . . Paris, 1968. 14 p.
  1. Type of microform: Microfilm.
  2. Availability: A copy of the film may be purchased.
  3. Orders: Service International de Microfilms, 9, rue du Commandant-Rivière, Paris VIIIᵉ, France.
  4. This guide to the microfilm of the *Epistolae Haereticorum* is a reprint of the detailed description of the manuscript taken from volume 2 of the *Catalogue des Manuscrits* of the Bibliothèque Sainte-Geneviève (Paris: Plon, Nourrit et Cie, 1896). The manuscript consists of five volumes (5,570 pages). The contents of each volume are given in great detail together with helpful notes.

438. Smith, Lester W.
Guide to the microfilm edition of the Peter B. Porter papers in the Buffalo and Erie County Historical Society. Lester W. Smith, project director; Arthur C. Detmers, Jr., editor. Buffalo, Buffalo and Erie County Historical Society, 1968. 22,[1] p.
  1. Type of microform: Microfilm.
  2. Availability: Thirteen rolls with pamphlet guide available. Individual rolls may also be purchased. The microfilm is also available on interlibrary

loan. A request for interlibrary loan should be addressed to the Library of the Historical Society at the address noted below.

3. Orders: Buffalo and Erie County Historical Society, 25 Nottingham Court, Buffalo, New York 14216.

4. The papers reproduced in this microfilm publication are those of Peter B. Porter (1773-1844), one of the influential national and local figures in the early history of Western New York—a Congressman, a major general of militia in the War of 1812, and Secretary of War. He played a significant role in the early transportation industry of the area and was a pioneer in other aspects of its economic development. Also included in the publication are papers of Peter B. Porter's grandson, Peter A. Porter (1853-1925), but the bulk of the collection consists of Peter B. Porter's papers covering the period from 1810 to 1844.

Following the introduction, which includes biographical sketches, there are explanations of the arrangement of the papers, the classification system used, the types and forms of documents, and the card catalogs (author and subject) for the collection. The content and provenance of the collection are discussed, and information or related materials in other collections and in published sources is given. Next there is an outline showing the contents of each roll of microfilm, followed by notes on the contents of each of the rolls.

This pamphlet and the microfilm of the Porter papers were made possible by a grant from the National Historical Publications Commission.

439. Snell, Joseph W.

Guide to the microfilm edition of the Anderson family papers, 1802-1905, in the Kansas State Historical Society. Editor: Joseph W. Snell; assistant editor: Mrs. Eunice L. Schenck; microfilm technician: George T. Hawley. Topeka, Kansas, Kansas State Historical Society, 1967. 7 p.

1. Type of microform: Microfilm.

2. Availability: Three rolls and pamphlet guide available. Individual rolls and guide may be purchased separately.

3. Orders: Microfilm Publications, Kansas State Historical Society, 120 West Tenth Street, Topeka, Kansas 66612.

4. The microfilm edition and the *Guide* were published with the aid of a grant from the National Historical Publications Commission. The *Guide* gives a brief sketch of the persons involved (John Anderson, John Byars Anderson, William C. Anderson, and John Alexander Anderson), a description of the collection, and contents of the rolls.

440. Snell, Joseph W.

Guide to the microfilm edition of the Chester I. Long papers, 1890-1928, in the Kansas State Historical Society. Editor: Joseph W. Snell; assistant editor: Mrs. Eunice L. Schenck; microfilm technician: George T. Hawley. Topeka, Kansas, Kansas State Historical Society, 1967. 10 p.

2. Type of microform: Microfilm.

2. Availability: Thirty-one rolls and pamphlet guide available. Individual rolls and guide may be purchased separately.

3. Orders: Microfilm Publications, Kansas State Historical Society, 120 West Tenth Street, Topeka, Kansas 66612.

4. The microfilm publication of the Long papers and the pamphlet guide were made possible by a grant from the National Historical Publications Commission. The *Guide* gives a brief sketch of Long's life, a description of the collection, and contents of the rolls.

441. Snell, Joseph W.
Guide to the microfilm edition of the Isaac McCoy papers, 1808-1874, in the Kansas State Historical Society. Editor: Joseph W. Snell; assistant editor: Mrs. Eunice L. Schenck; microfilm technician: George T. Hawley. Topeka, Kansas, Kansas State Historical Society, 1967. 9 p.
1. Type of microform: Microfilm.
2. Availability: Thirteen rolls and pamphlet guide available. Individual rolls and guide may be purchased separately.
3. Orders: Microfilm Publications, Kansas State Historical Society, 120 West Tenth Street, Topeka, Kansas 66612.
4. The microfilm publication of the McCoy papers, concerned mostly with Indian missions, and the pamphlet guide were made possible by a grant from the National Historical Publications Commission. The *Guide* gives a brief biographical sketch, a description of the collection, and contents of the rolls. A calendar of correspondence appears at the beginning of the first roll.

442. Snell, Joseph W.
Guide to the microfilm edition of the John G. Pratt papers, 1834-1899, in the Kansas State Historical Society. Editor: Joseph W. Snell; assistant editors: Mrs. Eunice L. Schenck, Eugene D. Decker; microfilm technician: George T. Hawley. Topeka, Kansas, Kansas State Historical Society, 1967. 9 p.
1. Type of microform: Microfilm.
2. Availability: Twelve rolls with pamphlet guide available. Individual rolls and guide may be purchased separately.
3. Orders: Microfilm Publications, Kansas State Historical Society, 120 West Tenth Street, Topeka, Kansas 66612.
4. The microfilm edition and the *Guide* were made possible by a grant from the National Historical Publications Commission. The *Guide* includes a biographical sketch of John G. Pratt, a description of the collection, and contents of the rolls.

443. Snell, Joseph W.
Guide to the microfilm edition of the John Stillman Brown family papers, 1818-1907, in the Kansas State Historical Society. Editor: Joseph W. Snell; assistant editor: Mrs. Eunice L. Schenck; microfilm technician: George T. Hawley. Topeka, Kansas, Kansas State Historical Society, 1967. 7 p.
1. Type of microform: microfilm.
2. Availability: Four rolls and pamphlet guide available. Individual rolls and guide may be purchased separately.
3. Orders: Microfilm Publications, Kansas State Historical Society, 120 West Tenth Street, Topeka, Kansas 66612.
4. The publication of the *Guide* and the microfilm was made possible by a grant from the National Historical Publications Commission. The *Guide*

gives a brief sketch of John Stillman Brown and his family, a description of the collection, contents of the rolls, and an index to the correspondence.

444. Snell, Joseph W.
Guide to the microfilm edition of the Joseph Little Bristow papers, 1894-1925, in the Kansas State Historical Society. Editor: Joseph W. Snell; assistant editor: Mrs. Eunice L. Schenck; microfilm technician: George T. Hawley. Topeka, Kansas, Kansas State Historical Society, 1967. 16 p.
1. Type of microform: Microfilm.
2. Availability: 119 rolls and printed guide available. Individual rolls and guide may be purchased separately.
3. Orders: Microfilm Publications, Kansas State Historical Society, 120 West Tenth Street, Topeka, Kansas 66612.
4. The publication of the microfilm and the *Guide* was made possible by a grant from the National Historical Publications Commission. The *Guide* provides a chronology of the life of Joseph L. Bristow, a description of the collection and contents by rolls.

445. Snell, Joseph W.
Guide to the microfilm edition of the Jotham Meeker papers, 1825-1864, in the Kansas State Historical Society. Editor: Joseph W. Snell; assistant editors: Mrs. Eunice L. Schenck [and] Don W. Wilson; microfilm technician: George T. Hawley. Topeka, Kansas, Kansas State Historical Society, 1967. [6] p.
1. Type of microform: Microfilm.
2. Availability: Two rolls and pamphlet guide available. Microfilm and guide also available on interlibrary loan.
3. Orders: Microfilm Publications, Kansas State Historical Society, 120 West Tenth Street, Topeka, Kansas 66612.
4. This brief *Guide* presents biographical information about the Rev. Jotham Meeker, Baptist minister, Indian missionary, and printer, and a description of his correspondence and papers, which are in the possession of the Kansas State Historical Society. Several helpful secondary works are cited and related manuscript collections of the Society are noted. The publication of this *Guide* and microfilm publication was made possible by a grant from the National Historical Publications Commission.

446. Snell, Joseph W.
Guide to the microfilm edition of the New England Emigrant Aid Company papers, 1854-1909, in the Kansas State Historical Society. Editor: Joseph W. Snell; assistant editor: Mrs. Eunice L. Schenck; microfilm technician: George T. Hawley. Topeka, Kansas, Kansas State Historical Society, 1967. 22 p.
1. Type of microform: Microfilm.
2. Availability: Nine rolls and pamphlet guide available. Individual rolls and guide may be purchased separately.
3. Orders: Microfilm Publications, Kansas State Historical Society, 120 West Tenth Street, Topeka, Kansas 66612.
4. The *Guide* and the microfilm publication were made possible by a

grant from the National Historical Publications Commission. The *Guide* gives a brief account of the New England Emigrant Aid Company, the official records and correspondence of which appear in the microfilm, a description of the collection, the contents of the rolls, and an index to correspondence. The index appears also on rolls one and two, preceding the correspondence.

447. Snell, Joseph W.
Guide to the microfilm edition of the private papers of Charles and Sara T. D. Robinson, 1834-1911, in the Kansas State Historical Society. Editor: Joseph W. Snell; assistant editor: Mrs. Eunice L. Schenck; microfilm technician: George T. Hawley. Topeka, Kansas, Kansas State Historical Society, 1967. 14 p.
  1. Type of microform: Microfilm.
  2. Availability: Thirteen rolls with pamphlet guide available. Individual rolls and guide may be purchased separately.
  3. Orders: Microfilm Publications, Kansas State Historical Society, 120 West Tenth Street, Topeka, Kansas 66612.
  4. The *Guide* and microfilm publication were made possible by a grant from the National Historical Publications Commission. The *Guide* gives brief biographical sketches of Charles Robinson and his wife, a description of the collection, the contents of the rolls, and an index to the correspondence.

448. Snell, Joseph W.
Guide to the microfilm edition of the Thaddeus Hyatt papers, 1843-1898, in the Kansas State Historical Society. Editor: Joseph W. Snell; assistant editors: Mrs. Eunice L. Schenck, Don W. Wilson; microfilm technician: George T. Hawley. Topeka, Kansas, Kansas State Historical Society, 1967. 10 p.
  1. Type of microform: Microfilm.
  2. Availability: Two rolls and pamphlet guide available. Individual rolls and guide may be purchased separately.
  3. Orders: Microfilm Publications, Kansas State Historical Society, 120 West Tenth Street, Topeka, Kansas 66612.
  4. The microfilm edition and the *Guide* were made possible by a grant from the National Historical Publications Commission. The *Guide* gives a very brief biographical sketch of Thaddeus Hyatt, a description of the collection, contents of the rolls, and index to the correspondence.

449. Snell, Joseph W.
Guide to the microfilm edition of the Thomas Ewing, Jr., papers, 1856-1908, in the Kansas State Historical Society. Editor: Joseph W. Snell; assistant editor: Mrs. Eunice L. Schenck; microfilm technician: George T. Hawley. Topeka, Kansas, Kansas State Historical Society, 1967. 6 p.
  1. Type of microform: Microfilm.
  2. Availability: Two rolls and pamphlet guide available. Individual rolls and guide may be purchased separately.
  3. Orders: Microfilm Publications, Kansas State Historical Society, 120 West Tenth Street, Topeka, Kansas 66612.
  4. The microfilm publication of the private and business correspondence of Thomas Ewing, Jr., the legal correspondence of the Leavenworth law

firms with which he was associated, and the pamphlet guide were made possible by a grant from the National Historical Publications Commission. The *Guide* gives a brief sketch of Ewing's life, a description of the collection, and contents of the rolls. An index to the addressees appears at the beginning of each roll.

450. Studley, Miriam V., ed.

Guide to the microfilm edition of the Stevens family papers, edited by Miriam V. Studley, Charles F. Cummings, and Thaddeus J. Krom. Newark, N.J., The New Jersey Historical Society, 1968. 32 p.

    1. Type of microform: Microfilm.

    2. Availability: Forty-six rolls and printed guide available. Individual rolls and guide may be purchased separately or borrowed through interlibrary loan.

    3. Orders: New Jersey Historical Society, 230 Broadway, Newark, New Jersey 07104.

    4. The *Guide* provides a brief account of the Stevens family, a discussion of finding aids to the papers, an explanation of the filming plan, and roll notes. Besides the papers of six generations of the Stevens family, the collection includes the papers of the Hoboken Land and Improvement Company. The preparation and filming were made possible by a grant from the National Historical Publications Commission.

451. U.S. Department of State. Historical Office.

A catalog of files and microfilms of the German Foreign Ministry archives, 1920-1945. Compiled and edited by George O. Kent, Historical Office, Department of State. Stanford, Calif., Hoover Institution, Stanford University, 1962-   (Hoover Institution Publications)

    v. 1-3 published, 1962-66. To be completed with v. 4.

    1. Type of microform: Microfilm.

    2. Availability: Available for use at the National Archives in Washington and at the Public Record Office in London. Positive copies of complete rolls available for purchase at prices listed in the "National Archives Supplement" appearing in each volume of the *Guide*.

    3. Orders: Orders accompanied by check or money order made payable to the General Services Administration should be sent to: Cashier, National Archives and Record Service, Washington, D.C. 20408.

    Orders from outside the United States and its possessions should be accompanied by an international money order or check drawn in United States dollars on a bank in the United States and made payable to the General Services Administration and sent to the address noted above.

    4. The *Catalog* lists all the files of the Politisches Archiv (1920-1945) which were seized by the American and British armies at the end of World War II and indicates which of the files are available on microfilm. It is a continuation of *A Catalogue of Files and Microfilms of the German Foreign Ministry Archives, 1867-1920*, published in 1959 by the Committee for the Study of War Documents of the American Historical Association.

452. U.S. Library of Congress.

A descriptive checklist of selected manuscripts in the monasteries of Mount Athos microfilmed for the Library of Congress and the International Greek New Testament project, 1952-53. Together with listings of photoreproductions of other manuscripts in monasteries of Mt. Athos, prepared by Harvard University, Cambridge, Massachusetts, Institut de Recherche et d'Histoire des Textes, Paris, France, and the Deutsche Akademie der Wissenschaften zu Berlin, Berlin, Germany. Compiled under the general direction of Ernest W. Saunders . . . Prepared for the press by Charles G. LaHood, Jr. . . . Washington, Library of Congress Photoduplication Service, 1957. 36 p.

1. Type of microform: Microfilm.

2. Availability: Positive copies of microfilms in the Library of Congress are available in quantities of one or more reels at currently published rates. Inquiries concerning copies of photoreproductions of manuscripts in other institutions should be made directly to the institutions.

3. Orders: Photoduplication Service, Library of Congress, Washington, D.C. 20540.

4. Lists and describes manuscripts belonging to the various monasteries on Mt. Athos, Greece, of which photoreproductions have been made. Part I describes the 209 Greek and Georgian Biblical manuscripts and selected portions of 44 other manuscripts containing apocrypha and writings of several of the early Church Fathers, which were microfilmed in 1952-53 for the Library of Congress and the International Greek New Testament Project.

Part II lists photocopies of manuscripts from monasteries on Mt. Athos available from: Deutsche Akademie der Wissenschaften, Berlin, Germany; Harvard University, Cambridge, Massachusetts; and the Institut de Recherche et d'Histoire des Textes, Paris, France. Arrangement of Part II is by name of monastery.

The bibliography lists three manuscript catalogs which were microfilmed and published catalogs of Mt. Athos manuscripts.

453. U.S. Library of Congress. Manuscript Division.

Calendar of the papers of Martin Van Buren, prepared from the original manuscripts in the Library of Congress, by Elizabeth Howard West, Division of Manuscripts. Washington, Govt. Print. Off., 1910. 757 p.

1. Type of microform: Microfilm.

2. Availability: Positive copies of the Van Buren papers may be purchased. A positive print is also available for interlibrary loan through the Chief, Loan Division, Library of Congress.

3. Orders: Photoduplication Service, Library of Congress, Washington, D.C. 20540.

4. Since no index for the microfilm edition of Van Buren's papers (35 reels) has been published, the *Calendar* of his papers prepared by Dorothy H. West will be useful in searching for specific documents. In the *Calendar*, documents are arranged chronologically with full descriptive notes, and there is a detailed name and subject index.

454. U.S. Library of Congress. Manuscript Division.

Index to the Abraham Lincoln papers. Washington, 1960. 124 p. (*Its Presidents' papers index series*)

1. Type of microform: Microfilm.

2. Availability: Positive copies of the microfilm of the Lincoln papers may be purchased. (A reedited microfilm made in 1959 supersedes the one made in 1947.) A positive print is also available for interlibrary loan through the Chief, Loan Division, Library of Congress.

3. Orders: Photoduplication Service, Library of Congress, Washington, D.C. 20540.

4. This *Index* provides access to the Lincoln papers (14,724 pieces on 97 reels) owned by the Library of Congress. The introduction to the *Index* gives a brief account of the provenance of the papers with reference to other accounts, instructions on how to use the *Index*, and a reel list. Mechanically reproduced by the use of key-punched cards, the *Index* is primarily a name index and not a subject index. Names of writers and recipients are alphabetically arranged. For each entry are given date, series, and number of pages, and in the last column, headed "Addenda," is recorded useful information which could not fit into the closely calculated spacing of the main entry. On pp. 122-23 is found a description of the three series in which the papers are arranged, plus a complete list of accessions showing sources of acquisition.

455. U.S. Library of Congress. Manuscript Division.

Index to the Andrew Jackson papers. Washington, 1967. 111 p. (*Its* Presidents' papers index series)

1. Type of microform: Microfilm.

2. Availability: Positive copies of the microfilm of the Jackson Papers may be purchased. A positive print is also available for interlibrary loan through the Chief, Loan Service, Library of Congress.

3. Orders: Photoduplication Service, Library of Congress, Washington, D.C. 20540.

4. This *Index* provides access to the Jackson papers (seventy-eight reels of microfilm) owned by the Library of Congress. The introduction to the *Index* includes an interesting essay on the provenance of the papers, a description of the contents of the eleven series in which the papers are arranged, a reel list, and instructions about how to use the *Index*. Produced electronically by the use of key-punched cards, the *Index* is basically a name index and not a subject index. Names of writers and recipients are alphabetically arranged. For each entry are given date, series, number of pages, and, in the last column, headed "Addenda," helpful information which could not fit into the closely calculated spacing of the main entry.

456. U.S. Library of Congress. Manuscript Division.

Index to the Andrew Johnson papers. Washington, 1963. 154 p. (*Its* Presidents' papers index series)

1. Type of microform: Microfilm.

2. Availability: Positive copies of the Andrew Johnson papers may be purchased. A positive print is also available for interlibrary loan through the Chief, Loan Division, Library of Congress.

3. Orders: Photoduplication Service, Library of Congress, Washington, D.C. 20540.

4. This *Index* provides access to the Andrew Johnson papers (fifty-five

reels of microfilm) owned by the Library of Congress. The introduction to the *Index* includes a brief essay on the provenance of the papers, instructions on how to use the *Index*, and a reel list. Produced by the use of key-punched cards, which were sorted and printed mechanically, the *Index* is primarily a name index and not a subject index. Names of writers and recipients are arranged alphabetically. For each entry are given date, series, number of pages, and, in the last column headed "Addenda," helpful information which could not fit in the closely calculated spacing of the main entry. On pp. 150-153 is found a description of the twenty series in which the papers are arranged and a list of accessions showing sources of acquisition.

457. U.S. Library of Congress. Manuscript Division.
     Index to the Benjamin Harrison papers. Washington, 1964. 333 p. (*Its* Presidents' papers index series)
     1. Type of microform: Microfilm.
     2. Availability: Positive prints of the Benjamin Harrison papers may be purchased. A positive print is also available for interlibrary loan through the Chief, Loan Division, Library of Congress.
     3. Orders: Photoduplication Service, Library of Congress, Washington, D.C. 20540.
     4. This *Index* provides access to the Benjamin Harrison papers (69,612 items reproduced on 151 reels of microfilm) which cover every aspect of Harrison's life and career. The introduction includes a brief essay on the provenance of the papers, a reel list, and instructions on the use of the *Index*. On pp. 328-332 is found a description of the papers as organized in 19 series, plus a complete list of accessions showing source of acquisition. Produced mechanically by the use of key-punched cards, the *Index* is basically a name and not a subject index. The names of writers and recipients are arranged in alphabetical order, and for each entry are given date, series, and number of pages. A column headed "Addenda" is used for helpful data that could not fit into the closely calculated spacing of the main entry.

458. U.S. Library of Congress. Manuscript Division.
     Index to the Calvin Coolidge papers. Washington, 1965. 34 p. (*Its* Presidents' papers index series)
     1. Type of microform: Microfilm.
     2. Availability: Positive copies of the microfilm of the Coolidge papers may be purchased. A positive print is also available for interlibrary loan through the Chief, Loan Division, Library of Congress.
     3. Orders: Photoduplication Service, Library of Congress, Washington, D.C. 20540.
     4. The introduction to the *Index* contains a brief essay on the provenance of the Coolidge papers (over 175,000 pieces on 190 reels) owned by the Library of Congress. Despite its large number of manuscripts, this collection does not provide enough material for a thorough study of Coolidge's long career of public service, nor does the smaller collection in the Forbes Library in Northampton contain many manuscripts of much value in this respect. "The evidence is . . . quite strong that Coolidge eliminated, if not quite all, at least a large part of his personal papers." Following the essay on the

provenance of the papers is a description of the contents of the three series in which they are arranged, followed by a reel list and instructions on how to use the *Index*. "The character of the surviving Coolidge Papers is such that it was decided that . . . [the] index would be organized around the 'case files' and subject titles of the collection's contents, together with cross references. In consequence, this index is much smaller than would be one which indexed every correspondent and every letter." The *Index*, mechanically produced by the use of key-punched cards, provides in columns: (1) an alphabetical list of case file titles and cross-references; (2) series; (3) case file number; (4) number of pages; and (5) "Addenda," helpful information which it was impossible to include in the closely calculated spacing of the first or main entry column.

459. U.S. Library of Congress. Manuscript Division.
    Index to the Chester A. Arthur papers. Washington, 1961 [i.e., 1962] 13 p. (*Its* Presidents' papers index series)
    1. Type of microform: Microfilm.
    2. Availability: Positive copies of the microfilm of the Arthur papers may be purchased. A positive print is also available for interlibrary loan through the Chief, Loan Division, Library of Congress.
    3. Orders: Photoduplication Service, Library of Congress, Washington, D.C. 20540.
    4. The introduction to the *Index* includes a brief essay on the provenance of the Arthur papers (1,413 items on 3 reels of microfilm) owned by the Library of Congress, instructions on how to use the *Index*, and a reel list. Produced by the use of key-punched cards which were sorted and printed mechanically, the *Index* is essentially a name index and not a subject index. Names of writers and recipients are arranged alphabetically. For each entry are given date, series, number of pages, and, in the last column headed "Addenda," helpful information which could not fit into the closely calculated spacing of the main entry. On p. 12 is a description of the contents of the three series in which the papers are arranged, plus a complete list of accessions showing sources of acquisition.

460. U.S. Library of Congress. Manuscript Division.
    Index to the Franklin Pierce papers. Washington, 1962. 16 p. (*Its* Presidents' papers index series)
    1. Type of microform: Microfilm.
    2. Availability: Positive copies of the microfilm of the Pierce papers may be purchased. A positive print is also available for interlibrary loan through the Chief, Loan Division, Library of Congress.
    3. Orders: Photoduplication Service, Library of Congress, Washington, D.C. 20540.
    4. This *Index* provides access to the Pierce papers (seven reels of microfilm) owned by the Library of Congress, plus photocopies of those owned by the New Hampshire Historical Society and the Henry E. Huntington Library. The introduction to the *Index* includes a concise essay on the provenance of the papers, instructions on how to use the *Index*, and a reel list. Produced mechanically by means of key-punched cards, the *Index* is basically a name

index and not a subject index. Names of writers and recipients are arranged alphabetically. For each document are given date, series, number of pages, and in the final column, headed "Addenda," helpful information that could not fit into the closely calculated spacing of the main entry. On p. 15 is found a description of the contents of the five series in which the papers are arranged, plus a complete list of acquisitions since 1902.

461. U.S. Library of Congress. Manuscript Division.
Index to the George Washington papers. Washington, 1964. 294 p. (*Its Presidents' papers index series*)
   1. Type of microform: Microfilm.
   2. Availability: Positive copies of the microfilm of the Washington papers may be purchased. A positive print is also available for interlibrary loan through the Chief, Loan Division, Library of Congress.
   3. Orders: Photoduplication Service, Library of Congress, Washington, D.C. 20540.
   4. This *Index* provides access to the Washington papers (64,786 original manuscripts reproduced on 124 reels of microfilm) owned by the Library of Congress. In addition to the original manuscripts, the Library of Congress also owns photocopies of a number of manuscripts. In the 1920s and 1930s, the Library made an intensive effort to assemble photocopies of Washington manuscripts in other institutions and in private hands. This supplementary photocopy material was not filmed but may be consulted in the Manuscript Division of the Library of Congress. The introduction to the *Index* includes an interesting essay on the provenance of the papers, a description of the contents of the seven series in which they are arranged, a reel list, and instructions about how to use the *Index* to locate a specific document. Mechanically produced by means of key-punched cards, the *Index* is basically a name index and not a subject index. Arranged alphabetically by the name of the writer or recipient, it provides date, series, and number of pages, and, in a fifth column headed "Addenda," gives helpful data which could not fit into the limited spacing of the main entry.

462. U.S. Library of Congress. Manuscript Division.
Index to the Grover Cleveland papers. Washington, 1965. 345 p. (*Its Presidents' papers index series*)
   1. Type of microform: Microfilm.
   2. Availability: Positive copies of the microfilm of the Cleveland papers may be purchased. A positive print is also available for interlibrary loan through the Chief, Loan Division, Library of Congress.
   3. Orders: Photoduplication Service, Library of Congress, Washington, D.C. 20540.
   4. This *Index* provides access to the Cleveland papers (87,027 manuscripts reproduced on 164 reels) owned by the Library of Congress. The introduction to the *Index* gives a brief essay on the provenance of the papers, a description of the contents of the ten series in which they are arranged, a reel list, and instruction on how to use the *Index* to locate a document. The *Index,* mechanically produced by means of key-punched cards, is primarily a name index and not a subject index. It gives reference to date, series, and

number of pages. The "Addenda" column lists helpful data which could not fit into the limited spacing of the main entry.

463. U.S. Library of Congress. Manuscript Division.
    Index to the James K. Polk papers. Washington, 1969. 91 p. (*Its* Presidents' papers index series)
    1. Type of microform: Microfilm.
    2. Availability: Positive copies of the microfilm of the Polk papers may be purchased. A positive print is also available for interlibrary loan through the Chief, Loan Division, Library of Congress.
    3. Orders: Photoduplication Service, Library of Congress, Washington, D.C. 20540.
    4. This *Index* is a means of access to the Polk papers (sixty-seven reels of microfilmed documents) owned by the Library of Congress. The introduction to the *Index* provides an interesting essay on the provenance of the papers, a brief description of the contents of the eleven series in which the papers are arranged, a reel list, and instructions on how to use the *Index*. Produced by use of electronic data processing equipment, the *Index* is primarily a name index and not a subject index. Names of writers and recipients are arranged alphabetically; for each document are given date, series, number of pages, and, in a column headed "Addenda," useful information which could not fit the closely calculated spacing of the main entry.

464. U.S. Library of Congress. Manuscript Division.
    Index to the James Madison papers. Washington, 1965. 61 p. (*Its* Presidents' papers index series)
    1. Type of microform: Microfilm.
    2. Availability: Positive copies of the microfilm of the Madison papers may be purchased. A positive print is also available for interlibrary loan through the Chief, Loan Division, Library of Congress.
    3. Orders: Photoduplication Service, Library of Congress, Washington, D.C. 20540.
    4. This *Index*, produced by means of electronic data processing, provides access to the papers of James Madison in the Library of Congress. (Madison letters in other manuscript collections in the Library of Congress or elsewhere are not included.) The *Index* provides a background essay on the "tangled story" of Madison's papers, describes the contents of the six series in which the papers are arranged, contents of the twenty-eight reels, and precise instructions about its use in finding what documents exist in the collection and where they are located on the microfilm reproduction. It is essentially a name index listing names of writers and recipients of letters, alphabetically first and chronologically when the same name appears more than once, with references to date, series, and number of pages. A column headed "Addenda" gives helpful information which did not fit the closely calculated spacing of the main entry.

465. U.S. Library of Congress. Manuscript Division.
    Index to the James Monroe papers. Washington, 1963. 25 p. (*Its* Presidents' papers index series)

1. Type of microform: Microfilm.

2. Availability: Positive copies of the microfilm of the Monroe papers may be purchased. A positive print is also available for interlibrary loan through the Chief, Loan Division, Library of Congress.

3. Orders: Photoduplication Service, Library of Congress, Washington, D.C. 20540.

4. This *Index* provides access to the Monroe papers (3,821 documents on 11 reels of microfilm) owned by the Library of Congress. Also included in the microfilm edition are 381 items of correspondence and related manuscripts owned by Mr. Laurence Hoes, deposited in the James Monroe Memorial Library in Fredericksburg. The introduction to the *Index* includes an interesting essay on the provenance of the papers, instructions on how to use the *Index,* and a reel list. Produced electronically by the use of key-punched cards, the *Index* is basically a name index and not a subject index. Names of writers and recipients are arranged alphabetically. For each item are noted date, series, number of pages, and, in the last column, headed "Addenda," is given helpful information which could not fit into the closely calculated spacing of the main entry. On p. 23 is a description of the contents of the four series in which the papers are arranged and on p. 24 is a complete list of original manuscripts acquired since 1901, showing source of acquisition.

466. U.S. Library of Congress. Manuscript Division.
Index to the John Tyler papers. Washington, 1961. 10 p. (*Its* Presidents' papers index series)

1. Type of microform: Microfilm.

2. Availability: Positive copies of the microfilm of the Tyler papers may be purchased. A positive print is also available for interlibrary loan through the Chief, Loan Division, Library of Congress.

3. Orders: Photoduplication Service, Library of Congress, Washington, D.C. 20540.

4. This *Index* provides access to the Tyler papers (1,410 documents reproduced on 3 reels) owned by the Library of Congress. The introduction includes an interesting essay on the provenance of the papers which explains the loss of the bulk of Tyler's papers and enumerates a number of collections possessing one or more Tyler documents, instructions on how to locate a specific document, and a reel list. Produced mechanically by means of key-punched cards, the *Index* is basically a name index rather than a subject index. Names of writers and recipients are alphabetically arranged; for each document are given date, series, number of pages, and in a column headed "Addenda," helpful information which would not fit the closely calculated spacing of the main entry. On p. 9 is a description of the papers as arranged in three series and a complete list of acquisitions since 1903, showing source of acquisition.

467. U.S. Library of Congress. Manuscript Division.
Index to the Theodore Roosevelt papers. Washington, 1962. 3 v. (*Its* Presidents' papers index series)

1. Type of microform: Microfilm.

2. Availability: Positive copies of the microfilm of the Theodore

Roosevelt papers may be purchased. A positive print is also available for interlibrary loan through the Chief, Loan Division Library of Congress.

3. Orders: Photoduplication Service, Library of Congress, Washington, D.C. 20540.

4. This three-volume *Index,* produced by means of electronic data-processing equipment, provides access to the voluminous papers of Theodore Roosevelt presented to the Library of Congress by former President and Mrs. Roosevelt between 1916 and 1939. The *Index* provides valuable background information about the collection, a concise description of the contents of the fifteen series in which the papers are arranged, a reel list, and clear-cut instructions concerning its use in finding what documents exist in the collection and where they are located on the microfilm reproduction. It is basically a "name index listing the last name and initials of writers and recipients of letters and other documents, alphabetically first, and then chronologically, when the same name appears more than once," with references to date, series, and number of pages. A column headed "Addenda" provides helpful data which would not fit the closely calculated spacing of the main entry.

468.　U.S. Library of Congress. Manuscript Division.

Index to the Ulysses S. Grant papers. Washington, 1965. 83 p. (*Its* Presidents' papers index series)

1.　Type of microform: Microfilm.

2.　Availability: Positive copies of the microfilm of the Grant papers may be purchased. A positive print is available for interlibrary loan through the Chief, Loan Division, Library of Congress.

3.　Orders: Photoduplication Service, Library of Congress, Washington, D.C. 20540.

4.　This *Index* provides access to the Grant papers (47,236 manuscripts reproduced on 32 reels) held by the Library of Congress. The introduction to the *Index* includes a brief essay on the provenance of the papers, a description of the contents of the seven series in which the papers are arranged, a reel list, and concise instructions about how to use the *Index* to locate a document. Produced mechanically by means of key-punched cards, the *Index* is primarily a name index and not a subject index. Besides the names of writers and recipients, arranged alphabetically, it provides date, series, and number of pages. An "Addenda" column is used for helpful data that could not fit into the closely calculated spacing of the main entry.

469.　U.S. Library of Congress. Manuscript Division.

Index to the William H. Harrison papers. Washington, 1960. 10 p. (*Its* Presidents' papers index series)

1.　Type of microform: Microfilm.

2.　Availability: Positive copies of the microfilm of the William H. Harrison papers may be purchased. A positive print is also available for interlibrary loan through the Chief, Loan Division, Library of Congress.

3.　Orders: Photoduplication Service, Library of Congress, Washington, D.C. 20540.

4.　This *Index* provides access to the William H. Harrison papers (984 pieces on 3 reels). The introduction to the *Index* includes a concise essay on the provenance of the papers, instructions on how to use the *Index*, and a reel list. Produced by the use of key-punched cards, which were mechanically sorted and printed, the *Index* is essentially a name index and not a subject index. Names of writers and recipients are arranged alphabetically. For each entry are given date, series, number of pages, and, in the last column headed "Addenda," useful information which could not fit into the closely calculated spacing of the main entry. On pp. 8-9 is a description of the contents of the four series in which the papers are arranged, plus a complete list of accessions since 1901, showing sources of acquisition.

470.   U.S. Library of Congress. Manuscript Division.
Index to the William McKinley papers. Washington, 1963. 482 p. (*Its* Presidents' papers index series)
   1.   Type of microform: Microfilm.
   2.   Availability: Positive prints of the microfilm of the McKinley papers may be purchased. A positive print is also available for interlibrary loan through the Chief, Loan Division, Library of Congress.
   3.   Orders: Photoduplication Service, Library of Congress, Washington, D.C. 20540.
   4.   This *Index* provides access to the McKinley papers (105,832 documents reproduced on 98 reels of microfilm) held by the Library of Congress. The only other large collection of McKinley manuscripts known is composed of the records created during the years when McKinley was governor of Ohio, now in the custody of the Ohio Historical Society at Columbus. The introduction to the *Index* includes a brief essay on the provenance of the McKinley papers, a reel list, and clear-cut instructions about how to locate a document. On pp. 478-481 is found a description of the contents of the 16 series in which the papers are arranged, plus a complete list of accessions, showing source of acquisition. Produced mechanically by the use of key-punched cards, the *Index* is primarily a name index and not a subject index. In addition to the names of writers and recipients, it provides references to date, series, and number of pages. A column headed "Addenda" is used for helpful data that could not fit into the carefully calculated spacing of the main entry.

471.   U.S. Library of Congress. Manuscript Division.
Index to the Zachary Taylor papers. Washington, 1960. 9 p. (*Its* Presidents' papers index series)
   1.   Type of microform: Microfilm.
   2.   Availability: Positive copies of the microfilm of the Taylor papers may be purchased. A positive print is also available for interlibrary loan through the Chief, Loan Division, Library of Congress.
   3.   Orders: Photoduplication Service, Library of Congress, Washington, D.C. 20540.
   4.   This *Index* provides access to the Taylor papers (631 documents reproduced on 2 reels of microfilm) owned by the Library of Congress. In the introductory pages of the *Index* are found a brief essay on the provenance of the papers, instructions on how to use the *Index* to locate a specific docu-

ment, and a reel list. Produced mechanically by means of key-punched cards, the *Index* is primarily a name index and not a subject index. Names of writers and recipients are arranged alphabetically; for each document are given date, series, number of pages, and, in a column headed "Addenda," helpful information which could not fit the closely calculated spacing of the main entry. On p. 8 is a brief description of the contents of the five series in which the papers are arranged and a complete list of acquisitions since 1904, showing source of acquisition.

472. U.S. Library of Congress. Manuscript Division.
    Kraus collection of manuscripts. *Not yet published.*
    1. Type of microform: Microfilm.
    2. Availability: When microfilming of the collection is completed, the Library of Congress will have available a master negative film from which scholars may order copies and a positive film which may be borrowed on interlibrary loan.
    3. Orders: For microfilms: Photoduplication Service, Library of Congress, Washington, D.C. 20540.
      For interlibrary loan: Interlibrary Loan, Chief, Loan Division, Library of Congress, Washington, D.C. 20540.
    4. An announcement that the Library of Congress planned to microfilm for purposes of preservation the Kraus Collection of Manuscripts appeared in its *Information Bulletin* of March 26, 1970. A letter of August 18, 1971, from the Photoduplication Service states that the microfilming is in process and that the Manuscript Division is preparing a guide to the microfilm edition of the collection. The collection, made up of letters, documents, rare books, and manuscripts relating to the history and culture of Spanish America in the colonial period, 1492-1819, was the gift of the well-known collector and bibliophile, Hans P. Kraus of New York City.

473. U.S. Library of Congress. Processing Department.
    British manuscripts project; a checklist of the microfilms prepared in England and Wales for the American Council of Learned Societies, 1941-1945. Compiled by Lester K. Born . . . Washington, Library of Congress, 1955. 179 p.
    1. Type of microform: Microfilm.
    2. Availability: Copies available for purchase at the cost of positive prints.
    3. Orders: Photoduplication Service, Library of Congress, Washington, D.C. 20540.
    4. Lists the "contents of the 2,652 reels of microfilm containing reproductions of nearly five million pages of manuscript and, in a few instances, rare printed materials found in some of the major public and private collections of England and Wales." Listing is in alphabetical order by name of depository; within a depository, alphabetically by collection; and within a collection, by numerical sequence of manuscripts. For each item, there is provided the accepted designation by depository name and number; a short enumeration of the contents of the item plus the number of the reel (together with the position on the reel) on which the item is reproduced. Each item is prefixed by a serial number which serves only for reference in the index

which is limited to personal and geographic names (see introduction for further limitations of the index).

474. Uyehara, Cecil H.
    Checklist of archives in the Japanese Ministry of Foreign Affairs, Tokyo, Japan, 1868-1945; microfilmed for the Library of Congress, 1949-1951. Compiled by Cecil H. Uyehara under the direction of Edwin G. Beal. Washington, Library of Congress Photoduplication Service, 1954. 262 p.
    1. Type of microform: Microfilm.
    2. Availability: Positive copies available for purchase at currently published rates.
    3. Orders: Photoduplication Service, Library of Congress, Washington, D.C. 20540.
    4. Lists the contents of 2,116 reels of microfilmed documents. Selection was based primarily on the relevance of the documents to events leading up to the Pacific War. Supplemented by the *Checklist of Microfilm Reproductions of Selected Archives of the Japanese Army, Navy and Other Government Agencies, 1868-1945.* (See Item 4481.)

475. Wainwright, Nicholas B.
    Guide to the microfilm edition of the Thomas Penn papers. Philadelphia, The Historical Society of Pennsylvania [1968] 16 p.
    1. Type of microform: Microfilm.
    2. Availability: Ten rolls and printed guide available. Individual rolls and guide may be purchased separately.
    3. Orders: Historical Society of Pennsylvania, 1300 Locust Street, Philadelphia, Pennsylvania 19107.
    4. The *Guide* provides a biographical sketch of Thomas Penn, origin and description of the collection, and list of dates covered in each roll. An alphabetical index for rolls 4-10 is included in roll 10. This microfilm edition was sponsored by the National Historical Publications Commission.

476. Washington University, St. Louis. Libraries. Library of the School of Medicine.
    Index to the Wm. Beaumont, M.D., (1785-1853), manuscript collection. Compiled by Phoebe A. Cassidy [and] Roberta S. Sokol. Introd. by Estelle Brodman. [St. Louis] Washington University School of Medicine, 1968. 165 p.
    1. Type of microform: Microfilm.
    2. Availability: Copies of the microfilm may be purchased.
    3. Orders: Library of the School of Medicine, Washington University, 4580 Scott Avenue, St. Louis, Missouri 63110.
    4. This *Index* produced by computer lists the documents in the Beaumont collection in chronological order and provides four points of access to them: places, names, dates, and subjects. A copy of the *Index* may be purchased with or without microfilm of the Beaumont Collection.

477. White, Helen McCann.
    Guide to a microfilm edition of the Ignatius Donnelly papers. St. Paul, Minnesota Historical Society, 1968. 34 p.

1. Type of microform: Microfilm.
2. Availability: 167 rolls and printed guide may be purchased. Guide and individual rolls may be purchased separately.
3. Orders: Manuscripts Department, Minnesota Historical Society, 690 Cedar Street, St. Paul, Minnesota 55101.
4. The *Guide* provides a biographical sketch of Donnelly, a chronological and analytical description of the papers, contents of the microfilm by rolls, a selected list of authors, and a list of subjects covered. The microfilm edition and the *Guide* were made possible by a grant of funds from the National Historical Publications Commission to the Minnesota Historical Society.

478. White, Helen McCann.
    Guide to a microfilm edition of the Lawrence Taliaferro papers. St. Paul, Minnesota Historical Society, 1966. 12 p.
    1. Type of microform: Microfilm.
    2. Availability: Four rolls and printed guide may be purchased. Guide and individual rolls may be purchased separately.
    3. Orders: Manuscripts Department, Minnesota Historical Society, 690 Cedar Street, St. Paul, Minnesota 55101.
    4. The Taliaferro papers include order books and other items related to his military service, 1813-1819, correspondence reflecting his service as Indian agent in Minnesota, 1820-1839, and an autobiography, 1864. The *Guide* provides a biographical sketch, a description of the papers and their origin, a selected list of correspondents, and a list of subjects covered. The microfilm edition and the *Guide* were made possible by a grant of funds from the National Historical Publications Commission to the Minnesota Historical Society.

479. Wiltse, Charles Maurice.
    Dartmouth College Library/University Microfilms microfilm edition of the Papers of Daniel Webster, a project organized at Dartmouth College under the direction of Edward Connery Lathem, Librarian of the College, sponsored in part by the National Historical Publications Commission and carried to completion under the editorship of Charles M. Wiltse, editor of the Papers of Daniel Webster. Guide and index to the microfilm. Ann Arbor, Michigan, University Microfilms, 1971. 175 p.
    1. Type of microform: Microfilm.
    2. Availability: Complete set of forty-one rolls and guide available; single rolls may be purchased; guide may be purchased separately.
    3. Orders: University Microfilms, 300 North Zeeb Road, Ann Arbor, Michigan 48106.
    4. Excluded from the microfilm edition of Webster's papers are the official files of the Department of State during his two terms as Secretary, since these papers are already available on microfilm from the National Archives and Record Service. Also excluded are most of Webster's legal papers. Records of the Supreme Court and many lower federal courts may be procured on microfilm from the National Archives. "Reports of cases argued by Webster in the county courts of New Hampshire and Massachusetts, as far

as they still exist, will constitute a separate microfilm publication, to be issued by University Microfilms in association with Dartmouth College, and it is hoped that reports of cases in various states may eventually be added.

"The overall arrangement of the microfilm edition follows a pattern of chronological sequence, within broad categories: general correspondence and miscellaneous documents; business papers; Congressional papers divided into House of Representatives and Senate; State Department papers; and finally papers in other departments of government." There is a description of each of these categories, followed by a Webster chronology and a Webster bibliography. Then comes a description of each reel of microfilm and the index to the microfilm in which for each item, a frame number is given; the reel number is determined from a frame and reel tabulation given on the page preceding the index.

480.   Yale University. Library.

Plato manuscripts: a catalogue of microfilms in the Plato microfilm project, Yale University Library. Edited by Robert S. Brumbaugh and Rulon Wells, with the assistance of Donna Scott and Harry V. Botsis. New Haven, 1962. 2 v.

————— ————— The Plato manuscripts; a new index. Prepared by the Plato microfilm project of the Yale University Library under the direction of Robert S. Brumbaugh and Rulon Wells. New Haven, Yale University Press, 1968. 163 p.

1. Type of microform: Microfilm.

2. Availability: Not available on interlibrary loan; copies not permitted without written authorization from the owning institution. With such a letter of authorization, positive microfilm may be supplied at standard price.

4. The *Catalogue,* a photographic reproduction of the card catalog prepared by the project, represents a new and accurate inventory of the older (pre- and post-1600) manuscripts (except the Paris A and Bodleian B which are available in photographic facsimile) and their contents, with leaf location. Issued in two installments or parts: Part I covers the manuscripts in Belgium, Denmark, England, Germany and Italy; Part II covers manuscripts in Austria, Czechoslovakia, France, Holland, and Spain, and post-1600 manuscripts in Belgium, Denmark, England, Germany, and Italy, plus addenda to Part I. While the project did not set out to acquire systematically microfilms of post-1600 manuscripts, it was decided to include those listed in L. A. Post's "List of Plato Manuscripts" in his *Vatican Plato and Its Relations* (Middletown, Conn., 1934).

Within each country, arrangement is by city and by library; within each library, manuscripts are given in the order in which they occur in it, with the leaf numbers of the several dialogues indicated. The manuscript Bodleian B. (Clark .39) is described in the same way, but separately in the appendix to Part I, while manuscript Paris A (Grecs 1807) is described in the appendix to Part II. Also in Part II is a "Cumulative Index by Dialogues."

Entries are numbered consecutively for easy reference and film and reel numbers are given. Also included for each entry is a number referring to L. A. Post's "List of Plato Manuscripts" in his *Vatican Plato and Its Relations,* which was used to check orders and accessions. Although Post did not number his entries, the enumeration used in the *Catalogue* follows his order of listing.

A third and final part of the *Catalogue* will be published as soon as all cards have been processed.

The *Index*, based on a new cataloging from microfilm of the extant pre-1500 manuscripts containing Plato's works in whole or in part, is in two sections: "Manuscripts Listed by Library" and "Manuscripts Listed by Dialogue." Two useful supplementary indexes, "Index of Collated Manuscripts (Arranged by Library Location)" and an "Index of Collators' Abbreviations" are followed by three appendixes, "List of Papyri," "An Epigraphic Note," and "Bibliography."

481. Young, John.
Checklist of microfilm reproductions of selected archives of the Japanese Army, Navy and other government agencies, 1868-1945. Washington, Georgetown University Press, 1959. 144 p.

1. Type of microform: Microfilm.

2. Availability: Positive prints are in the National Diet Library in Tokyo, the National Archives, and the Library of Congress. The Library of Congress copy is available on interlibrary loan. Positive copies are also available for purchase in quantities of one or more reels at currently published prices.

3. Orders: Photoduplication Service, Library of Congress, Washington, D.C. 20540.

4. A guide to microfilm copies of some 400,000 pages of material of historical value selected from the archives of the Japanese Army and Navy ministries and other government agencies. The documents, in Japanese, deal primarily with events in Eastern Asia between 1900 and 1945; a few deal with events outside this area, while a portion pertain to the years of the Meiji period before 1900. The collection supplements that listed in *Checklist of Archives in the Japanese Ministry of Foreign Affairs* (Tokyo, Japan, 1868-1945) (see Item 474).

482. Yushodo Film Publications, Inc.
Uesugi Monjo. Documents of the Uesugis, feudal lords of the Yonezawa domain (Yamagata Pref., Northeast Japan) in the modern age. (In Yushodo Film Publications, Ltd. General catalog 1970-71)

1. Type of microform: Microfilm.

2. Availability: Complete set of 236 reels with printed explanation and index may be purchased.

3. Orders: Yushodo Film Publications, Ltd., 29 Sanei-cho, Shinjuku-ku, Tokyo, Japan.

4. The documents of the Uesugis form a complete record of the economy, politics, customs, and culture of the Yonezawa-Han, a feudal clan, in the Edo era. The original manuscripts, 5,000 items, are in the Yonezawa City Library. The microfilm edition is accompanied by an explanation and index (102 p.) by Dr. M. Tokoro and Dr. Y. Fuse.

IV. REFERENCE BOOKS

483. Guide to microforms in print. 1961-   Washington, Microcard Editions, 1961-   Annual
    Latest edition: 1972
    1. Type of microform: All types.
    2. Availability: All publications and sets listed may be purchased. Prices are given in many instances, but in the case of large sets and long runs of back issues of journals, newspapers, government documents, etc., it is necessary to write to the publisher of the material in question concerning price and the availability of single volumes or units.
    3. Orders: Orders should be addressed to publisher indicated. A directory of publishers and addresses by the alphabetic designations used in the *Guide* appears in each edition.
    4. "An annual cumulative guide, in alphabetic order, to books, journals, and other materials, which are available on microfilm and other microforms from United States publishers. Theses and dissertations are not listed ... *not a union list of microforms* ... essentially a listing of microform publications offered for sale on a regular basis."

Subject guide to microforms in print. 1962-63-   Washington, Microcard Editions, 1962-   Annual
    Latest edition: 1970-71
    A companion volume to the publication listed as Item 483. Lists materials under 135 subject classifications derived from the *Outline of the Library of Congress Classification* (Washington: Library of Congress, Subject Classification Division, 1942). "The Subject Classifications" and an "Index to the Subject Classifications" plus "Special Notes" appear on pp. viii-xii.

485. Hale, Richard Walden.
    Guide to photocopied historical materials in the United States and Canada. Ithaca, N. Y., Published for the American Historical Association [by] Cornell University Press [1961] 241 p.
    1. Types of microform: Microfilm primarily.
    2. Availability: In general, the materials listed are accessible to all qualified persons. Positive copies of negative films may be purchased, and positive films are available on interlibrary loan. If an institution does not follow this general policy, this fact is indicated in the listing of "Holders of Photocopies." Prices are not given but must be secured from institutions holding material.
    3. Orders: Inquiries or orders should be addressed to the institution holding the desired material.
    4. Provides information about photocopies of 11,137 bodies of historical manuscript records held by some 285 institutions in the United States and Canada, indicating type of photocopy and location. The body of the *Guide* is arranged according to the sequence used in the American Historical Association's *Guide to Historical Literature* (New York: Macmillan, 1961) and is followed by an index, primarily of personal and institutional names.

486. Hixon, Donald L.
    Music in early America; a bibliography of music in Evans. Metuchen, N.J., Scarecrow Press, 1970. 607 p.

"This bibliography is an index to the music published in seventeenth and eighteenth century America as represented by Charles Evans' *American Bibliography* and the Readex Corporation's microprint edition of *Early American Imprints, 1639-1800.*" Part one, the bibliography, contains about 800 items arranged alphabetically by composer (or other main entry). For each item are given: composer, title, place, publisher, date, collation, notes, and Evans number. Contents of collections are listed. Part two is an alphabetical composer-editor-compiler arrangement of those items not yet reproduced in the *Early American Imprints* microprint edition, some of which will undoubtedly turn up in the future. Part three provides brief biographical sketches; Part four is a composer-compiler index; Part five is a title index and Part six is an index to the Evans numbers cited in Parts one and two. The bibliography will be useful to the scholars interested in American musical history, enabling them to exploit the Readex Microprint edition of *Early American Imprints*.

487. National register of microform masters. Sept. 1965-   Washington, 1965-
      1. Type of microform: All types.
      2. Availability: Type of negative indicated by abbreviations following the location symbol.
      3. Orders: Orders should be addressed to institution owning the negative.
      4. The *Register* lists titles for which master negatives exist and identifies those which are designated "master preservation negatives." Included are foreign and domestic books, pamphlets, serials, and foreign doctoral dissertations; excluded are technical reports, typescript translations, foreign and domestic archival manuscript collections, and United States doctoral dissertations and master's theses.

488. New Mexico. University. Library.
      Union list of Southwestern materials on microfilm in New Mexico libraries. [Albuquerque?] 1957. 8 p.
      1. Type of microform: Microfilm.
      2. Availability: Although policies governing interlibrary loan of films may vary, the preface of this union list indicates that most libraries listing material will also lend.
      3. Orders: Orders should be addressed to the Interlibrary Loan Service of the institution holding the desired material.
      4. Eleven libraries submitted material for inclusion in this *Union List*. First are listed newspapers, arranged alphabetically by title, and then other materials, arranged alphabetically by author. Included in the latter category are books, manuscript material, theses, and journal articles. There is no indication whether the film is negative or positive.

489. Ontario Council of University Librarians.
      Union list of microform sets in O.C.U.L. libraries. 1st ed. Edited by Anni Leibl and Jean S. Yolton. Hamilton, Ont., Printed by the University of Toronto Press, distributed by the Mills Memorial Library, McMaster University Libraries, 1971. 23 p.
      This union list, the cooperative effort of the fourteen provincially supported universities, includes microform editions of composite sets and collec-

tions of separately published works made by microform publishers. It does not include individual titles of newspapers, serials, or monographs.

The listing is by series title, giving location symbols, type of microform, availability on interlibrary loan or in printed copy, and citations to available guides.

490. South Asian Microform Union List of Citations in South Asia Microform Newsletter [and] South Asian Library and Research Notes. Edited by Joan M. and Henry Ferguson. Educational Resources Center, University of the State of New York, State Education Department. [1969] 151 p. (South Asian library and research notes. v. 6, no. 1-4 [1969])

1. Type of microform: Type of microform not indicated.

2. Availability: Questions concerning availability, price, etc., should be directed to the owner of the microform.

3. A union list of bibliographic data on microform holdings originally published in issues of the *South Asian Microform Newsletter* and its successor, *South Asian Library and Research Notes* through 1966 only. This combined list includes the holdings of several commercial publishers of microforms as well as those of libraries.

491. Tilton, Eva Maude, comp.

A union list of publications in opaque microforms. 2d ed. New York, Scarecrow Press, 1964. 744 p.

This publication is not at all a union list in the usual sense (i.e., library locations are not given), but rather a compilation of titles from publishers' lists and catalogs in one alphabet by main entry. Among the titles listed are many master's theses and doctoral dissertations. Listings of European, as well as American, publishers are represented.

492. U.S. Library of Congress. Union Catalog Division.

Newspapers on microfilm. [1st]-   ed. Washington, Library of Congress, 1948-

1. Type of microform: Microfilm.

2. Availability: The symbol "N:" is used to indicate the source (library or commercial firm) from which positive microform copies are available. Prices must be secured by applying to the holder of the negative. Information relative to availability on interlibrary loan likewise must be secured from the library holding the film.

3. Orders: See above.

4. The latest edition of *Newspapers on Microfilm* (6th, 1967) contains approximately 21,700 entries, representing 4,600 foreign and nearly 17,000 domestic newspapers. Locations of both positive and negative microfilm copies are indicated. Bibliographic data given are minimal, but adequate for identification purposes.

Arrangement is geographical by state and city for the United States, by province and city for Canada and the French West Indies, and simply by city for other countries. American Samoa, Guam, Okinawa, Puerto Rico, the Virgin Islands appear alphabetically among the states of the United States.

493. Wisconsin. State Historical Society.

Labor papers on microfilm; a combined list. Madison, 1965. 66 p. (*Its Guides to historical resources*)

1. Type of micorform: Microfilm.

2. Availability: Positive copies available from the library holding the master negative. When a price is stated, it is for the full span of years given in the entry. If no price is indicated, or if only a portion of a film is wanted, inquiries should be directed to the library holding the negative.

The Society takes continuing subscriptions to microfilm copies of currently published titles with the understanding that they will be filmed only in three-year cumulations. Master negatives are not available on interlibrary loan from the Society, but it does lend positive copies for a fee of $1.00 per reel borrowed.

3. Orders: State Historical Society of Wisconsin, 816 State Street, Madison, Wisconsin 53706.

4. A combined list of holdings of thirteen libraries owning master negatives. It does not presume to give complete coverage of the field, but listings were solicited from all libraries known to have filming programs. Limited in general to titles published in the United States. Canadian labor journals are being filmed by the Department of Labour of Canada (Item no. 19).

Organization of the list follows closely that used by Bernard G. Naas and Carmelita Sakr in their *American Labor Union Periodicals, a Guide to Their Location* (Ithaca, 1956). Entries provide only a minimum of bibliographic information, since details are available in the above *Guide*.

Included are union periodicals, general labor periodicals and newspapers, state and local periodicals and newspapers, socialist and communist periodicals, anarchist periodicals, liberal and reform periodicals, farmer organization periodicals, and eighteen general periodicals.

Index to a Microform Bibliography

French resistance, 175
German, 12, 146
Greenland, 6
Indochinese, 5
Japanese, 82, 107-108, 169
Jewish, 39
Malaysian, 89, 135, 165
Philippine, 119
Prisoners of war, 174
Russian, 13-14, 146, 230, 275
Singapore, 135
South African, 96
Spanish, 146
Underground, 179
Newspapers on microfilm, 492
New York (City) Public Library, 106, 150-152
Talleyrand Collection, 250
New York (State) University, Education Research Center, 490
New York Historical Society, 423
New York University, 423
Nicholson, John, papers, 420
Nielsen, Lauritz, 222
Niermann, Eleanor, 399
Nihon Maikuro Shashin, 107-108
Nineteenth-century American literature, 240
Nineteenth-century fiction, 270
Nippon shakai rodo undoshi shiryo, 313
Non-GPO imprints received in the Library of Congress, July 1967-December 1969, 289
North Carolina
University, 293
Library, 109, 402-418
North Dakota University, 433
Notre Dame University, 354, 383-386
Nuclear science abstracts, 286
Nussbaum, Frederick Louis, 400

Oberlin College Library, Oberlin, Ohio, 252
Oceania, 152
Ohio Historical Society, 320, 382
Oklahoma State University Library, 84
Old Dominion Foundation, 323
One thousand scientific manuscripts in the Ambrosiana Library, Milan, 354
Ontario Council of University Librarians, 489
Opaque microforms, publications in, 491
Oregon Improvement Company records, 1880-1896, 335
Oregon, University, School of Health, Physical Education and Recreation, 231
Orion Books, 110
Országos Széchényi Könyvtar, Budapest, 18
Ottawa, National Library, 111
Outlaw, David, papers, 406

Ouvrages cyrilliques concernant les sciences sociales, 112

PCMI library collections, 113
PKI, *see* Communist party of Indonesia
Pan American Institute of Geography and History, Commission on History, 114-116
Paoletti, Odette, 117
Parral, Mexico, Archivo, 401
Partai Komunis Indonesia, *see* Communist party of Indonesia
Pascoe (W. & F.) Pty., Ltd., 118
Patton, James Welch, 402-418
Peirce, Charles S., papers, 432
Penn, Thomas, papers, 475
Pennsylvania
Historical and Museum Commission, 340, 379, 419-420
Provincial Council, Records, 1682-1776, 379
State Archives, 379
University, 267
Library, 253
Pennsylvania Abolitionist Society, 430
Periodicals, 1, 17-18, 29, 94, 106, 157, 163
African, 146
Agriculture, 64
American, 172, 227, 302
Art, 45, 55
Australian, 118, 125
Black, 226-227
Botanical, 46-47, 56
Canadian, 19, 26
Central Asian, 68
Chinese, 4, 50, 142, 164
Congolese, 61
English, 17, 143, 192-194, 208, 227, 302
European, 52
French, 5, 63, 143
German, 102, 143
Geological, 53, 65
Greenland, 6
Humanities, 117
Indonesian, 60
Japanese, 35, 50, 169
Jewish, 39
Labor, 19
Latin American, 146, 237
Legal, 62
Malaysian, 134
Medical, 66-67, 266
Middle Eastern, 146
Military, 281
Musical, 70
Philippine, 119
Radical, 163
Religious, 206

Bibliography of Literature Used

ALA Bul, American Library Association Bulletin
Am Archivist, American Archivist
Am Documentation, American Documentation
Bibl Soc of Am Papers, Bibliographical Society of America Papers
Bkmark, Bookmark
CRL, College and Research Libraries
Canad Lib, Canadian Library
Canad Lib J, Canadian Library Journal
Canadian Lib Assn Bul, Canadian Library Association Bulletin
Cath Lib W, Catholic Library World
Ill Lib, Illinois Libraries
J Cat & Class, Journal of Cataloging and Classification
J Doc, Journal of Documentation
J Doc Repr, Journal of Documentary Reproduction
LRTS, Library Resources and Technical Services
Law Lib J, Law Library Journal
Lib J, Library Journal
Lib Q, Library Quarterly
Lib Trends, Library Trends
Libn and Bk W, Librarian and Book World
Music Lib Assn Notes, Music Library Association Notes
NMA Proceedings, National Microfilm Association Proceedings
New Zealand Lib, New Zealand Libraries
Ont Lib R, Ontario Library Review
Pub Wkly, Publishers Weekly
Rev Int Doc, Revue Internationale de la Documentation
Sp Lib, Special Libraries
Tid Dok, Tidskrift för Dokumentation
Un B L, Unesco Bulletin for Libraries
Z Bibl und Bibliog, Zeitschrift für Bibliothekswesen und Bibliographie
Zentr Bibl, Zentralblatt für Bibliothekswesen

American Association of Junior Colleges. *Microform project, a research project to determine the student acceptability and learning effectiveness of microforms in community junior colleges.* Washington, D.C., The Association, 1970.
American Association of Law Libraries. Committee for Microfilming. "United States Supreme Court records and briefs. Report, 1939-40" *Law Lib J*, XXXIII, 1940, 209-10.
American Library Association. Copying Methods Section. Library Standards for Microfilm Committee. *Microfilm norms; recommended standards for libraries.* Chicago, A. L. A., 1966.

Applebaum, Edmond L. "Implications of the *National register of microform masters* as part of a national preservation program" *LRTS,* IX, 1965, 489-94.

Ardern, L. L. *John Benjamin Dancer.* London, Library Association, 1960. (Library Association Occasional Papers no. 2)

———. "Council for microphotography and document reproduction" *Libn and Bk W,* L, 1961, 157-59.

Aschenborn, H. J. "International standardization of microfiche" [Guildford, Eng., IPC Science and Technology Press, Ltd., 1971] 12 p. (Preprint from *Proceedings* of the 3d Congress on Reprography, London, 1971)

Asleson, Robert. "Microforms, where do they fit?" *LRTS,* XV, 1971, 57.

AUPELF [Association des universités partiellement ou entièrement de langue francaise]. "Microfiche service" *Un B L,* XXI, 1967, 224-25.

Avedon, Don M. *Computer output microfilm.* 2d ed. Silver Spring, National Microfilm Association, 1971.

Ballou, Hubbard W. and John Rather. "Microfilming and microfacsimile publications" *Lib Trends,* IV, 1955, 182-94.

Barker, Ronald E. *Photocopying practices in the United Kingdom.* London, Faber and Faber, 1970.

Barton, Walter. "Bibliothek und Mikrofilm" *Z Bibl und Bibliog,* XI, 1964, 127-47.

Belda, Luis S. "Actividades del Servicio Nacional de Microfilm en 1959" [Work of the National Microfilm Service in 1959] Spain. Servicio Nacional de Microfilm. *Boletín,* IX (53), January-March 1960, 125-35.

——— [and] Pilar Léon Tello. "Inventario de fondos fotocopiados, año 1959-60" [List of books reproduced, 1959-60] Spain. Servicio Nacional de Microfilm. *Boletín,* X (58), March-April 1961, 105-11.

Bernstein, George B. *A fifteen-year forecast of information processing technology.* Prepared by Research and Development Division, Naval Supply Systems Command. Detroit, Management Information Services, 1969. Based on the author's thesis, George Washington University. Also available from National Technical Information Service as AD 681752.

Blum, Fred. "Catholica on microforms" *Cath Lib W,* XL, 1969, 551-57.

———. *Guide to selected research material on microforms.* 1968, Thesis, Catholic University of America. 135 p.

Born, Lester Kruger. "History of microform activity" *Lib Trends,* VII, 1960, 348-58.

———. "Literature of microreproduction, 1950-55" *Am Documentation,* VII, 1956, 167-87.

———. "National plan for extensive microfilm operations" *Am Documentation,* I, 1950, 66-75.

———. "A synthesis on "Microfilm" at the Library of Congress" *J Doc,* VIII, 1952, 1-13.

Boyd, Julian P. "A new guide to the indispensable sources of Virginia history" *William and Mary Quarterly,* 3d ser., XV, 1958, 3-15.

Brockway, Duncan. "New look at the cataloging of microfilm" *LRTS,* IV, 1960, 323-30.

Campbell, B. W. "A successful microfiche program" *Sp Lib,* LXII, 1971, 136-42.

Canadian Library Association (Association canadiènne des bibliothèques). "Canadian newspapers microfilmed . . . A union list of available files" *Canadian Lib Assn Bul,* X, 1953, x-xiii of Microfilm Section following p. 64.

———. "Other Canadian newspapers on microfilm: a union list of negatives" *Canadian Lib Assn Bul,* X, 1953, xiii-xvi of Microfilm Section following p. 64.

Carruthers, Ralph H. "New York Public Library changes treatment of microfilm serials" *Lib J,* LXII, 1947, 880-82.

——— and Wyllis E. Wright. "Library methods of handling microfilm" *ALA Bul,* XXXII, 1938, 385-87.

Clapp, Verner W. and R. T. Jordan. "Reevaluation of microfilm as a method of book storage" *CRL,* XXIV, 1963, 5-15.

Cornell, George W. *A survey of microfilm in some Ohio college and university libraries.* 1949, Dissertation, Western Reserve University.

Custer, Arline. "Archives of American art: a manuscript and microfilm collection requires unusual techniques for control" *LRTS,* II, 1958, 197-208.

Deighton, L. C. "The future of printing in a data hungry society" *Pub Wkly,* CLXXXIX, 1966, 55-60.

Delks, Patricia J. *Microfilm classification.* 1954, Thesis, Western Reserve University. 37 p.

Dennis, Faustine. "Cataloging in the microfilm reading room of the Library of Congress" *J Cat & Class,* VIII, 1952, 17-20.

Diaz, A. J. "Microreproduction information sources" *LRTS,* XI, 1967, 211-14.

Diefenbach, Dale A. "Conference on Southeast Asian research material, Puntjak, Indonesia, 1969" *LRTS,* XV, 1971, 76.

Dunning, A. "The growth of the microfilm industry" *NMA Proceedings,* 14th annual meeting and convention, 1965, 25-35.

Frank, Otto. *Die Mikrofilm Technik.* Stuttgart, Dorothea-Verlag, 1961. 328 p.

Freedman, Samuel B. "Microphotography of source documents for the proposed national science library system" (*In* Kent, Allen, ed. *Library planning for automation.* Washington, Spartan [1965] p. 35-53)

Fussler, Herman Howe. "Microfilms and libraries" (*In* Randall, William Madison, ed. *Acquisitions and cataloging of books.* Chicago, University of Chicago Press [c1940] p. 331-54)

———. "Microphotography and the future of interlibrary loans" *J Doc Repr,* II, 1939, 3-10.

———. *Photographic Reproduction for libraries; a study of administrative problems.* Chicago, University of Chicago Press, 1942.

———. "Photographic reproduction of library materials" *Lib Trends,* II, 1954, 532-44.

———. "Some implications of microphotography for librarians" *J Doc Repr,* II, 1939, 184-88.

Gerould, Albert C. "Cataloging of microfilm at Stanford" *Lib J,* LXII, 1937, 682-83.

Great Britain. National Library Committee. *Report of the National Libraries Committee presented to Parliament by the Secretary of State Education and Science by command of Her Majesty,* June 1969. London, H. M. S. O. [1969] (Cmnd. 4028)

Gregory, Roma S. "Acquisitions of microforms" *Lib Trends,* XVIII, 1970, 373.

Guide to microforms in print. 1961-   Washington, Microcard Editions. Annual.

Hale, Richard W., Jr. "Cataloging of microfilm" *Am Archivist,* XXII, 1969, 11-13.

Hawkin, William R. *Copying methods manual.* A. L. A., Library Technology Program, 1966. (LTD Publications. No. 11)

———. "Microform standardization; its problems and prospects in the international field" *MICRODOC,* VI, 1967, 94-96.

Hawkins, Reginald. *Production of microforms.* Rutgers University Press, 1960. (Rutgers University. Graduate School of Library Service. *State of the library art.* v. 5, no. 1)

Hensel, Evelyn M. "Microcard cataloging being solved at Penn State" *Lib J,* LXXV, 1950, 344-45.

Henshaw, Francis G. "A brief history of the LC microreproduction projects" *NMA Proceedings,* 8th meeting, 1959, 211-27.

Hirsch, Rudolf. "Distribution analysis of the union list of microfilms" *J Doc Repr,* V. 1942, 110-11.

———. "Union list of microfilms" *Am Documentation,* I, 1950, 88-90.

Holmes, Donald C. *Determination of the environmental conditions required in a library for the effective utilization of microforms.* Final report. ARL for HEW, 1970.

———. *Determination of user needs and future requirements for a systems approach to microform technology.* Interim report. ARL for HEW, 1969.

Horn, Andrew H. *Southern California list of microtext editions.* Los Angeles, Issued by the Libraries of Occidental College and the University of California in Los Angeles, 1959.

Jägerskiöld, Olof. "Microphotography in Swedish archives and libraries" *Tid Dok,* VII, 1951, 46-47.

Jenkins, William S. "Legislative documents microfilm project" *Ill Lib* XXX, 1948, 466-70.

———. "State documents microfilms as research resources for law libraries" *Law Lib J,* XLI, 1948, 77-87.

Jones, H. G. "Carolina's newspaper microfilming program" *North Carolina Library,* XIX, 1960, 14-17.

Jones, Helen Jane and Jeannette Hagan. "Microfilm cataloging lacks system" *Lib J*, LXXII, 1947, 505-07.
Jones, Polly T. "Cataloging of microfilm; a bibliography" *J Cat & Class*, X, 1954, 155-57.
Kaser, David, C. W. Stone, C. K. Byrd. *Library developments in eight Asian countries.* Metuchen, N. J., Scarecrow, 1969.
Keenleyside, Mrs. Marjorie (Culver). "Microcards" (In American Theological Library Association Conference, 3d, 1949, Chicago. *Proceedings*, p. 10-15)
Knight, Kenneth C. "Union list of projected book holdings" *Lib J*, LXXVI, 1951, 1997.
Kottenstette, J. P. "Student reading characteristics: comparing skill-levels demonstrated on hardcopy and microfilm presentations" (In American Society for Information Sciences. Conference, 1969, San Francisco. *Proceedings*, v. 6: Cooperating information societies. Greenwood, 1969, p. 345-51)
Kuhlman, Augustus F. "Are we ready to preserve newspapers on films? A symposium" *Lib Q*, V, 1935, 189-214.
Lapsley, Eleanor M. *Study of use and care of microfilm in the library.* 1949, Thesis, Carnegie Institute of Technology. 111 p.
Leisinger, Albert H. "The microfilm committee of the International Council of Archives" [Guildford, Eng., IPC Science & Technology Press, Ltd., 1971] [14] p. (preprint from *Proceedings* of the 3d Congress on Reprography, London, 1971)
——. "The microfilm programs of the National Archives" *NMA Proceedings*, 8th meeting, 1959, 229-38.
Leuris, Chester M. and William H. Offenhauser. *Microrecording; industrial and library applications.* New York, Interscience, 1956.
Lewis, Ralph W. "User's reaction to microfiche" *CRL*, XXXI, 1970, 260.
Linares, Emma. "Microfilm services and their use in Argentina" (In *Acquisitions of Latin American library materials* [Seminar, 3d, 1958, Berkeley] Final report and papers. University of California Library, 1959. p. 92-99)
Litchfield, D. H. and M. A. Bennett. "Teaching microphotography to librarians" *Lib J*, LXX, 1945, 734-37.
Luther, Frederick. *Microfilm; a history, 1839-1900.* Annapolis, National Microfilm Association, 1959.
——. "100 years of microfilm technology" *NMA Proceedings*, 8th meeting, 1959, 13-19.
Macgregor, I. K. "Cataloging microfilm" *New Zealand Lib*, XII, 1948, 163-66.
MacKinney, Loren C. "Manuscript photoreproductions in classical, mediaeval, and renaissance research" *Speculum*, XXI, 1946, 244-52.
——. "Postwar microfilming of mediaeval research material" *Speculum*, XXXVII, 1962, 492-96.
Metcalf, Keyes D. "Care and cataloging of microfilms" *ALA Bul*, XXXI, 1937, 72-74.
——. "Microphotography and bibliography" *Bibl Soc of Am Papers*, XXXII, 1938, 65-70.
"La microcopie en France dans les bibliothèques, archives et centres de documentation," *Bulletin des Bibliothèques de France*, IV, 1959, 161-82, 229-48.
Microform utilization: the academic library environment. Report of conference held at Denver, Colorado, 7-9 December 1970. Sponsored by the University of Denver. Supported by U. S. Office of Education. Conference chairman: James P. Kottenstette. Editor: Alta Bradley Morrison. [Denver University, 1971]
Micropublishing for learned societies. [Proceedings of the Seminar held at Hatfield, England, 1968] Hatfield, Herts, 1968.
National Microfilm Association. *Glossary of terms for microphotography and reproductions made from micro-images.* Edited by Donald M. Avedon. 4th edition. Annapolis, National Microfilm Association, 1966. (NMA Informational Monograph No. 2)
"National reprographic centre for documentation in the United Kingdom." *Un B L*, XXI, 1967, 164.
Nelson, Carl E. *Microfilm technology: engineering and related fields.* New York, McGraw-Hill, 1965.

Nitecki, Joseph Z. "Simplified classification and cataloging of microforms" *LRTS,* XIII, 1969, 79-85.

Otten, Klaus W. "A hypothesis, microform will become the major medium for 'New Information' in reference libraries" *Journal of Micrographics,* IV, 1971, 265.

Paris. Bibliothèque Nationale. *"Bibliographical control of microcopies" Un B L,* XIX, 136-60+.

Parmelee, Margaret E. "Cataloging microfilms at the University of Michigan Library" *J Doc Repr,* III, 1940, 232-37.

Pelcowa, Janina. "Normes polonaises concernant les microfilms" *Rev Int Doc,* XXXI, 1964, 111.

Pflug, Günther. "Mikrofilm und Xerographie" *Nachrichten für Dokumentation,* XII, 1962, 83-85.

"Photographic reproduction" (*In* Conference on international, cultural, educational, and scientific exchanges, Princeton University, November 25-26, 1946 . . . Chicago, American Library Association, 1947. p. 43-54)

"Planning for scholarly photocopy, a report prepared by the American Council of Learned Societies" *Modern Language Assn. Publications,* LXXIX, 1964, 77-90.

Plante, Julian G. "Monastic manuscript microfilm library" *Music Lib Assn Notes,* XXV, 1968, 12-14.

Plumb, Philip W., ed. *The economics of microfilming and document reproduction.* Papers given at seminars held by the Microfilm Association of Great Britain, Cambridge, 1968. The Microfilm Association of Great Britain, 1969.

Pons, Wei-ta. "Technical services of microfilms at Columbia University libraries: a case study" *LRTS,* II, 1958, 127-32.

Raney, M. Llewellyn. "Film of French revolution journals" *ALA Bul,* XXXII, 1938, 426.

Ready, W. B. "Catalogue retrieval: a library economy" *LRTS,* XIV, 1970, 439-44.

Reichmann, Felix. "Bibliographical control of reprints" *LRTS,* XI, 1967, 415-35.

—— and Josephine Tharpe. *Determination of an effective system of bibliographic control of microform publications.* Interim report. ARL for HEW, 1970.

Rider, Fremont. *The scholar and the future of the research library, a problem and its solution.* New York, Hadham Press, 1944.

Rundell, Walter. *In pursuit of American history; research and training in the United States.* Norman, University of Oklahoma Press, 1970.

Salem, A. *India: mobile microfilm unit (13 June - 13 September 1967).* Paris, UNESCO, 1967. 3 p.

Schatz, S. "Facsimile transmission in libraries, a state-of-the-art survey" *LRTS,* XII, 1968, 5-15.

Schneider, Linda and D. W. Schneider. "Microform masters, a national need" *Southeastern Librarian,* XX, 1970, 106.

Schwegmann, George A., Jr. "Bibliographic control of microforms" *Lib Trends,* VIII, 1960, 380-90.

Scott, P. R. "Present and future of government documents in microform" *Lib Trends,* XV, 1966, 72-86.

——. "Scholars and researchers and their use of microforms" *NMA* [National Microfilm Association] *Journal,* II, 1969, 121-26.

Sevillano Colom, Francisco. "Lista del contenido de los volumenes microfilmados del Archivo Nacional de Asunción" *Hispanic American Review,* XXXVIII, 1958, 60-120.

——. "Mision de la UNESCO en Panama. Materiales microfilmados" *Boletín del Comité de Archivos* [of the Commission on History, Pan American Institute of Geography and History] I, 1958.

——. "The UNESCO microfilm unit in Latin America" *Un B L,* XVI, 1962, 182-86.

——. "UNESCO's microfilm project in Latin America" (In *Acquisitions of Latin American library materials* [Seminar, 3d, 1958, Berkeley] Final report and papers. University of California Library, 1959. p. 125-31)

Shaw, R. R. "Machines and the bibliographic problems of the twentieth century" (*In* Ridenour, L. N., et al. *Bibliography in the age of science.* Urbana, Ill., University of Illinois Press, 1951. p. 37-71)

Shelley, Fred. "Presidential papers program of the Library of Congress" *Am Archivist,* XXV, 1962, 429-33.

Shera, Jesse H., ed. *Bibliographic organization,* edited by Jesse H. Shera and Margaret E. Egan. Chicago, University of Chicago Press [1951].

Sherlock, Marjorie. "Cataloging unorthodoxies at Queen's University Library" *Ont Lib R,* XXVIII, 1944, 58-60.

Simonton, Wesley C. "Bibliographic control of microforms" *LRTS,* VI, 1962, 29-40.

———. "Library handling of microforms" *NMA Proceedings,* 11th meeting, 1962, 277-82.

Sontag, Raymond J. "The German diplomatic papers: publication after two world wars" *American Historical Review,* LXVIII, 1962, 57-68.

Subject guide to microforms in print. 1962-63- Washington, Microcard Editions. Annual.

Sullivan, Robert C. "Developments in photoreproduction of library material, 1970" *LRTS,* XV, 1971, 158. (See also previous reports)

Talman, James J. "Twenty-two years of the microfilm newspaper project" *Canad Lib,* XXV, 1968, 140-48.

Tate, Vernon D. "Documentary reproduction—post war" (In Inter-American library conference, *Papers and addresses.* Washington, D.C., 1946. p. 17-23)

Tauber, Maurice F. "Cataloging and classifying microfilms" *J Doc Repr,* III, 1940, 10-25.

———. *Technical services in libraries.* New York, Columbia University Press, 1954.
New edition will be published shortly. With permission of the author we were able to consult relevant parts.

Taylor, Dorothy K. "State of microfilming programs" *Am Archivist,* XXII, 1959, 59-82.

Teare, Robert Foster. "Microphotography and cataloging: a forecast" *CRL,* VII, 1946, 231-36.

Teplitz, Arthur. "Microfilm and reprography" *Annual review of information science and technology,* V, 1970, 87-111.

Thomson, June. "Cataloging of large works on microform in Canadian university libraries" *Canad Lib J,* XXVI, 1969, 446-52.

United Nations Educational, Scientific and Cultural Organization. Division of Libraries, Documentation and Archives. "List of micropublishers" *Un B L,* XVI, 1962, 198-205.

U. S. Business and Defense Services Administration. *Microforms: a growth industry.* Washington, U. S. Govt. Print. Off., 1969. 18 p.

U. S. Library of Congress. General Reference and Bibliography Division. *Microfilms and microcards, their use in research;* a selected list of references, compiled by Blanche Prichard McCrum. Washington, 1950.

Veaner, Allen B. "Crisis in micropublication" *Choice,* V, 1968, 448-53.

———. "Developments in reproduction of library materials and graphic communications" *LRTS,* XII, 1968, 203-14, 467.

———. *The evaluation of microreproductions.* Chicago, American Library Association, 1971. (LTP 17)

———. "On the need for improved communications between producers and users of research microfilm" (In *Reprographie II,* Bericht über den II internationalen Kongress für Reprographie. Darmstadt, Helwich, 1969)

Veenstra, John G. "Microimages and the library: a review of the most recent trends in the spreading use of microimage materials in libraries of all types" *Lib. J,* XCV, 1970, 3443.

Veit, Fritz. "Microforms, microform equipment and microform use in the educational environment" *Lib Trends,* XIX, 1971, 447.

Verry, Herbert R. *Microcopying methods.* rev. ed. revised by Gordon H. Wright. London, Focal Press, 1967. 183 p.

Waller, Jean M. "Our library in microform; the holdings of the library of the University of Malaya in Singapore" *Majaltah Perpustakaan Singapura* (Singapore Library Journal), I, 1961, 5-8.

Watson, Peter G. *Great Britain's National Lending Library.* Los Angeles, University of California, School of Library Service, 1970.

Whitney, William T. "Miniatures and microforms—a reference librarian looks ahead" (*In*

Moore, Everett LeRoy, ed. *Junior college libraries: development, needs, and perspectives.* Papers presented . . . 1969. (ACRL Monograph, no. 30) p. 47-56)

Williams, Bernard J. S. *Microform based communication systems, a review.* December 1968, FLA thesis. 268 p. on 6 microfiches.

——. "Micropublication and dissemination: a review paper" [Guildford, Eng., IPC Science & Technology Press, Ltd., 1971] [11] p. (Preprint from *Proceedings* of the 3d Congress on Reprography, London, 1971)

——. *Miniaturized communications, a review of microforms.* London, Library Association, 1970.

——. *Thesaurus of microform terms.* London, NRCd, 1969.

—— and Gordon H. Wright. "Microforms; an active tool for library systems" *MICRODOC,* VI, 1967, 3-14.

Williams, Edwin E. "Microbibliography; a possible alternative to microcards" *ALA Bul,* XXXIX, 1945, 450-52.

Wilson, William J. "Manuscript in microfilm; problems of cataloger and bibliographer" *Lib Q,* XIII, 1943, 293-309.

——. "A plan for a comprehensive medico-historical library: problems of scope and coverage" *Lib Q,* XXI, 1950, 249.

Wooster, Harold. *Microfiche 1969: a user survey.* Arlington, Va., Air Force Office of Scientific Research, 1969. 211 p.

——. "Towards a uniform federal report numbering system and a cuddly microfiche reader—two modest proposals" *NMA Journal,* II, 1969, 63-67.

Wright, Wyllis E. "Cataloging of microfilm" *Lib J,* LXIII, 1938, 530-32.

Zimmerman, Erich. "Die bibliotekarische Behandlung von Mikrofilmen" *Zentr Bibl,* LXIV, 1950, 91-1000.

—— "Regeln für die alphabetische Titelaufnahme von Mikrofilmen" *Nachrichten für Wissenschaftliche Bibliotheken,* VI, 1953, 61-67.

Zimmerman, Lee Franklin. "Newspaper microfilming project in Idaho" *Bkmark* (Idaho), VII, 1955, 48-51.